given their grave democratic deficits. Best of all, the book offers a subtle and ingenious answer." —John Fabian Witt, *Washington Post*

"A fantastic book. . . . A masterpiece."

—Daniel A. Cotter, *Chicago Daily Law Bulletin*

"Foner has a knack for looking at past conflicts through the lens of the present, without allowing the present to distort the past. . . . [He tells] a compelling story with dramatic incidents, colorful historical figures, and a sense of compassion. [*The Second Founding*] will provide [readers] with a clear view of a fractious past, and encourage them, in the words of the Civil Rights movement, 'To keep your eyes on the prize.' " —Jonah Raskin, *New York Journal of Books*

"Timely and important. . . . [Foner] has written many books about the Civil War, Reconstruction and slavery, but this one seems particularly attuned to the current political moment." —Ann Levin, *Associated Press*

"A timely reminder that these amendments could be transformative if used in broader ways in legal and Supreme Court decisions."

—Jane Ciabattari, *BBC Culture*

"Eric Foner . . . contends that the endeavour [of Reconstruction] is still under way. The aftermath of the civil war and the three Reconstruction amendments have not, Mr. Foner writes, set everything right for 'the world's first biracial democracy.' . . . [T]he Supreme Court often betrayed the promise of Reconstruction in the final decades of the 19th century. . . . The drive for a fairer, more just America, Mr. Foner aptly concludes, is 'a work in progress.' " —*Economist*

"Eric Foner has done it again: his concise, superbly researched, beautifully written history of the Civil War amendments chronicles a revolution in law and moral sensibility." —David W. Blight, Yale University,
author of the Pulitzer prize–winning
Frederick Douglass: Prophet of Freedom

"How are voter suppression, mass incarceration, and jeopardy to the American-born children of undocumented immigrants possible in the land of the free? Eric Foner brings his masterful knowledge of Reconstruction to illuminate the transformative constitutional amendments following the Civil War, and powerfully conveys the ongoing struggles over their meaning."

—Martha Minow, 300th Anniversary University Professor,
Harvard University, author of *In Brown's Wake:
Legacies of America's Educational Landmark*

ALSO BY ERIC FONER

Free Soil, Free Labor, Free Men:
The Ideology of the Republican Party Before the Civil War (1970)

America's Black Past: A Reader in Afro-American History (editor, 1971)

Nat Turner (editor, 1971)

Tom Paine and Revolutionary America (1976)

Politics and Ideology in the Age of the Civil War (1980)

Nothing But Freedom: Emancipation and Its Legacy (1983)

Reconstruction: America's Unfinished Revolution 1863–1877 (1988)

A Short History of Reconstruction (1990)

A House Divided: America in the Age of Lincoln (with Olivia Mahoney, 1990)

The New American History (editor, 1990; rev. ed. 1997)

The Reader's Companion to American History (editor, with John A. Garraty, 1991)

Freedom's Lawmakers: A Directory of Black Reconstruction Officeholders
(1993; rev. ed. 1996)

Thomas Paine (editor, 1995)

America's Reconstruction: People and Politics after the Civil War
(with Olivia Mahoney, 1995)

The Story of American Freedom (1998)

Who Owns History? Rethinking the Past in a Changing World (2002)

Give Me Liberty! An American History (2004)

Voices of Freedom: A Documentary History (editor, 2004)

Forever Free: The Story of Emancipation and Reconstruction (2005)

Herbert Aptheker on Race and Democracy: A Reader
(editor, with Manning Marable, 2006)

Our Lincoln: New Perspectives on Lincoln and His World (editor, 2008)

The Fiery Trial: Abraham Lincoln and American Slavery (2010)

American History Now (editor, with Lisa McGirr, 2011)

Gateway to Freedom: The Hidden History of the Underground Railroad (2015)

Battles for Freedom: The Use and Abuse of American History (2017)

ERIC FONER

THE SECOND FOUNDING

How the Civil War and Reconstruction Remade the Constitution

W. W. NORTON & COMPANY

Independent Publishers Since 1923

For information about permission to reproduce selections from this book, write to
Permissions, W. W. Norton & Company, Inc., 500 Fifth Avenue, New York, NY 10110

For information about special discounts for bulk purchases, please contact
W. W. Norton Special Sales at specialsales@wwnorton.com or 800-233-4830

Manufacturing by LSC Communications, Harrisonburg
Book design by Brooke Koven
Production manager: Anna Oler

Library of Congress Cataloging-in-Publication Data

Names: Foner, Eric, 1943–
Title: The second founding : how the Civil War and Reconstruction remade the
constitution / Eric Foner.
Description: First edition. | New York, NY : W. W. Norton & Company, 2019. |
Includes bibliographical references and index.
Identifiers: LCCN 2019014793 | ISBN 9780393652574 (hardcover)
Subjects: LCSH: Constitutional history—United States—19th century. | United States.
Constitution. 13th–15th Amendments | Reconstruction (U.S. history, 1865–1877)—
Influence. | United States—History—Civil War, 1861-1865—Law and legislation.
Classification: LCC KF4541 .F68 2019 | DDC 342.73—dc23
LC record available at https://lccn.loc.gov/2019014793

ISBN 978-0-393-35852-0 pbk.

W. W. Norton & Company, Inc., 500 Fifth Avenue, New York, N.Y. 10110
www.wwnorton.com

W. W. Norton & Company Ltd., 15 Carlisle Street, London W1D 3BS

3 4 5 6 7 8 9 0

For Daria

CONTENTS

LIST OF ILLUSTRATIONS

The Reconstruction Amendments

THIRTEENTH AMENDMENT

SECTION I.

Neither slavery nor involuntary servitude, except as a punishment for crime whereof the party shall have been duly convicted, shall exist within the United States, or any place subject to their jurisdiction.

SECTION 2.

Congress shall have power to enforce this article by appropriate legislation.

FOURTEENTH AMENDMENT

SECTION 1.

All persons born or naturalized in the United States, and subject to the jurisdiction thereof, are citizens of the United States and of the State wherein they reside. No State shall make or enforce any law which shall abridge the privileges or immunities of citizens of the United States; nor shall any State deprive any person of life, liberty, or property, without due process of law; nor deny to any person within its jurisdiction the equal protection of the laws.

SECTION 2.

Representatives shall be apportioned among the several States according to their respective numbers, counting the whole number of persons in each State, excluding Indians not taxed. But when the right to vote at any election for the choice of electors for President and Vice President of the United States, Representatives in Congress, the executive and judicial officers of a State, or the members of the legislature thereof, is denied to any of the male inhabitants of such State, being twenty-one years of age, and citizens of the United States, or in any way abridged, except for participation in rebellion, or other crime, the basis of representation therein shall be reduced in the proportion which the number of such male citizens shall bear to the whole number of male citizens twenty-one years of age in such State.

SECTION 3.

No person shall be a Senator or Representative in Congress, or elector of President and Vice President, or hold any office, civil or military, under the United States, or under any State, who, having previously taken an oath, as a member of Congress, or as an officer of the United States, or as a member of any State legislature, or as an executive or judicial officer of any State, to support the Constitution of the United States, shall have engaged in insurrection or rebellion against the same, or given aid or comfort to the enemies thereof. But Congress may by a vote of two-thirds of each House, remove such disability.

SECTION 4.

The validity of the public debt of the United States, authorized by law, including debts incurred for payment of pensions and bounties for services in suppressing insurrection or rebellion, shall not be questioned. But neither the United States nor any State shall assume or pay any debt or obligation incurred in aid of insurrection or rebellion against the United States, or any claim for the loss or emancipation of any slave; but all such debts, obligations and claims shall be held illegal and void.

SECTION 5.

The Congress shall have power to enforce, by appropriate legislation, the provisions of this article.

FIFTEENTH AMENDMENT

SECTION 1.

The right of citizens of the United States to vote shall not be denied or abridged by the United States or by any State on account of race, color, or previous condition of servitude.

SECTION 2.

The Congress shall have the power to enforce this article by appropriate legislation.

PREFACE

T HE CIVIL War and the Reconstruction period that followed
form the pivotal era of American history. The war destroyed
the institution of slavery, ensured the survival of the Union,
and set in motion economic and political changes that laid the foundation for the modern nation. During Reconstruction, the United States
made its first attempt, flawed but truly remarkable for its time, to build
an egalitarian society on the ashes of slavery. Some of the problems of
those years haunt American society today—vast inequalities of wealth
and power, terrorist violence, aggressive racism. But perhaps the era's
most tangible legacies are the Thirteenth, Fourteenth, and Fifteenth
Amendments to the United States Constitution. The Thirteenth irre-
vocably abolished slavery. The Fourteenth constitutionalized the principles of birthright citizenship and equality before the law and sought
to settle key issues arising from the war, such as the future political role
of Confederate leaders and the fate of Confederate debt. The Fifteenth
aimed to secure black male suffrage throughout the reunited nation.

Together with far-reaching congressional legislation meant to
provide former slaves with access to the courts, ballot box, and public accommodations, and to protect them against violence, the

Reconstruction amendments greatly enhanced the power of the federal government, transferring much of the authority to define citizens' rights from the states to the nation. They forged a new constitutional relationship between individual Americans and the national state and were crucial in creating the world's first biracial democracy, in which people only a few years removed from slavery exercised significant political power. All three amendments end with a clause empowering Congress to enforce their provisions, guaranteeing that Reconstruction would be an ongoing process, not a single moment in time. This in itself was a significant innovation. The Bill of Rights said nothing about how the liberties it enumerated would be implemented and protected. Introducing into the Constitution the words "equal protection of the law" and "the right to vote" (along with the qualifying "male," to the outrage of the era's women's rights activists), the amendments both reflected and reinforced a new era of individual rights consciousness among Americans of all races and backgrounds. So profound were these changes that the amendments should be seen not simply as an alteration of an existing structure but as a "second founding," a "constitutional revolution," in the words of Republican leader Carl Schurz, that created a fundamentally new document with a new definition of both the status of blacks and the rights of all Americans.[1]

The chapters that follow examine the origins, enactment, and objectives of the Reconstruction amendments and the contest over their meaning that followed ratification. This brief volume does not purport to present a full account of Reconstruction, a task I have assayed elsewhere.[2] But to understand the constitutional changes it is necessary to have some knowledge of this period immediately following the Civil War.

Reconstruction has conventionally been dated from the war's end in 1865 to 1877, when the last southern state came under the control of the white supremacist Democratic party. Lately, scholars have been writing of a "long Reconstruction" that lasted into the 1880s and even beyond. But whatever its chronological definition, Reconstruction can also be understood as a historical process without a fixed end point—

the process by which the United States tried to come to terms with the momentous results of the Civil War, especially the destruction of the institution of slavery. One might almost say that we are still trying to work out the consequences of the abolition of American slavery. In that sense, Reconstruction never ended.

I have devoted much of my career to the study of Reconstruction, but I must acknowledge that this part of our history is unfamiliar to many, perhaps most Americans. As a result, the Reconstruction amendments do not occupy the prominent place in public consciousness of other pivotal documents of our history, such as the Bill of Rights and Declaration of Independence. But even if we are unaware of it, Reconstruction remains part of our lives, or to put it another way, key issues confronting American society today are in some ways Reconstruction questions. Who is entitled to citizenship? Who should enjoy the right to vote? Should the laws protect the rights of aliens as well as citizens? How should the "equal protection of the laws" be defined and guaranteed? What should be the balance of power between the federal government and the states? How should Americans be protected from the depredations of terrorists? All of these questions were intensely debated during Reconstruction. Every term of the Supreme Court, moreover, adjudicates cases requiring interpretation of the Fourteenth Amendment. Some of the most transformative decisions of the modern era, from *Brown v. Board of Education* outlawing school segregation to *Obergefell v. Hodges*, establishing the right of gay persons to marry, were based on that amendment. It is impossible to understand American society today without knowing something about the Reconstruction period a century and a half ago.

Reconstruction is also a prime example of what we sometimes call the politics of history—the ways historical interpretation both reflects and helps to shape the time in which the historian is writing. For most of the twentieth century, an account of Reconstruction known as the Dunning School, named for Columbia University professor William A. Dunning and his students, dominated historical writing, legal scholarship, and popular consciousness. These scholars, who published their major works in the 1890s and early 1900s, were among the first generation of university-trained historians in the United States, and they developed insights that remain valuable, for example, that slavery was the fundamental cause of the Civil War, and that regional and class differences within white society helped to shape Reconstruction politics. Anticipating recent scholarship, they insisted that Reconstruction must be understood in a national context, as an example of nineteenth-century nation building. The Dunning School also pioneered the use of primary sources (at least those emanating from whites) to tell the story of Reconstruction.[3]

Nonetheless, ingrained racism undermined the value of the Dunning School's scholarship. Convinced that blacks lacked the capacity to participate intelligently in political democracy, they condemned Reconstruction, in the words of Dunning's Columbia colleague John W. Burgess, for imposing the rule of "uncivilized Negroes" over the whites of the South, inevitably producing an orgy of corruption and misgovernment. This portrait of Reconstruction became part of the Lost Cause ideology that permeated southern culture in the first part of the twentieth century and was reflected in the proliferation of Confederate monuments that still dot the southern landscape and have lately become a source of strident debate. Along with a nostalgic image of the Confederacy, the idea of the Lost Cause rested on a view of slavery as a benign, paternalistic institution and of Reconstruction as a time of "Negro rule" from which the South was rescued by the heroic actions of the self-styled Redeemers who restored white supremacy. This view of history reached a mass national audience in the film *The Birth of a Nation*, which had its premiere in 1915 in Woodrow Wilson's White House, and Claude Bowers's bestseller of the 1920s, *The Tragic Era*.[4]

This was a portrait of Reconstruction meant to justify the times in which it was written. It provided an intellectual foundation for Jim Crow, the racial system of the South and in many ways the United States as a whole, from the 1890s until the civil rights era of the 1960s. Indeed, it had a powerful impact beyond the nation's borders as a legitimation of colonial rule over nonwhite peoples in far-flung places from South Africa to Australia.[5] Its political lessons were very clear. First, biracial democracy was impossible. Since it had been a cardinal error to give black men the right to vote, the white South was justified in taking away the suffrage around the turn of the twentieth century. Any effort to restore African-Americans' political rights would lead to a replay of the supposed horrors of Reconstruction. Second, Reconstruction was imposed on the South by northerners. Some of them may have been motivated by humanitarian ideals, but the outcome proved that outsiders simply do not understand race relations in the southern states. The white South, therefore, should resist outside calls for change in its racial system. The third lesson of this view, which seems arcane today, was that because Reconstruction was brought into existence by the Republican party, the white South should remain solidly Democratic.

During the 1930s and 1940s, as criticism of the South's Jim Crow system mounted among racial liberals within and outside the region, the "memory" of Reconstruction purveyed by the Dunning School "gave shape and meaning to white supremacist politics" in the South. In 1944, Gunnar Myrdal noted in his influential work *An American Dilemma* that when pressed about the black condition, white southerners "will regularly bring forward the horrors of the Reconstruction governments and of 'black domination.'"[6]

For many years, the outlook of the Dunning School was also incorporated into Supreme Court decisions that interpreted the Reconstruction amendments, producing a jurisprudence that allowed the white South essentially to abrogate many of the provisions of the second founding. In a dissent in a 1945 case arising from the death of a black man at the hands of Georgia law enforcement officers, Justices Owen Roberts, Felix Frankfurter, and Robert H. Jackson wrote that it was "familiar history" that Reconstruction legislation was motivated by a "vengeful spirit" on the part of northerners. So familiar, in fact, that these justices felt no need to cite any work of historical scholarship to justify their claim. Eight years later, Jackson attributed the "race problem" in the South to whites' "historical memory" of Reconstruction and their identification of blacks with "offensive measures" of that "deplorable" era. This was not an outlook likely to produce a robust interpretation of the Reconstruction amendments as vehicles for promoting racial justice.[7]

The civil rights revolution destroyed the pillars of the Dunning School, especially its overt racism, and historians completely overhauled the interpretation of Reconstruction. If the era was tragic, we now think, it was not because it was attempted but because in significant ways it failed, leaving to subsequent generations the difficult problem of racial justice. Today most historians see Reconstruction, as W. E. B. Du Bois argued three-quarters of a century ago, as a key moment in the history of democracy and its overthrow as a setback for the democratic principle in the United States and throughout the world. This outlook casts the second founding in a different light.[8]

For the historian, seeking to understand the purposes of the Reconstruction amendments is not the same as attempting to identify, as a matter of jurisprudence, the "original intent" of those who drafted and voted on them or the original meaning of the language used. Whether the courts should base decisions on "originalism" is a political, not a historical, question. But no historian believes that any important document possesses a single intent or meaning. Numerous motives inspired the constitutional amendments, including genuine idealism, the desire to secure permanently the North's victory in the Civil War, and partisan advantage. Even on its own terms, the quest for original meaning often leads to disappointment. Members of Congress during the Civil War and Reconstruction had the irritating habit of not debating at length, or at all, concerns that have driven recent jurisprudence relating to the amendments, among them school segregation, affirmative action, marriage equality, and corporate personhood. Moreover, as in all crises, the meaning of key concepts embedded in the Reconstruction amendments such as citizenship, liberty, equality, rights, and the proper location of political authority—ideas that are inherently contested—were themselves in flux. In other words, the creation of meaning is an ongoing process. Freezing the amendments at the moment of their ratification misses this dynamic quality.

The Reconstruction amendments can only be understood in terms of the historical circumstances and ideological context in which they were enacted. These include how they were approved by Congress and the states; what those who framed, debated, and ratified them hoped to accomplish; and how other Americans understood and attempted to use them. In the chapters that follow my purpose is not so much to identify the one "true" intent of the Reconstruction amendments, as to identify the range of ideas that contributed to the second founding; to explore the rapid evolution of thinking in which previously distinct categories of natural, civil, political, and social rights merged into a more diffuse, more modern idea of citizens' rights that included most or all of them; and to suggest that more robust interpretations of the amendments are possible, as plausible, if not more so, in terms of the historical record, than how the Supreme Court has in fact construed them.

The crucial first section of the Fourteenth Amendment is written in the language of general principles—due process, equal protection, privileges or immunities of citizenship—that cry out for further elaboration, making it inevitable that their specific applications would be the subject of never-ending contention. Indeed, the very "indefiniteness of meaning," as George S. Boutwell, a key member of Congress, put it, was a "charm" to Congressman John A. Bingham of Ohio, who, more than any other individual, was responsible for that section's wording.[9] The Thirteenth Amendment did not clearly define "involuntary servitude" and the Fifteenth did not explain how to judge whether a state's voting restrictions were enacted "on account of race."

Congress built future interpretation and implementation into the amendments. But this ran the risk that their purposes could be defeated by narrow judicial construction or congressional inaction. That is what in fact happened in the decades between Reconstruction and the civil rights era. At the same time, unanticipated outcomes ended up subverting some of the amendments' purposes.[10] The

Thirteenth allows involuntary servitude to survive as a punishment for crime, seemingly offering constitutional sanction to the later emergence of a giant system of convict labor. The Fourteenth can be understood as protecting citizens' rights against violations by the states but not by private individuals (although this is not the only possible interpretation of its language). The Fifteenth leaves the door open to forms of disenfranchisement that while not explicitly based on race, bar most blacks from voting.

The very fact that the amendments were compromises means that they are open to what one member of Congress called "conflicting constructions." But rather than lamenting this ambiguity we should, in the spirit of John A. Bingham, embrace it. Ambiguity creates possibilities. It paves the way for future struggles, while giving different groups grounds on which to conduct them. Who determines which of a range of possible meanings is implemented is very much a matter of political power.

Abolitionists and many Republicans saw the second founding as the beginning of an even deeper transformation—what today would be called "regime change," the substitution of a regime committed to the idea of equality for the previous proslavery one. Over the course of the century and a half since their ratification, however, with a range of interpretations available, the Supreme Court has too frequently chosen a narrow reading of the amendments, with little thought about the practical consequences of its decisions. This began during Reconstruction itself as the Court (and nation) retreated from the ideal of equal citizenship and the empowerment of the federal government. These early decisions, which will be discussed in Chapter Four, created a series of precedents later reinforced by judicial adherence to the Dunning School view of Reconstruction. Historical interpretation has changed dramatically, but earlier decisions resting in part on a now repudiated understanding of the era remain embedded in established jurisprudence. The recent history of the amendments reveals their ongoing expansion to protect the rights of new groups—most recently, gay men and women, and gun owners—

yet a restricted application in questions involving race. This reflects, in part, the enduring impact of earlier decisions limiting the amendments' scope and enforcement.[11]

In the pages that follow I devote considerable attention to debates in Congress that focused directly on the language and implications of the amendments and to subsequent court decisions interpreting the newly revised Constitution. But constitutional meaning also arises from sites outside Congress and the courts, including popular conventions, newspapers, and actions in the streets. The protagonists included ordinary Americans of all backgrounds. For example, the Fourteenth Amendment was only ratified by a sufficient number of states because Congress had mandated the implementation of black male suffrage throughout the South, resulting in the election of legislatures that included black members for the first time in American history. Without black suffrage in the South, there would be no Fourteenth Amendment. Yet since no blacks served in Congress when the amendment was approved, the ways black Americans understood its provisions are almost never considered when "intent" is discussed and were consistently ignored by the Supreme Court during and after Reconstruction. To take another example, the campaign for the adoption of the Thirteenth Amendment was initiated by the Women's Loyal National League, founded by Elizabeth Cady Stanton and Susan B. Anthony, who firmly believed that abolition was the route to civil and political equality for blacks and all women. "A true republic," they insisted, would "surely rise from this shattered Union."[12] Even though they would be sorely disappointed, their intentions, as well as those of the broad abolitionist movement that embraced their proposal, constitute one dimension of the amendment's original purposes.

In her memoirs written in the 1890s, Stanton recalled that Reconstruction "involved the reconsideration of the principles of our government and the natural rights of man. The nation's heart was thrilled with prolonged debates in Congress and state legislatures, in the pulpits and public journals, and at every fireside on these vital questions." These debates threw open to question traditional conceptions of citizenship, property rights, democracy, state and national sovereignty, and the connections between public power and individual liberty. They unleashed an upsurge of claims to new rights by all sorts of Americans. The era's "popular constitutionalism" must form part of our understanding of the Reconstruction amendments. And that understanding changed over time as Americans sought to use the amendments for their own purposes and to expand their impact, often in ways not anticipated by those who wrote them. The second founding made it possible for movements for equality of all kinds to be articulated in constitutional terms. And demands that proved unsuccessful not only provide insights into grassroots political outlooks, but sometimes laid the groundwork and established the agenda for subsequent efforts that eventually prevailed.[13]

Shortly after the ratification of the Fifteenth Amendment, Carl Schurz summarized the meaning of the second founding. The "constitutional revolution," he declared, "found the rights of the individual at the mercy of the states . . . and placed them under the shield of national protection. It made the liberty and rights of every citizen in every state a matter of national concern. Out of a republic of arbitrary local organizations it made a republic of equal citizens." Unfortunately, a retreat soon followed, in which Schurz himself participated. By the turn of the century, a new regime of inequality took the place of the old, and full enjoyment of citizens' rights was indefinitely postponed. But not everything achieved after the Civil War could be taken away. The families, schools, and churches established and consolidated during Reconstruction survived, springboards for future struggles. The fact that African-Americans outside the South retained the right to vote would be of enormous political consequence when the Great Migration of the twentieth century redrew the nation's racial map. The amendments remained in place, "sleeping giants" to borrow a phrase from Massachusetts senator Charles Sumner, that continued to inspire those who looked to the Constitution to support their efforts to create a more just social order.[14] Decades later they would be awakened to provide the constitutional foundation for the civil rights revolution, sometimes called the Second Reconstruction. It is worth noting that no significant change in the Constitution took place during the civil rights era. The movement did not need a new Constitution; it needed the existing one enforced.

More recently, we have experienced a slow retreat from the ideal of racial equality. We live at a moment in some ways not unlike the 1890s and early twentieth century, when state governments, with the acquiescence of the Supreme Court, stripped black men of the right to vote and effectively nullified the constitutional promise of equality. "Principles which we all thought to have been firmly and permanently settled," Frederick Douglass observed, were "boldly assaulted and overthrown." [15] As history shows, progress is not necessarily linear or permanent. But neither is retrogression.

By themselves, the constitutional amendments that emerged from the Civil War cannot address all the legacies of slavery. Sumner remarked of the Thirteenth Amendment that rewriting the Constitution was not an end in itself but "an incident in the larger struggle for freedom and equality." But the Reconstruction amendments remain, in the words of one Republican newspaper, "a declaration of popular rights." They retain unused latent power that, in a different political environment, may yet be employed to implement in new ways the Reconstruction vision of equal citizenship for all. [16]

THE
SECOND
FOUNDING

INTRODUCTION

Origins of the Second Founding

T HE PROFOUND changes that American society experienced during the Civil War and Reconstruction and how they reshaped the Constitution and the broad legal and political culture cannot be understood without reminding ourselves of the status of African-Americans when the war began. There were a little under four million slaves and half a million free blacks in the United States in 1860. Slavery was politically powerful and economically thriving. Slave-grown cotton was by far the nation's most important export, and the profits generated by slavery enriched not only planters in the South but also merchants, manufacturers, and bankers in the free states.

Slavery's growth and power depended, in part, on protections provided by the Constitution. In 1787, at the time of the Constitutional Convention, around 700,000 slaves lived in the United States. They made up 40 percent of the population of the states from Maryland to Georgia. Of the fifty-five delegates nearly half, including a number of northerners, possessed slaves. George Washington, who presided, owned over two hundred, three of whom accompanied him to Philadelphia, where the convention took place. The Constitution did not mention the word "slavery," but clearly referred to slaves in such circumlocutions as "other persons" and "person held to service or labor." Nonetheless, many of the framers, including slaveholders from the Upper South, hoped that the institution would eventually die out, and they successfully resisted efforts to place an explicit national recognition of property in man in the document. Yet they did include clauses requiring the return of fugitive slaves to their owners, allowing states to import slaves from abroad for at least the next twenty years, and according southern states extra power in the House of Representatives by counting three-fifths of their slave population in apportioning its members. This last provision also enhanced southern power in the Electoral College that chooses the president.[1]

Most importantly, perhaps, it was almost universally agreed that the Constitution left slavery beyond the reach of the national government. State law established and maintained slavery and states could abolish slavery or prohibit its establishment, as northern states did during and after the War of Independence. But debates over slavery nearly always acknowledged what came to be called the "federal consensus"—that the national government had no power to take direct action against the institution in the states. As the country expanded, a rough balance was maintained between free states and slave. Since changes to the Constitution require approval by two-thirds of Congress and three-quarters of the states, an amendment abolishing slavery was clearly out of the question. The historian Linda Colley has observed that written constitutions often function as "weapons of control" rather than "documents of liberation and rights." As far as slaves were concerned, this certainly applies to the original Constitution. Of course, no black persons took part in the Constitutional Convention; nor did women, Native Americans, or poorer whites. Perhaps the second founding can be seen as a step toward making the Constitution what it might have been if "We the People" (the document's opening words) had been more fully represented at Philadelphia.[2]

Slavery shaped the definition of American citizenship before the

Civil War, giving it a powerful racial dimension. A nation, in Benedict Anderson's celebrated phrase, is more than a political entity—it is also "an imagined political community," whose borders are as much intellectual as geographic. Slavery rendered blacks all but invisible to those imagining the American community. When J. Hector St. John de Crèvecoeur, an immigrant from France who gained renown for popularizing facts and myths about the new republic during the era of the Revolution, posed his famous question, "What then is the American, this new man?" he answered, "a mixture of English, Scotch, Irish, French, Dutch, Germans, and Swedes.... He is either a European, or the descendant of a European." At the time, fully one-fifth of the population (the highest proportion in our history) consisted of Africans and their descendants.[3]

In British law, the American colonists, like persons in Great Britain, were "subjects" of the crown, entitled to protection and required to provide allegiance. Independence transformed British subjects into American citizens. Yet despite the enormous "cultural currency" that the idea of citizenship acquired in the United States in the first half of the nineteenth century, it was not until the constitutional revolution of Reconstruction that a commonly agreed-upon understanding of the rights it entailed and the role of the federal government in defining and guaranteeing those rights developed. Before the Civil War, as one member of Congress noted during Reconstruction, a person seeking enlightenment about American citizenship "must have been pained by the fruitless search in the law books and the records of our courts for a clear and satisfactory definition of the phrase 'citizen of the United States.'" During the early days of Reconstruction, members of Congress asked Horace Binney, a prominent lawyer and a former congressman, to explore the meaning of citizenship. "The word citizen," he responded, "is found ten times at least in the Constitution of the United States, and no definition of it is given anywhere."[4]

The Constitution's "Comity Clause" states that the citizens of each state are "entitled to all privileges and immunities of citizens in the several states," language that seems to suggest that the rights of citizens are determined by the states, not the federal government. The Constitution does require the president to be a "natural-born Citizen," that is, a person born in the country. This implies, but does not state explicitly, that citizenship derives either from birth in the United States or, for immigrants from abroad, a "naturalization" process. On occasion, the federal government created American citizens by purchasing the land on which they lived, for example the Louisiana Territory acquired from France, or via conquest, as in the Mexican-American War. In both cases, the residents (except, in the latter case, members of "savage tribes") could choose to become American citizens if they so desired.

Citizenship certainly did not imply equality. Whites, male and female, born in the United States were commonly assumed to be citizens, but white women lacked basic rights enjoyed by men. Slaves were not citizens, but the status of free black Americans remained highly controversial. The first Naturalization Act, approved by Congress in 1790, limited the process of becoming a citizen from abroad to white persons. What of free blacks born in the United States? At the time of ratification, most of the original states, including some in the South, allowed free black men to vote if they met the property or other qualifications. As time went on, however, the slave states placed severe restrictions on their lives and increasingly refused to recognize them as citizens. Some northern states did, however, and all accorded them basic rights such as property ownership, trial by jury, and the ability to hold public meetings, publish newspapers, and establish their own churches. But nowhere did free African-Americans enjoy full equality before the law. Their situation was anomalous—one jurist referred to free blacks as "quasi citizens."[5]

In the decades before the Civil War, the Constitution's Comity Clause did not seem to apply to African-Americans. A number of states, northern as well as southern, prohibited free black persons from entering their territory. In the 1790s and early nineteenth century, the federal government issued certificates of citizenship to black sailors, to prevent their impressment by the British navy. But several southern states incarcerated free black sailors whose vessels docked in the state, even though they had not been accused of any crime. The enforcement of South Carolina's draconian law led to a strong protest from Massachusetts, which recognized blacks as citizens, and also from Great Britain, to whose black seamen it also applied, but to no avail. The Comity Clause became an issue during the 1820–21 debates over the admission of Missouri, whose constitution not only established slavery but barred the entry of free blacks. Many northerners objected to the latter provision. As part of the Missouri Compromise, the state was admitted on the condition that its constitution should not be construed as denying to any citizens the privileges and immunities to which they were entitled, without enumerating what these might be or whether they applied to free blacks.[6]

In a country that lacked more traditional bases of nationhood—long-established physical boundaries; historic ethnic, religious, and cultural unity; a powerful and menacing neighbor—American political institutions became a point of unity and self-definition. Those denied the suffrage, wrote one advocate of democratic reform, were "put in the situation of slaves of Virginia." Increasingly, the right to vote became the emblem of American citizenship, if not in law (since suffrage qualifications were determined by the individual states) then in common usage and understanding. Noah Webster's *American Dictionary* noted that in the United States, but not in Europe, the word "citizen" had, by the 1820s, become synonymous with the right to vote. Of course, Webster was writing about men; white women were certainly citizens although denied the suffrage. But with the exception of Maine, every state that entered the Union between 1800 and the Civil War limited the suffrage to white men, and over time some of the original states rescinded blacks' right to cast a ballot. On the eve of conflict, black men enjoyed the same right to vote as their white counterparts in only five of the thirty-four states, all in New England. The identification of the polity—and citizenship itself—as a realm for white men became "so natural and necessary as to be self-evident," as one historian has put it.[7]

As Alexis de Tocqueville observed, a passion for equality animated

American democracy. But the concept of equality before the law—something enjoyed by all persons regardless of social status—barely existed before the Civil War. Belief in equality coexisted with many forms of second-class citizenship. Individuals' rights were determined by numerous factors, including race, ethnicity, gender, and occupation. Unequal status relations were built into the combination of local laws, judicial rulings, and customs known as the common law. In "a common law court," Senator Jacob M. Howard of Michigan declared during the Civil War, the idea of equality before the law was "not known at all." In accordance with the common law of coverture, most of the rights of married women were exercised by their husbands. The common law of master and servant distinguished sharply between the rights and powers of employers and employees. Rights often included the ability to exercise authority over others—as in the case of slaveholders, employers, fathers, and husbands. This is one reason why the extension of rights to African-Americans during Reconstruction was seen by many whites as taking something away from them.[8]

Antebellum political and legal discourse divided rights into distinct categories, not all of which every citizen enjoyed. Most basic were natural rights, such as the "unalienable" rights enumerated by Thomas Jefferson in the Declaration of Independence. Every person, by virtue of his or her human status, was entitled to life, liberty (even though this principle was flagrantly violated by the existence of slavery), and the pursuit of happiness (often understood as the right to enjoy the fruits of one's own labor and rise in the social scale). Civil rights, the second category, included legal entitlements essential to pursuing a livelihood and protecting one's personal security—the right to own property, go to court, sue and be sued, sign contracts, and move about freely. These were fundamental rights of all free persons, but they could be regulated by the state. Married women, for example, could not engage in most economic activities without the consent of their husbands, and many states limited the right of blacks to testify in court in cases involving whites. Then there were political rights. Legally, despite Webster's dictionary, access to the ballot box was a privilege or "franchise," not a right. It was everywhere confined to men, and almost everywhere to white men. Finally there were "social rights," an amorphous category that included personal and business relationships of many kinds. These lay outside the realm of governmental supervision. Every effort to expand the rights of blacks was attacked by opponents as sure to lead to "social equality," a phrase that conjured up images of black-white sexual intimacy and interracial marriage.[9]

During the 1850s, as the Republican party emerged as a northern sectional organization demanding that slavery's westward expansion be halted, Democrats persistently accused its partisans of favoring "Negro equality." While this was essentially political invective, by 1860 most northern Republicans seem to have concluded that free blacks were entitled to natural and civil rights; far fewer, however, supported political equality and almost none equality of social rights. In writing about Abraham Lincoln, the *New York Times* in 1860 articulated a rough consensus within the party: "He declares his opposition to negro suffrage, and to everything looking towards placing negroes upon a footing of political and social equality with the whites,—but he asserts for them a perfect equality of civil and personal rights under the Constitution."[10]

During the second founding, a new definition of American citizenship, incorporating equal rights regardless of race, was written into the Constitution. Indeed, one scholar has recently proposed that Reconstruction be reconceptualized as "The Era of Citizenship." Nonetheless, significant obstacles confronted those seeking to implement the idea of equal rights for black Americans. Racism, perhaps slavery's most powerful legacy, was one. Another was the long-standing tradition of local self-government, embodied in the authority of the states within the federal system and the "police" powers of local governments. In the legal culture of antebellum America, all sorts of activities—economic, political, personal—were subject to regulation by localities and states with the aim of securing not equality but public order, health, safety, and morality. Anti-black laws represented one component of a panoply of legislation restricting the rights of various groups, among them paupers, prostitutes, vagrants, and immigrants. Inequality, as noted above, was built into the common law. As long as citizenship remained subject to local definition and regulation, citizens would be manifestly unequal.[11]

Before Reconstruction the federal government played almost no role in defining or protecting Americans' rights. Most of the matters addressed by the second founding had traditionally been dealt with by the states and municipalities. No "political idea," wrote Frederick Douglass, the escaped slave who rose to become perhaps the most prominent abolitionist orator, was "more deeply rooted in the minds of men in all sections of the country [than] the right of each state to control its own affairs." But many Republicans, like Douglass, identified the idea of states' rights as second only to slavery itself as a cause of the war and an obstacle to any "general assertion of human rights," and wanted it sharply curtailed. Reconstruction was a key moment in the process by which a hierarchical, locally based legal culture was transformed into one committed, at least ostensibly, to the equality of all Americans, protected by the national government. "In the revolution we have gone through," the staunchly Democratic *New York World* observed in 1872, "the political equality of man has been substituted for the equality of the sovereign states." But it took a long time for a legal system grounded in autonomous local communities to be superseded by one oriented around the relationship of individual citizens to the nation-state. Even as the second founding transformed the federal system, the persistence of traditional respect for the authority of the states would hamper national efforts at enforcement and provide justification for Supreme Court rulings limiting the amendments' effectiveness.[12]

❦

THE REWRITING OF the Constitution only became possible because of the unprecedented crisis of Civil War and Reconstruction. But many of the ideas that took center stage during these years emerged from decades of debate in places far from formal sites of law-making, including the antislavery crusade and the "Colored Convention" movement, in which free blacks articulated a claim to recognition as equal citizens of the republic. Not that slavery's opponents saw eye to eye on constitutional issues. A wide spectrum of opinion existed within the antislavery movement. William Lloyd Garrison, the editor of the Boston weekly *The Liberator*, condemned the Constitution as a proslavery document, "null and void before God." Garrison insisted that principled foes of slavery could not in good conscience vote under such a system. Four years after the passage of the Fugitive Slave Act of 1850, Garrison publicly burned a copy of the Constitution, calling it "a covenant with death and an agreement with hell." Many abolitionists, however, disagreed with Garrison and his followers. A few, including Alvan Stewart and Lysander Spooner, produced treatises arguing that under the Fifth Amendment, which declared that no person could be deprived of liberty without due process of law, slavery actually had no legal existence. Slaves, said Stewart, should go to court and obtain writs of habeas corpus ordering their release from bondage. Frederick Douglass, after several years of adhering to the Garrisonian position, changed his mind and declared the Constitution "a glorious liberty document." "I am for strict construction," he declared, and the word "slavery" could not be found in the Constitution's text. Nor did it contain language allowing for "discrimination in favor of, or against, any class of people." In the mid-1850s, Douglass embraced the view that the federal government possessed the power, without any change in the Constitution, to abolish slavery throughout the nation.[13]

Few inside or outside the antislavery crusade found this last argument convincing. Far more common was an outlook that came to be known as "freedom national." This was based on the idea that the Constitution was neither explicitly proslavery nor a vehicle for immediate abolition, but that it did make possible a kind of antislavery politics—not abolitionism, but one nonetheless deeply threatening to the South. Already articulated in the debates over the admission of Missouri, fully developed as a legal doctrine by the Ohio antislavery lawyer Salmon P. Chase in the 1840s, and adopted by a large segment of the Republican party in the following decade, this doctrine insisted that the Constitution regarded slavery as a local institution, confined to the states where it was recognized by law. The federal government had no constitutional power to attack slavery in these states, but all persons in areas of federal jurisdiction (other than fugitive slaves) must be regarded as free. According to this view, slavery had no right to exist in the District of Columbia, the western territories, or in federal forts and arsenals. Were "freedom national" enacted into law, a "cordon of freedom" would surround the slave states, eventually producing abolition there (although it was never explained precisely how this would happen).[14]

Freedom national was embodied in the platform of the Free Soil party in 1848 and 1852, and the Republican platforms of 1856 and 1860, which called for separating the federal government entirely from the institution of slavery. Antislavery spokesmen scoured the Constitution for clauses useful for their cause, beginning with the Preamble itself, which said the document's purpose was to "secure the blessings of liberty." Other such clauses included the provisions guaranteeing a republican form of government, granting Congress power over the territories, and prohibiting the denial of liberty without due process of law. In his celebrated Cooper Union speech of 1860, Abraham Lincoln examined debates at the Constitutional Convention and early sessions of Congress to argue that the Constitution's intent was antislavery, but that its purposes had been distorted by southern domination of successive national administrations and the federal courts. Thus the Republican party could pursue antislavery politics—especially, barring slavery's expansion into the territories, the issue that brought on the Civil War—not only without violating the Constitution but with confidence that it was following the original policy of the founders. This antislavery interpretation of the Constitution fell on deaf ears at the Supreme Court, which rejected it outright on a number of occasions. But it would strongly influence the second founding.[15]

The crusade against slavery gave birth to a new understanding of citizenship and the rights it entailed. The movement, wrote Angelina Grimké, the daughter of a South Carolina slaveholder who became a Quaker and embraced abolitionism while living in Philadelphia, was "the school in which human rights are ... investigated." Long before the Civil War, abolitionists black and white put forward an understanding of national citizenship severed from the concept of race, with citizens' rights enforced by the federal government. Abolitionists (but not, before the war, most Republicans) demanded not simply an end to slavery but also the incorporation of the freed people as full members of the polity and society. Abolitionists "hitched their politics to black citizenship," in the words of the historian Manisha Sinha. The first legal treatise on the rights of free black Americans came from the pen of a white abolitionist, William Yates, in 1838. As abolitionists battled for the right of northern blacks to vote, enjoy access to public education, and receive equal treatment in transportation and public accommodations, they put forward an idea that would be incorporated into the laws and Constitution during Reconstruction: that all persons born in the United States were American citizens who should enjoy full equality, regardless of race. And the abolitionist critique of the Fugitive Slave Act of 1850, which provided that the status of an accused runaway would be determined by a federal commissioner, not a jury, and that the alleged fugitive could not testify in his or her own behalf, led to the elevation of "due process of law" as essential to equitable judicial proceedings.[16]

Some of the language of the Reconstruction amendments—due process, privileges or immunities of citizens, the right to vote—already existed in the Constitution or were commonplace in legal language. But not "equal protection," the heart of the first section of the Fourteenth Amendment. It was, however, a staple of abolitionist discourse. As early as 1832, Garrison's *Liberator*, referring to free blacks, insisted that "they have as good and true a right to the equal protection of the law as we have." Four years later, an abolitionist convention declared: "We must bring back the lost rights of the citizen, under the Constitution, to equal protection and privileges in every state." Key figures in the draft-ing of the Reconstruction amendments—including Henry Wilson of Massachusetts, Thaddeus Stevens of Pennsylvania, and James Ashley and John A. Bingham of Ohio—were veterans of antislavery politics and of prewar struggles for the citizenship rights of free blacks. They and others carried ideas honed in the antislavery movement into the process of rewriting the Constitution after the Civil War.[17]

Most insistent in promoting egalitarian constitutionalism were free blacks, whose newspapers, orations, and state and national Colored Conventions advanced claims to full equality in the land of their birth. The rise of the American Colonization Society intensified black claims to equal citizenship. Founded in 1816, the society advo-cated the removal from the country of blacks already free, although many members advocated a long-term goal of ending slavery and expelling the entire black population to Africa or the Caribbean. The idea won the support of numerous political leaders, including Henry Clay, Andrew Jackson, Chief Justice Roger B. Taney, and, for a time, Abraham Lincoln, not to mention surviving founders of the nation including Thomas Jefferson and James Madison. While a few black leaders, including John Russwurm, the editor of *Freedom's Journal*, the nation's first black-owned newspaper, embraced colonization, most redoubled their efforts to gain recognition as citizens with the same right to remain in the land of their birth as white Americans. William Lloyd Garrison's forthright condemnation of colonization was one reason for the high regard in which he was held by free black communities. "This Country is Our Only Home," declared an edito-rial in the *Colored American* in 1840. "It is our duty and privilege to claim an equal place among the *American* people." During the decades before the Civil War, black conventions, which commonly described themselves as gatherings of "colored citizens," condemned coloniza-tion and promoted the principle of "birthright citizenship" (language used by the black abolitionist Martin R. Delany in 1852). "Nothing could be plainer," insisted the National Convention of Colored Citizens in 1843, "than that native free born men must be citizens."

Free blacks seized upon the Constitution's requirement that the president be a "natural born Citizen" to argue that American citizenship derived from place of birth, not ancestry or race.[18]

Equality—expressed in such language as equal liberty, equal justice, equal rights, and equal citizenship—was the hallmark of antebellum black politics. Moving well beyond the meticulously parsed distinction between natural, civil, political, and social rights, black leaders insistently claimed them all as "immunities" of American citizenship. They disassembled the fraught category of "social rights" into private and intimate personal relations, a matter of individual choice, not law, and a new category, "public rights," which encompassed equal access to businesses serving the public such as hotels, theaters, streetcars, steamships, and railroads. Throughout the country, these businesses regularly excluded blacks. Though flagrantly violated by states such as Indiana, Illinois, and Oregon, which barred black persons from entering their territory, free blacks insisted that mobility was a key element of citizenship. Free blacks and their white allies used a variety of tactics to press for citizenship rights. They launched campaigns for the vote, sued streetcar companies that excluded black passengers, and challenged discriminatory laws in local, state, and federal courts. Their efforts usually failed, but they did win a few victories, such as the repeal of Ohio's discriminatory Black Laws in 1849 and the racial integration of Boston's public schools in 1855. These pre–Civil War campaigns helped to establish a discourse of rights that would flourish in Reconstruction. They form an essential part of the background to the second founding.[19]

Before the Civil War, black spokesmen, like abolitionists more generally, tended to ground their claims in the preamble of the Declaration of Independence rather than the Constitution. As early as the era of the Revolution, slaves petitioning for freedom cited the Declaration's words about liberty and equality, seeing the document as a charter of individual rights rather than an assertion of national sovereignty. "The colored people," the Rev. James Hood, a North Carolina political leader, would declare during Reconstruction, "had read the declaration until it had become part of their natures." But some also claimed the Constitution, despite its protections for slavery, as their own. "As Americans," insisted the president of the Indiana black convention of 1851, "we are entitled to all the rights, privileges, and immunities of citizenship, ... according to the letter and spirit of the Constitution."[20]

Generally speaking, antebellum judges did not agree. Relatively few cases related to slavery and the rights of individual citizens came before the federal courts in the years from independence to the Civil War. Most such issues were settled at the local and state levels. When the Supreme Court did deal with slavery, however, its rulings nearly always sided with the institution. On the eve of the war, in the infamous *Dred Scott* decision, Chief Justice Roger B. Taney declared that the Constitution "expressly" protected the right of property in slaves and that no black person could be a citizen of the United States or part of the national "political community." Blacks, Taney insisted, were permanent aliens. States could make free blacks citizens if they wished, but neither the federal government nor other states must recognize that status (in other words, the Comity Clause did not apply to them). Ironically, one reason for Taney's ruling was his expansive understanding of what citizenship entailed. Being a citizen, he declared, meant freedom from legal discrimination and full enjoyment of the rights specified in the Constitution, among them the ability to travel anywhere in the country and the right "to keep and carry arms wherever they went." These were not rights that he thought black people, free or slave, ought to enjoy.[21]

The *Dred Scott* decision caused a furor in the North and put the question of black citizenship on the national political agenda. James McCune Smith, a black physician, author, and antislavery activist, carefully dissected Taney's reasoning, citing legal precedents going back to "the annals of lofty Rome" to demonstrate that all free persons born in the United States, black as well as white, "must be citizens." Many Republicans also rejected Taney's reasoning. In a stinging dissent, Justice John McLean of Ohio insisted that regardless of race, "birth on the soil of a country both creates the duties and confers the rights of citizenship." His state's legislature adopted a resolution declaring that "every free person, born within the limits of any state of this Union, is a citizen thereof." During the Civil War and Reconstruction, Republicans would take steps toward recognizing the citizenship of free blacks. Their actions would powerfully affect the rights of all Americans.[22]

The Civil War greatly enhanced the power of the national government, imposed unprecedented demands (especially conscription) upon Americans, and led Congress to enact measures previously beyond the scope of federal authority, including laws relating to banking, currency, and taxation. Among Republicans, the war severely weakened belief in state sovereignty. "There is and can be . . . only one paramount sovereign authority," declared the governor of Michigan in 1864. More than any other single act, emancipation announced the existence of a new kind of national state, one capable of abolishing the largest concentration of property in the country (slaves as property were worth nearly four billion 1860 dollars), and identified that state with the expansion of freedom and human rights. Even before Lincoln issued the Emancipation Proclamation, abolitionists insisted that the war should produce a new nation, "with one law impartial over all." As the federal government committed itself to the destruction of slavery and began enlisting black men into the Union army, the question of the postwar status of African-Americans inevitably moved to the center of political debate. "Everything among us," wrote a black Californian, "indicates a change in our condition. . . . Our relation to this government is changing daily. . . . The revolution has begun, and time alone must decide where it is to end."[23]

Late in 1862, Salmon P. Chase, now serving as Lincoln's secretary of the Treasury, requested an opinion from Attorney General Edward Bates as to whether free black men were authorized to pilot ships on coastal waterways. The answer hinged on whether such men were American citizens. Previous attorneys general, including Taney himself, had ruled in the negative. But Bates, audaciously declaring that *Dred Scott* had been wrongly decided, affirmed the citizenship of all free persons born in the United States, regardless of race. Bates added, however, that "eighty years of practical enjoyment of citizenship, under the constitution" had failed to clarify "the exact meaning of the word, or [its] constituent elements." Other than piloting vessels, he declined to specify the rights that came with citizenship. He did note that the status was compatible with legal "degradation," citing the example of female citizens excluded from voting.[24]

For Bates, citizenship was essentially a symbolic category, not a guarantee of specific rights. But African-Americans and their allies, drawing on prewar campaigns for equality and now invoking blacks' wartime loyalty to the nation and service in the Union army, seized the opportunity to press demands for recognition as American citizens and an expansive definition of citizens' rights. As a member of one of the first black units, the famed 54th Massachusetts regiment, wrote in 1864, "if we fight to maintain a republican government, we want republican privileges. . . . All we ask is the proper enjoyment of the rights of citizenship." Another black soldier declared that he and his companions were fighting for "the exercise of our political, free, civil and public rights" (although he hastened to add that this did not mean that "the black man's son should marry the white man's daughter"). Demands for political and civil equality by the free black community of New Orleans gained a sympathetic hearing among Radical Republicans in Congress and influenced Lincoln's decision to call for partial black voting rights in his last speech, in April 1865. During the war Congress for the first time required the desegregation of public transportation in the nation's capital, repealed the ban on black testimony in federal courts, and mandated that black and white soldiers receive equal pay.[25]

"We are slowly approaching a clearer understanding of . . . the rights of persons," one member of Congress proclaimed in 1869 during debates on the Fifteenth Amendment. During Reconstruction the language of rights suffused political debates—people spoke of the rights of citizens, fundamental rights, the rights of free men, women's rights, the rights of free labor. Moreover, while the Fifteenth Amendment connects the right to vote directly to citizenship, the Thirteenth and Fourteenth reflect a growing commitment to the idea that some rights transcend national identity. After the Thirteenth, no one in the United States, regardless of his or her citizenship status, could be held as a slave. The crucial first section of the Fourteenth extends the enjoyment of life, liberty, and property and the equal protection of the law to all "persons," citizen or alien. At the same time, the deeply ingrained distinction between various categories of rights began to break down. In a letter to the British reformer John Bright in 1867, Charles Sumner, perhaps the most principled egalitarian in Congress, explained how his thinking had evolved: "For a long time I was perplexed by the subtlety so often presented, that the suffrage is a 'privilege' and not a 'right,' and being a 'privilege,' it was subject to such limitations as the policy or good will of the legislature chose to impose. The more I think of it, the more it seems to me an essential right." But it was not only the radical Sumner whose concept of rights expanded during Reconstruction. The Civil War crystallized in the minds of northerners the idea of a powerful national state protecting the rights of citizens. The second founding not only put abolition, equal rights, and black male suffrage into the Constitution, but in its provisions for national enforcement made the federal government for the first time what Sumner called "the custodian of freedom."[26]

❧

THE SECOND FOUNDING began during the Civil War with congressional passage of the Thirteenth Amendment. But the very progress of wartime abolition underscored the challenges that lay ahead. As evidenced by the New York City Draft Riots of 1863, when blacks were murdered on the streets of the nation's largest city, racism remained deeply entrenched in the North as well as the South. After Frederick Douglass delivered his impassioned "Mission of the War" speech at Cooper Union in February 1864, calling for the abolition of slavery to be accompanied by full equality before the law and suffrage for black men, the *New York Times* (edited by Henry J. Raymond, the head of the Republican National Committee) published a letter insisting that

Douglass's demand to "place the slaves of the South on an immediate civil equality with the white citizens of the country, ought not and will not be gratified." The city's *Journal of Commerce*, which spoke for New York merchants far more interested in a rapid revival of the plantation economy than in elevating blacks' condition beyond ending slavery, declared Douglass's idea the "road to ruin."[27]

When the war ended, blacks remained on the margins of northern society, deprived almost everywhere of the right to vote, and largely relegated to low-wage unskilled labor. Moreover, during the war new governments in a number of slave states abolished slavery but gave little thought to the freed people's rights and prospects. Conventions that drafted new constitutions for Louisiana and Maryland offered almost nothing to blacks beyond abolition, and delegates strenuously denied "any sympathy with Negro equality." Their actions reinforced a growing conviction in the Republican North that the protection of citizens' rights could not be left in the hands of the states.[28]

Given the persistence of racism and respect for the traditional authority of the state and local governments, not to mention the numerical obstacles to ratification, amending the Constitution posed a daunting challenge. So did the reverence with which most Americans viewed the document. Long before the Civil War, a "cult of the founders" had become embedded in American culture. Tom Paine called the Constitution America's "political bible." The fact is, however, that the framers did not foresee a situation in which eleven states waged war against the nation. Nor does the Constitution specify how states that claim to have seceded should be reincorporated into the Union, or what would happen in peacetime to actions (such as emancipation) undertaken as war measures. During the conflict, Lincoln felt obligated to stretch constitutional authority to its limits and beyond. He raised money and troops without congressional authorization, suspended the writ of habeas corpus, and, in the Emancipation Proclamation, drew on a vaguely defined "military necessity" to liberate, without compensation to the owners, over three million slaves. "The whole rebellion is beyond the Constitution," wrote the political scientist Francis Lieber in 1864.

But rather than concluding that a document that had palpably failed ought to be replaced, most Americans sought to square policy initiatives with the Constitution either by reinterpreting or rewriting it.[29]

Some Radicals insisted that Congress could take all necessary actions without going through the arduous amendment process. Thaddeus Stevens claimed that the southern states had, in fact, left the Union; they were conquered provinces, with no surviving constitutional rights. Sumner maintained that the Declaration of Independence ought to enjoy equal legal standing with the Constitution; as a result, "anything for human rights is constitutional." The Radicals, commented Gideon Welles, who served as secretary of the navy under Lincoln and his successor, Andrew Johnson, were "humanitarians and not constitutionalists." The legalistic Welles did not mean this as a compliment.[30]

Yet what is striking is the enduring power of constitutionalism itself—the widespread desire to find a secure constitutional basis for public policy. The Reconstruction journalist E. L. Godkin (who like Paine came to the United States from Great Britain, which lacks a written constitution) derided what he called Americans' "Constitution-worship."[31] Godkin believed that excessive regard for a document nearly a century old formed a serious obstacle to creative thinking in an unprecedented crisis. Yet that very adulation underscored the importance of the second founding. Writing changes into the Constitution automatically gives them a powerful claim not only on the legal system but also on the public imagination, which is why the Reconstruction amendments provoked widespread debate and violent opposition.

The second founding took place in response to rapidly changing political and social imperatives at a moment when definitions of citizenship, rights, and sovereignty were in flux. The amendments were accompanied by unprecedented legislation to define and secure Americans' civil, political, and public rights. "These are no times of ordinary politics," the abolitionist Wendell Phillips wrote to Sumner in 1866, urging him to remain steadfast in support of black suffrage, despite defeats. "They are formative hours; the national purpose grows and ripens in thirty days as much as ordinary years bring it forward. . . . You can afford to wait that verdict."[32]

As Phillips predicted, the amendments, and the legislation implementing them, went far beyond what most white Americans had thought possible or desirable in 1865. People who entered the Civil War as moderates emerged committed to remaking the South's political, economic, and social system. Opponents of black suffrage in 1865 came to support it a few years later. Those who rejected federal prohibition of discrimination by private businesses at the outset of Reconstruction voted for the Civil Rights Act of 1875, which did precisely that. Some Republicans came to insist that access to education was as fundamental to citizenship as other rights. The second founding can only be understood as part of a much longer debate about rights, democracy, and equality, one that continues to this day.

1

WHAT IS FREEDOM?

The Thirteenth Amendment

I N HIS second inaugural address, delivered on March 4, 1865, as
the Civil War drew to a close, Abraham Lincoln described the
destruction of American slavery as "astounding." Lincoln, who
always chose his language carefully, was justified in using so dramatic
and uncommon a word (it appears only three other times in his entire
Collected Works). To be sure, in retrospect the abolition of slavery
seems inevitable, a preordained result of the evolution of American
society or, in some tellings, a logical outgrowth of the ideals of the
American Revolution. Yet it is important to remember that despite
decades of antislavery agitation there were more slaves in the United
States when the war began than at any point in the nation's history.
Slaveholders and their allies had controlled the federal government
for nearly the entire period since the founding of the republic. In
1858, the *Chicago Tribune*, a major journalistic voice of antislavery
sentiment, flatly declared that "no man living" would see the end of
American slavery.[1]

Yet abolition did come. Like all great historical transformations, it
was a process, not a single event. It played out over time, arose from
many causes, and was the work of many individuals. It began at the

war's outset when slaves, eager to seize the opportunity presented by the presence of northern armies and ignoring Lincoln's insistence that the struggle was solely about national unity, began to seek refuge behind Union lines. The Emancipation Proclamation, issued on January 1, 1863, which made the destruction of slavery an objective of the Union war effort, was the crucial step in the process, but by itself did not abolish slavery. As the *New York Times* noted, while the proclamation "set free" all the slaves in areas to which it applied, many were not in fact "made free." That could only be accomplished by the presence of the Union army. On April 9, 1865, when Robert E. Lee surrendered at Appomattox Court House, the majority of the slaves were still being held in bondage. The final, irrevocable abolition of slavery throughout the reunited nation did not come until December 1865, with the ratification of the Thirteenth Amendment. Without the amendment, slavery might well have lingered for years in some parts of the United States.[2]

As early as 1827, *Freedom's Journal* had called for an amendment abolishing slavery. But the path to abolition by constitutional amendment was neither smooth nor predictable. Changing the Constitution is a complex, cumbersome process. It had last been accomplished in 1804. Roughly 150 amendments to resolve the secession crisis were proposed during the winter of 1860–61. One, known as the Corwin Amendment after the Ohio political leader Thomas Corwin, would have prohibited future federal interference with slavery in the states. Intended to stave off the secession of the Upper South, this proposed Thirteenth Amendment won congressional approval on the morning of Lincoln's inauguration and was mentioned favorably by the president in his address later that day. But with the outbreak of war it became moot. When Lincoln assumed office, the institution existed in fifteen of the thirty-four states, so if one assumed that approval by three-quarters of all the states, including the eleven that eventually became the Confederacy, was needed for ratification, abolishing slavery by constitutional amendment was clearly impossible.[3]

"I have always hated slavery, as much as any abolitionist," Lincoln declared in 1858. But Lincoln was not an abolitionist, and never claimed to be one. He did not share the abolitionists' commitment to ending slavery immediately nor their belief that free blacks and emancipated slaves should become equal members of American society. Nonetheless, in the 1850s Lincoln emerged as a major spokesman for the newly created Republican party, committed to halting the westward expansion of slavery. In speeches of eloquence and power, he condemned slavery as a fundamental violation of the nation's founding principles as enunciated in the Declaration of Independence. Yet Lincoln was also a lawyer, a politician, and a constitutionalist. He believed that the North must abide by provisions of the Constitution that protected slavery, including distasteful ones such as the Fugitive Slave Clause, lest the entire edifice fall.[4]

Lincoln, however, did speak of a future without slavery. The aim of the Republican party, he insisted, was to put the institution on the road to "ultimate extinction," a phrase he borrowed from his political idol Henry Clay. Ultimate extinction could take a long time: Lincoln once said that slavery might survive for another hundred years. But to the South, Lincoln seemed as dangerous as an abolitionist, because he was committed to the eventual end of slavery. His election provided the catalyst for secession, civil war, and, eventually, abolition.[5]

Slavery can be abolished in a number of ways. One is individual manumission, some of which occurred in the United States but not nearly enough to threaten the system's viability. Manumission frees slaves but unless it applies to all does not abolish the institution of slavery. Second is emancipation by legal means. Even without the Corwin Amendment, the Constitution was almost universally understood to bar national interference with slavery in the states. But slavery is created by state law and the law can be changed, as happened in the northern states after the American Revolution. Legal emancipation is feasible in "societies with slaves," to borrow the formulation of historian Ira Berlin (and before him, Moses I. Finley), where slavery is one element of the social and economic order, not its foundation, and owners lack the political power to prevent the passage of abolition laws. In "slave societies," where slavery is central to the economy and slaveowners therefore more powerful, "the persons who make all the laws . . . ," as Adam Smith put it, "are persons who have slaves themselves." The Old South was the largest, most powerful slave society in modern history. Lincoln long believed that abolition there could only be accomplished with the cooperation of owners. To secure this, Lincoln advocated a program of gradual emancipation coupled with monetary compensation for the loss of property in slaves and "colonization"—encouraging blacks to emigrate to Africa, Haiti, or Central America—since slaveholders would never consent to the creation of a vast new population of free African-Americans.[6]

A third mode of attacking slavery is military emancipation. War destabilizes; it strips away constitutional protections. Contending sides make slavery a military target to weaken their opponents. They urge slaves of the enemy to run away and to enlist as soldiers, usually promising them freedom. This happened many times in wars in the Western Hemisphere. During the American Revolution and the War of 1812, for instance, thousands of slaves gained their freedom by escaping to British lines. But these events, while freeing many slaves, did not destroy slavery, which survived and expanded in the early republic. Moreover, slaves freed through military action sometimes suffered reenslavement when the fortunes of war shifted. This happened to some slaves in the aftermath of the Haitian Revolution, and later in the United States when Confederate forces drove Union soldiers from areas containing newly liberated men, women, and children.[7] Military emancipation freed numerous slaves during the Civil War. But it eventually required a constitutional amendment—a form of legal emancipation—to destroy the system for good. War did break the power of slaveholders, so that they were unable to block ratification.

For most of the Civil War, a constitutional amendment was not the most widely preferred route to abolition. The war, of course, did not begin as a crusade to abolish slavery. Almost from the beginning, however, abolitionists and Radical Republicans pressed for action against the institution as a war measure, and slaves began escaping to Union lines. Faced with this pressure, Lincoln put forward his own ideas. He began by returning to the plan of gradual, compensated emancipation coupled with colonization—a plan that would make slaveowners partners in abolition. He proposed this in November 1861, only a few months into the war, to political leaders in Delaware, and the following spring pressed it on Congress and the other border slave states (Maryland, Kentucky, and Missouri) that remained in the Union. The plan envisioned abolition by the states, with federal funding. The border states, intent on retaining slavery, were not interested. Lincoln's plan also failed to win support among African-Americans. Very few were willing to leave the land of their birth, which rendered colonization impossible as Lincoln always insisted it must be voluntary. Meanwhile, military emancipation and emancipation by statute proceeded. By 1862 the army was no longer returning fugitive slaves to their owners. With the South no longer represented, Congress freed all slaves who came within Union lines. It also abolished slavery in Washington, D.C., and the nation's western territories. These measures freed many slaves, but did not abolish the institution of slavery.[8]

A powerful combination of events moved Lincoln to adopt a new policy toward slavery. They included the congressional enactments of 1862; the failure of conventional military strategy to win the war; the desire to forestall European intervention; the need to enlist black soldiers; and the growing numbers of slaves escaping to Union lines. In September 1862, in the Preliminary Emancipation Proclamation, Lincoln announced his change in policy. This was, in effect, a warning to Confederates that if they did not lay down their arms, Lincoln would decree emancipation. Yet that December, in his annual message to Congress, he again presented his old plan for state-by-state abolition. He asked for changes in the Constitution, not to abolish slavery immediately but to authorize the appropriation of funds for any state that provided for abolition by the year 1900. The money would help compensate the former owners and colonize the emancipated slaves outside the country. It was a final offer of abolition with the cooperation of slaveowners. Neither Congress, the border states, nor the Confederacy paid any attention to these proposals.[9]

With the Emancipation Proclamation, national policy toward slavery changed dramatically. The proclamation was an act of military emancipation, grounded in Lincoln's constitutional authority as commander in chief. Despite popular legend, Lincoln did not free four million slaves with a stroke of his pen. The proclamation had no bearing on the slaves in the border states (which now numbered five after the admission of West Virginia). Since they were not at war with the Union, "military necessity" did not apply to them. Lincoln also exempted certain areas of the Confederacy that had fallen under Union military control, including parts of Virginia and Louisiana and the entire state of Tennessee. (This last exemption was made for political, not military or constitutional, reasons, at the request of military governor Andrew Johnson, to attract the support of slaveholders for the regime he headed. It required a vivid imagination to believe that all of Tennessee was in Union hands.) All told, perhaps 800,000 of the nearly four million slaves were not covered by the proclamation. But 3.1 million were. Despite its limitations, this was the largest act of slave emancipation in world history. Never before had so many slaves been declared free on a single day.

The proclamation did not immediately end slavery but it sounded the institution's death knell—assuming that the Union won the war. (Had the Confederacy emerged victorious, slavery would undoubtedly have lasted for a long time.) Why, then, was the Thirteenth Amendment necessary? As a presidential decree, the proclamation could presumably be reversed by another president. Even apart from its exemptions, moreover, the proclamation emancipated people; it did not abolish the legal status of slave, or the state laws establishing slavery. Emancipation, in other words, is not quite the same thing as abolition. Something more would be necessary to rid the country entirely of slavery. As Frederick Douglass put it, in calling for a constitutional amendment, the proclamation was "a vast and glorious step in the right direction. But unhappily, excellent as that paper is, it settles nothing. It is still open to decision by courts, canons, and Congresses."[10]

Nonetheless, the Emancipation Proclamation was a dramatic departure from Lincoln's previous statements and policies regarding slavery. It was immediate, not gradual, contained no mention of compensation for slaveowners, and made no reference to colonization. Since emancipation no longer required the consent of slaveholders, these inducements were now irrelevant. Also, the proclamation authorized the enrollment of black soldiers into the armed forces, setting in motion the process by which 200,000 black men served in the Union army and navy. They played a critical role in achieving Union victory and staking a claim to citizenship in the postwar world. Putting black men in the armed forces suggested a different racial future than encouraging them to leave the country. The proclamation, in other words, placed on the national agenda the question of the civil and political status of the emancipated slaves.[11]

Overall, by making the destruction of slavery an objective of the Union army, the Emancipation Proclamation fundamentally altered the character of the Civil War. But it did not mean the end of Lincoln's quest for state-by-state abolition. Military and legal emancipation now proceeded together. As the army occupied territory and freed slaves, Lincoln redoubled his efforts to create Unionist state governments in portions of the South, partly as a war measure, since detaching states from the Confederacy would be a powerful aid to the Union cause, but also so that these governments could rid their states of the laws that established slavery. Lincoln's Proclamation of Amnesty and Reconstruction, issued in December 1863, envisioned abolition by state action. It required southern states that desired readmission to the Union to adopt new constitutions abolishing slavery.

Despite the Emancipation Proclamation's unequivocal language stating that the slaves affected "are and henceforward shall be free," Lincoln seemed to assume that the only slaves truly emancipated were those who physically came within Union lines. This is why in August 1864, when he believed he would not win reelection, Lincoln urged

Frederick Douglass to organize a group of "scouts" who would venture behind enemy lines and encourage slaves to run off to the Union army. Moreover, Lincoln feared that the proclamation's constitutionality might be called into question after the war ended. Indeed, his proposed amnesty oath for Confederates who wished to return to loyalty to the Union required support of congressional acts and presidential proclamations relating to slavery, unless "modified or declared void by decision of the Supreme Court." The Supreme Court still had a Democratic majority and until his death late in 1864, Roger B. Taney, of what one Republican newspaper called "Dred Scott infamy," remained chief justice. Litigation challenging the proclamation was inevitable and could certainly cause problems for federal policy makers after the war ended.[12]

◦◦◦

ALL THESE CONSIDERATIONS led to an increase in support for a constitutional amendment abolishing slavery. As soon as the Thirty-eighth Congress convened in December 1863, plans for amending the Constitution began to circulate. Representative James M. Ashley, a longtime activist in the antislavery movement in Ohio, introduced the first such proposal on December 14. Francis Lieber, a professor at Columbia University and one of the nation's leading political scientists, composed a set of no fewer than seven amendments. In keeping with Lieber's intense nationalism, the first four had to do with the primacy of the national government and the punishment of treason. Not until his proposed Seventeenth Amendment did Lieber get around to "slavery shall be forever abolished." His Eighteenth established the principles of birthright citizenship and equality before the law regardless of race. Widely circulated in pamphlet form by the Loyal Publication Society, Lieber's proposals seem to have influenced discussions of both the Thirteenth and Fourteenth amendments.[13]

Meanwhile, abolitionists launched a "fresh moral agitation" toward the goal of an amendment abolishing slavery. The campaign was coordinated by the Women's Loyal National League, founded in 1863. For the time being women activists suspended the movement for woman suffrage to press for an end to slavery, the route, they believed, to blacks and white women obtaining their "rights and privileges as free and equal citizens of a common republic." By early 1864, some two thousand men, women, and children were at work circulating petitions. Initially, they called for Congress to legislate complete abolition, something most members believed was beyond their constitutional authority. Subsequent iterations, at the suggestion of William Lloyd Garrison, "added the Constitutional amendment to their prayer."[14]

In February 1864, two tall black men carried a "monster" petition with 100,000 signatures onto the Senate floor and deposited it on Charles Sumner's desk. Sumner thereupon introduced an amendment based on the 1791 French Declaration of the Rights of Man and of the Citizen: "Everywhere within the limits of the United States, . . . all persons are equal before the law, so that no person can hold another as a slave." The proposal went on to give Congress the power to "make all laws" necessary to carry the prohibition into effect. Abolitionists and Radical Republicans such as Sumner were already looking beyond the end of slavery to purging the statute book of racially biased discriminatory laws. Wendell Phillips, for example, called for two amendments, one abolishing slavery and another barring any state from making "any distinction among its citizens on account of race and color." Later that spring, Sumner again urged his colleagues to incorporate "the equality of all persons before the law" into the Thirteenth Amendment. "The language may be new in our country," he acknowledged, "but it is already well known in history." This led him to deliver a history lesson about the French Revolution—a typical Sumner speech that annoyed many of his Senate colleagues.[15]

The final wording, modeled on the Northwest Ordinance, of 1787, which prohibited slavery in the territories north of the Ohio River, was hammered out in the Senate Judiciary Committee, headed by Senator Lyman Trumbull of Illinois: "Neither slavery nor involuntary servitude, except as a punishment for crime whereof the party shall have been duly convicted, shall exist within the United States, or any place subject to their jurisdiction." Thus, in the act of abolition, the amendment for the first time introduced the word "slavery" into the Constitution. Trumbull also incorporated a second clause drawing on language proposed by Sumner and by Congressman James F. Wilson of Iowa: "Congress shall have power to enforce this article by appropriate legislation." This wording was influenced by John Marshall's famous decision in *McCulloch v. Maryland*, which upheld the power of Congress to pursue constitutional ends by "all means which are appropriate." [16]

When he presented the amendment to the Senate, Trumbull pointed out that while various acts of Congress and the Emancipation Proclamation had freed many slaves, they had not destroyed slavery's legal foundations. Trumbull rejected the idea, espoused by Sumner and other Radicals, that the war power itself, or the Constitution's clause guaranteeing to each state a republican form of government, gave Congress the power to abolish slavery by statute and that it should do so immediately rather than going through the cumbersome amendment process. "I am as anxious to get rid of slavery as any person," Trumbull declared, but "it has been an admitted axiom from the foundation of this government, among all parties, that Congress had no authority to interfere with slavery in the states where it existed." He also rejected the idea of seeking "the proper words for a constitution" in the French experience: "We all know that their constitutions were failures." Senator Jacob Howard of Michigan also urged Sumner to "dismiss all reference to French constitutions or French codes, and go back to . . . good old Anglo-Saxon language employed by our fathers in the ordinance of 1787." The wording of the Northwest Ordinance, he added, was familiar and "well understood" by the people of the United States. It was particularly appealing to Republicans because during the 1850s they had frequently cited the ordinance's prohibition of slavery in the Old Northwest as evidence of the founders' supposed hostility to slavery. [17]

Not all Republicans initially supported the proposed amendment. Some, including Lincoln himself, preferred abolition to take place through action by the states. But the party soon rallied around the Thirteenth Amendment. Much of the congressional discussion covered familiar ground. Slavery, nearly all Republicans believed, had caused the war; it was responsible, said Senator Henry Wilson, for "every dollar sacrificed, for every drop of blood shed." It not only violated the fundamental rights of its victims, but put the liberties of whites in jeopardy. Abolition would ensure that the sectional conflict that had dogged the nation since its founding would not reemerge after the end of the war. The amendment would destroy the Slave Power that had so often shaped national policy. One element, however, was new, reflecting the ideological changes unleashed by the war. Republicans condemned slavery not simply as a violation of basic human rights but as an affront to the nation. "The defiant pretensions of the master, claiming control of his slave," declared Sumner, "are in direct conflict with the paramount rights of the national government."[18]

The amendment's second section, granting enforcement power to Congress, embodied this new sense of national empowerment. It was "not less significant," the *New York Herald* observed, than the section abolishing slavery. "These words," the paper continued, "record in the Constitution the results of a great war. . . . They are the constitutional guarantee that Congress shall have the power to arrange the new conditions of society in the South, especially so far as it relates to the condition of the Negro race." Traditionally, the federal government had been seen as the greatest threat to individual liberty. But, as the *Chicago Tribune* observed, "events have proved that the danger to . . . freedom is from the states, not the federal government." The second clause gave Congress seemingly unlimited authority to prevent actions by states, localities, businesses, and private individuals that sought to maintain or restore slavery.[19]

The Fourteenth Amendment has often been viewed as instituting a dramatic change in the federal system and a substantial enhancement of the authority of the central government. But it was the Thirteenth, the first amendment in the nation's history to expand the power of the federal government rather than restraining it, that initiated this redefinition of federalism.[20] No one in 1864, of course, anticipated the future—Lincoln's death, the conflict with Andrew Johnson, white southern intransigence after the war's end, national civil rights legislation, and further changes to the Constitution to protect the basic rights of the freed people. But the second clause certainly envisioned future action to secure the end of slavery and the advent of freedom, however those goals were defined. "By this amendment," James G. Blaine would later write, "the relation between the national and state governments, respecting the question of human liberty, was radically changed. . . . Freedom of the person became henceforth a matter of national concern."[21]

Like the Emancipation Proclamation, the amendment was immediate, not gradual, provided no monetary compensation for the abrogation of property in slaves, and said nothing about colonizing the former slaves outside the country. (Indeed, to the extent that it guaranteed to the former slaves the basic rights of free Americans, it could be viewed as prohibiting their involuntary colonization outside the United States.) Unlike the proclamation, it applied to the entire country and for the first time made the abolition of slavery an essential part of the nation's legal order. Few countries, and certainly none with as large a slave population, have experienced so radical a form of abolition. The original Constitution had specified only three things neither the state nor federal governments could do—grant titles of nobility, pass bills of attainder, and enforce ex post facto laws. The Thirteenth Amendment added a fourth—allow the existence of slavery. The amendment created a new fundamental right to personal freedom, applicable to all persons in the United States regardless of race, gender, class, or citizenship status.[22]

Given that the irrevocable abolition of slavery appears in retrospect an unavoidable consequence of the Civil War, the depth and rancor of Democratic opposition to the amendment may seem surprising. Early in 1864, it appeared that the amendment might garner some support from northern Democrats anxious to sever their party from association with slavery. But as election-year politics moved to the fore, Democratic support waned. With the South unrepresented in Congress, few members directly defended slavery. Instead, the party's congressmen fell back on familiar arguments against abolition, notably the alleged incapacity of blacks. "The wooly-headed Negro," declared Senator Lazarus Powell of Kentucky, was "an inferior man . . . and no fanaticism can raise him to the level of the Caucasian race." Some Democrats warned that future congresses would wield the "revolutionary power" of Section 2 to force black citizenship, black suffrage, racial "amalgamation," and black land ownership upon the states. Others claimed that abolition threatened private property in general. If the Constitution could be amended to abolish one form of property without monetary compensation, why not others? In the future, asked Senator Willard Saulsbury of Delaware, would Congress confiscate the factories of New England? Fernando Wood, the former mayor of New York City now a member of the House of Representatives, painted a lurid picture of the amendment's consequences: "It involves the extermination of the white men of the southern States, and the forfeiture of all the land and other property belonging to them."[23]

Much of the debate focused on the scope of congressional power. In both houses of Congress, Democrats saw the amendment as overturning essential principles that had governed the nation since its founding and had made the Constitution's ratification possible in the first place. They condemned it as a revolution in federal-state relations, which violated the original understanding that states should decide for themselves whether or not to establish slavery. Indeed, even though the Constitution provides for its own alteration, some opponents condemned the Thirteenth Amendment as unconstitutional. The issue, declared Anton Herrick of New York, was not slavery but "the right of the states to control their domestic affairs." "Give up our right to have slavery," proclaimed Robert Mallory of Kentucky, "and in what rights are we secure? One after another will be usurped . . . until all state rights will be gone" and the white population reduced to "abject submission and slavery." "It strikes at the root of all state institutions," declared Samuel J. Randall of Pennsylvania. Democrats still spoke of restoring the Union "as it was"—that is, with slavery intact.[24]

On April 8, 1864, the Senate approved the Thirteenth Amendment by a vote of thirty-three to six. The four senators from the border slave states of Kentucky and Delaware voted against it, as did two northern Democrats. But three Democrats from the North, along with five Unionists and Republicans from the border, cast votes in favor. Because the amendment envisioned immediate, nationwide abolition, the *New York Herald* called the vote a rebuke to Lincoln's preference for a state-by-state approach, a declaration by Congress that "his petty tinkering devices of emancipation will not answer." The *Herald*'s mercurial editor James Gordon Bennett, who had earlier strongly criticized the Republican Congress, now supported passage as "the only way in which this slavery question may be decisively and firmly settled by universal emancipation," although, he added, "our amiable president, in his rustic simplicity, may still imagine that his way is better." But in June, in a vote almost entirely along party lines, the amendment mustered only ninety-three votes in the House, thirteen short of the necessary two-thirds majority.[25]

As these events unfolded, Lincoln remained noncommittal. Shortly before the president sent his annual message to Congress in December 1863, Congressman Isaac N. Arnold of Illinois had urged him to include a recommendation for a change in the Constitution to rid the nation of slavery. Lincoln chose not to do so. What finally moved him to a public embrace of the amendment was the nomination of John C. Frémont for president in late May 1864 by a convention in Cleveland that brought together critics of the administration from the left, including Radical Republicans, abolitionists, and a smattering of Democrats. Their platform called for a constitutional amendment not only abolishing slavery but also establishing "absolute equality before the law" (although it avoided taking a position on black suffrage). As part of his response, Lincoln directed Edwin D. Morgan to make the pending Thirteenth Amendment the "key note" of his speech opening the party's national convention, which assembled in July in Baltimore. The Republican platform demanded the "utter and complete extirpation" of slavery via constitutional amendment. It said nothing about equality before the law—"Baltimore has not dared to rise to the level of Cleveland," Wendell Phillips complained. The *New York Times*, which in February had condemned "hot-headed men" for pressing an amendment it deemed premature, now rejoiced that "the logic of the war itself, silent but irresistible," had turned public sentiment in favor of complete abolition.[26]

During the campaign of 1864 some Republicans saw the Thirteenth Amendment as a winning issue, insisting that abolition was necessary to win the war and prevent another one, but others shied away from it, fearing that it might "frighten some voters" otherwise inclined to support the president. In the aftermath of his reelection, however, Lincoln declared that "the voice of the people" had been heard and called on the House to vote again on the amendment. Lincoln threw his support to the effort to secure passage, intervening more directly in the legislative process than at any other point in his presidency. He pressured border Unionists and lame-duck Democrats, most of whom had opposed the amendment in June, to change their votes. Lincoln also authorized Speaker of the House Schuyler Colfax to announce that if the amendment failed again, a special session of the next Congress would be called in March, as soon as the current one expired. The newly elected Thirty-ninth Congress had an expanded Republican majority, enough to ensure approval.[27]

The result hung in the balance until the very end. On January 12, 1865, the Washington correspondent of the *New York Times* reported that there was "no hope" of the amendment passing in the House. Nonetheless, a little over two weeks later, on January 31, the House approved the Thirteenth Amendment by a vote of 119–56, slightly more than the required two-thirds majority. Every Republican voted in favor, along with sixteen Democrats, all but two of them lame ducks who had been defeated in the recent election or had chosen not to run. During these debates, border congressmen who had previously opposed passage explained their change of heart. The conduct of blacks during the war, including their military service, said John A. Creswell of Maryland, had disproved the idea that "the Negro race" was unfit for freedom. James S. Rollins of Missouri, who described himself as once "a large owner of slaves," declared, "we can never have an entire peace in this country as long as the institution of slavery remains." The five border states produced nineteen votes for the amendment and only eight against. Ratification, of course, still lay in the future. But an old nightmare of the Lower South had come to pass: the northern tier of slave states joined the North in bringing about the abolition of slavery.[28]

The outcome was greeted with wild celebration and visions of millennial change. Cheers erupted in the House galleries, while members on the floor threw their hats in the air. Some congressmen embraced one another; others "wept like children." "The scene," wrote one northern correspondent, "was entirely without precedent in all our national history." In the distance, a barrage of fire by three batteries of artillery heralded the result. "What a grand jubilee," wrote George W. Julian of Indiana, "for the old battle-scarred abolitionists.... I have felt, ever since the vote, as if I were in a new country." Passage, wrote the always exuberant *New York Herald*, was "one of the most remarkable, important, desirable, decisive and momentous events in the records of this or any other nation of modern or ancient times." The rather more staid *Boston Daily Advertiser* proclaimed that ratification would be "the crowning event of the war, indeed of the century." The vote, wrote the *New York Times*, had finally made the United States "what it has never been hitherto, thoroughly *democratic*—resting on human rights as its basis."[29]

Lincoln offered impromptu remarks to a group that came to the White House to celebrate. The Thirteenth Amendment, he declared, went well beyond the Emancipation Proclamation as a way to "eradicate slavery." The proclamation, he explained, was "inoperative" on slaves who did not come within Union lines and might have no effect on their children. (This was an odd interpretation of the language of a document he himself had written, which declared free all slaves in most of the South, whatever their ages and whether they remained on the plantations or not. It seems to have reflected fear that once peace came, courts might rule that the proclamation, based on the "war power," had lapsed, except for slaves who had fully taken advantage of it.) "But this amendment," Lincoln continued, "is a King's cure for all the evils." Even though the Constitution does not envision the president playing any role in the enactment of an amendment, Lincoln affixed his signature to an official copy. Whereupon the Senate, mindful of congressional prerogatives, passed a resolution declaring the president's approval unnecessary.[30]

❦

TO BECOME PART of the Constitution, the Thirteenth Amendment required ratification by three-quarters of the states. The admission of Nevada on the eve of the 1864 election (when some Republicans thought its three electoral votes might be needed to provide Lincoln's margin of victory) had increased the number of states to thirty-six, including the eleven of the Confederacy. Thus, were the seceded states counted, ratification required twenty-seven approvals. It seemed unlikely that the three northern and border states (Kentucky, Delaware, and New Jersey) carried by George B. McClellan, Lincoln's Democratic opponent in 1864, would ratify. On the other hand, by early 1865 seven former slave states had abolished slavery by statute, constitutional amendment, or popular convention. Three were the border states Maryland, Missouri, and West Virginia; four— Tennessee, Arkansas, Louisiana, and Virginia—were Confederate states where wartime Reconstruction had produced pro-Union governments. Assuming that every other northern state ratified, approval by these border and southern states would bring the total precisely to twenty-seven. Whether other former Confederate states would ratify depended on the progress of Reconstruction.

Lincoln's home state of Illinois was, appropriately, first to ratify.

Delaware, the border state where Lincoln had begun his emancipation initiative in 1861, became the first to reject the amendment; not until 1901, long after it had become part of the Constitution, would the amendment abolishing slavery gain Delaware's approval. Kentucky also refused. The place of Lincoln's birth would have the distinction of being the only state to reject the Thirteenth, Fourteenth, and Fifteenth Amendments. It finally decided to ratify them in 1976.

When Lincoln was assassinated in April 1865, twenty-one of the required twenty-seven states had approved the amendment. His vice president and successor, Andrew Johnson, secured final ratification. A sometime owner of a few slaves, Johnson had made his career in prewar politics as a spokesman for the yeoman farmers of East Tennessee and a fierce critic of the state's "slaveocracy." During the Civil War, he persuaded Lincoln to exempt his entire state from the Emancipation Proclamation. But Johnson soon came to embrace emancipation, promising to be a Moses to Tennessee's black population, leading it to a promised land of freedom.

Johnson, however, possessed few of Lincoln's qualities of greatness. He was incorrigibly racist, and his plan of Reconstruction, announced in May 1865, offered the former slaves no protection for their newly won freedom and no voice in creating new governments in the South. Under its terms, conventions elected by and composed of white southerners who had taken oaths of future loyalty were to write new constitutions for the southern states. Johnson insisted that these conventions abolish slavery in their own states and strongly urged the new legislatures to ratify the Thirteenth Amendment. He added that any Confederate seeking an individual pardon—which he required of well-to-do southerners—must take an oath not only to defend the Constitution but to support "all laws and proclamations . . . with reference to the emancipation of the slaves." Unlike Lincoln, Johnson did not include a caveat in his plan of Reconstruction anticipating a possible Supreme Court decision invalidating the Emancipation Proclamation. With the war over, the antislavery radical Salmon P. Chase now chief justice, and slavery effectively dead in most of the South, such a ruling was inconceivable.[31]

Johnson's requirements led to unseemly wrangling. The amendment's second section, conferring enforcement power on Congress, sparked considerable alarm in the South. As blacks held mass meetings and conventions to demand civil and political equality and conflicts over land and labor swept across the defeated Confederacy, whites insisted that the only way to secure social tranquillity and productive labor was the restoration of states to the Union "with the right and power to govern our population in our own way ... as under the old Constitution," in the words of a Georgia plantation agent. Slavery was dead, observed New York Democratic leader Samuel L. M. Barlow, and there would be no objection to the amendment in the South were it not for fear that the second section gave "control of the *Negro* question to Congress." Mississippi altered its prewar constitution so as to abolish slavery in the state, but rejected the Thirteenth Amendment entirely. In a formal message, its legislative Committee on Federal and State Relations explained why: the second section might in the future be interpreted to authorize Congress "to legislate in respect to freedmen in this state. [We] can hardly conceive of a more dangerous grant of power." Mississippi did not get around to ratifying the Thirteenth Amendment until 1995. Several former Confederate states ratified with the "understanding" that the amendment did not empower Congress to determine the future of the former slaves and did not preclude monetary compensation for the former owners. Such provisos, of course, had no legal standing. When Georgia ratified early in December 1865, the required twenty-seven states was reached.[32]

On December 18, 1865, Secretary of State William H. Seward certified that the Thirteenth Amendment had become part of the Constitution. That date, the final end of slavery throughout the United States, proclaimed the *New York Times*, "will be forever memorable in the annals of the republic." In fact, black communities long celebrated January 1—the date of the Emancipation Proclamation—instead. Some still mark "Juneteenth," commemorating June 19, 1865, when Union General Gordon Granger, having arrived in Texas the previous day, proclaimed the end of slavery there. In 1948, at the urging of President Harry S. Truman, Congress established February 1 (the anniversary of Lincoln's signing of the text of the Thirteenth Amendment) as National Freedom Day, and some communities continue to commemorate that holiday. But December 18 has long been forgotten.[33]

"The one question of the age is *settled*," declared Congressman Cornelius Cole of California. But if the Thirteenth Amendment resolved one question—the fate of slavery—it opened a host of others. The amendment, said Senator Henry Wilson, would "obliterate . . . everything connected with [slavery] or pertaining to it." Was this possible? Plantation slavery was a total institution, the foundation of comprehensive systems of labor, politics, and race relations. In the House, James F. Wilson described slavery as an "aggregation of enormities." Which would fall along with the right to property in man? The racial inequality inseparable from slavery? The structure of political and economic power based on slavery? What did it mean to be a free person in post-slavery America? The amendment inevitably raised these issues, but no clear answer emerged from the congressional debates. "Questions of the consequences of emancipation," said John F. Farnsworth of Illinois, would "be settled" in the future "by justice and expediency."[34]

Nonetheless, Democratic attacks in the spring of 1864 and again in early 1865 had forced Republicans to try to delineate the basic rights that belonged to all Americans—rights slavery had denied and emancipation would restore—a discussion that continued throughout postwar Reconstruction. All agreed that contractual relations must be substituted for the discipline of the lash and the master's authority over the personal and family lives of the former slaves ended. Many insisted that civil rights—access to the courts, security in the ownership of property, freedom of movement, and so on—were essential to the enjoyment of freedom. At this early stage, nearly all Republicans denied Democratic charges that freedom would lead inexorably to the right to vote; this, they insisted, was a matter for individual states to regulate.

The deceptively straightforward language of the Thirteenth Amendment raised profound questions about American society. The substantive meaning of freedom was extensively discussed in 1864 and early 1865 when Congress considered the amendment. The border Unionist John Henderson declared that the abolition of slavery carried with it nothing at all, at least as far as the federal government was concerned: "We give him no rights except his freedom and leave the rest to the states." But even Congressman William Holman, an Indiana Democrat hardly known as an advocate of emancipation, noted that "mere exemption from servitude is a miserable idea of freedom." (His point, however, was not that blacks' rights deserved protection but that black suffrage, which he strongly opposed, was an inevitable consequence of abolition.) "In the language of America," said Holman, freedom meant "the right to participate in government."[35]

Most Republicans assumed that freedom meant more than not being chained and that abolition would expand the rights of whites as well as blacks. Trumbull noted that freedom of speech and the press had long been suppressed in parts of the country "by reason of slavery." As for the freedpeople, "a new nation" had emerged from the war, declared Isaac N. Arnold, in which "liberty, *equality before the law* is to be the great cornerstone." James Harlan of Iowa offered a long list of the "incidents of slavery," including denial of the rights to marry, own property, testify in court, and enjoy access to education. Presumably abolition would carry with it these essential entitlements. Most Republicans believed that the amendment's enforcement clause empowered Congress to protect these and other basic rights of the former slaves.[36]

These speeches drew on the prewar antislavery constitutionalism that envisioned a unified nation-state with a single national citizenship enjoying equality before the law regardless of race. But they also remained within the framework of traditional distinctions between natural, civil, political, and social rights. Republicans tended to speak vaguely of "fundamental rights," the inalienable rights of man, "the sacred rights of human nature," and the rights of free labor. There was little discussion of whether abolition conferred citizenship on blacks. Rights, not citizenship, was the language of the amendment's supporters (partly because before the war, citizenship had not carried with it many clearly defined entitlements). On the other hand, it was evident that the former slaves would be part of American society. No one spoke of sending them out of the country—the idea of colonization was dead.[37]

By 1865, the war had vindicated the social vision of free labor essential to the Republican party's outlook since its founding. No phrase was repeated more often in discussions of the amendment than one Lincoln himself had long emphasized—the right to the fruits of one's labor, an essential distinction between slavery and freedom. Lincoln alluded to this in his second inaugural when he referred pointedly to the slaves' "two hundred and fifty years of unrequited toil." As early as 1862, Harlan had insisted that although abolition did not necessarily imply social or political equality, it did mean that blacks "shall be equal with the white race in their right to themselves and the enjoyment of the proceeds of their own labor . . . in their right to justice and . . . [in] the right to apply the proceeds of their own labor to the promotion of their own welfare and the welfare of their dependent families." Ebon C. Ingersoll of Illinois spoke of "a right to till the soil, to earn his bread by the sweat of his brow, and to enjoy the rewards of his own labor . . . without regard to color or race." Republicans believed that the Thirteenth Amendment prevented states or individuals from denying freed slaves these opportunities.[38]

The free-labor vision of a reconstructed South imagined a vast social transformation. Emancipated slaves, enjoying the same opportunities for advancement as northern workers and motivated by the same quest for self-improvement, would labor more productively than as slaves. Northern capital would help to regenerate the region. The South would eventually come to resemble the free society of the North, with public schools, small towns, and independent producers. "Abolish slavery," proclaimed Ingersoll, "and school-houses will rise upon the ruins of the slave mart, intelligence will take the place of ignorance, wealth of poverty." The Thirteenth Amendment by itself could not accomplish all these goals, but it was an essential first step in that direction.[39]

✺

DERIVED FROM THE Northwest Ordinance, the amendment's language may have been familiar, but it was not entirely self-explanatory. Most Republicans no doubt believed that they understood what slavery was. But "involuntary servitude"? That phrase covered multiple relationships and institutions. In colonial America, numerous immigrants had arrived as indentured servants, who obtained passage to the New World by agreeing to labor for a certain number of years for an employer. In the late eighteenth century, gradual emancipation laws in the North required children born to slaves to labor for up to twenty-eight years for their parents' owners—far longer than white apprentices—before gaining their freedom.

By the time of the Civil War, these forms of servitude had pretty much died out. But particularly in the West, multiple systems of semi-free labor continued to flourish. They included peonage (forced labor to satisfy a debt), especially in the Southwest; long-term contract labor for Native Americans, Mexicans, and immigrants from China; and court-designated "wards"—Indian women and children required to labor for white families. There was little discussion in Congress of the amendment's impact on these forms of servitude, although the language undoubtedly opened the door to congressional action against them. Indeed, less than two years after ratification, Congress approved the Anti-Peonage Act of 1867, which, under authority of the Thirteenth Amendment, prohibited both "voluntary" and involuntary peonage. In California the movement against Chinese immigration paradoxically fused racism and antislavery rhetoric to define Chinese contract laborers as unfree "coolies" too servile to become upstanding free laborers. Chinese exclusion, enacted into national law in 1882, was promoted, in part, as a fulfillment of the Thirteenth Amendment.[40]

The Thirteenth Amendment originated with a group of feminist abolitionists who hoped it would pave the way to greater rights for American women. The amendment itself made no mention of gender; the right to freedom applied to men and women equally. Yet some contemporaries raised the question whether the end of involuntary servitude affected the family status of emancipated black women. In the legal structure of nineteenth-century America, one pillar of which was the common law of coverture, adult white men were the "paradigmatic legal individuals." The end of slavery meant that black women entered a social and legal world in which men were deemed to be the heads of families, with wives and children subordinate to them. This was not necessarily the kind of freedom all black women had in mind. Like black men who served in the Union army, black women had found ways to support the Union cause, working as cooks, laundresses, and nurses for the military, passing along information about southern forces, depriving the Confederacy of their labor by seeking refuge behind Union lines, and forming organizations aimed at "ameliorating the miseries of our colored soldiers in their struggle for freedom," as one group in North Carolina put it. Like their male counterparts, they asserted a claim to recognition by the postwar nation. Most relished the opportunity to consolidate stable marriages immune to supervision and breakup by a white owner and to devote more time to their families than was possible under slavery. But many also desired a degree of autonomy within family life. The persistence of coverture meant that the constitutional revolution of Reconstruction did not end the subordination of black women, although it did give them more leverage in dealing with the authority of husbands, fathers, and former masters. During Reconstruction they would take part in mass political meetings, sign labor contracts on their own, and open individual accounts with the Freedman's Savings Bank, an institution chartered by Congress toward the war's end to encourage thrift among the former slaves. Black women's voices, however, were rarely heard in Congress or the national press.[41]

A few opponents of the amendment charged that the abolition of "involuntary servitude" threw into question the legality of a husband's common law right to sexual relations with his wife and to her unpaid labor in the household. Yet most Republicans saw abolition not as reorienting traditional family relations but as restoring to blacks the natural right to family life so grievously undermined by slavery. In these free families, men would take their rightful place as heads of the household and women theirs in the domestic sphere from which slavery had unnaturally removed them. Restoring the freedman's "manhood" and women's right to raise their children without white interference was central to conceptions of emancipation. Within this context, unpaid female labor at home was natural, not oppressive, and certainly not a form of involuntary servitude. "A husband has a right of property in the service of his wife," said one Republican member of Congress, which the abolition of slavery was not intended to destroy. Along with the right to "personal liberty," declared another, the "right of a husband to his wife" and of a "father to his child" comprised the "three great fundamental natural rights of human society." The amendment was intended to restore these rights, not undermine them.[12]

One form of involuntary labor was explicitly authorized by the Thirteenth Amendment. Like the Northwest Ordinance, the amendment allowed involuntary servitude, and perhaps, depending on how one read the first section, slavery itself, to continue for those convicted of crime. The criminal exemption, almost unmentioned in the debates of 1864 and 1865, would later take on baleful significance as a constitutional justification for the exploitation of the labor of convicts.

The provision referring to those found guilty of crime is an excellent illustration of the aphorism that historians write with one eye (at least) fixed on the present. For decades, scholars of the Thirteenth Amendment paid absolutely no attention to this clause. But with mass incarceration and the widespread use of prison labor suddenly having become national issues, the provision has attracted considerable discussion. The Hollywood documentary *13th*, for example, draws a straight line from the Thirteenth Amendment to the exploitation for profit of prisoners today. To be sure, setting prisoners to work long predated the Civil War and Reconstruction. A large number of convicts—30,000 or more—had been transported from the British Isles to the colonies in the decades before the American Revolution, and upon arrival sold to labor for a number of years as punishment for crime. (After losing its American colonies, Britain found another destination for convicts, Australia, which received 150,000 between the American Revolution and the Civil War.) "Forced, hard productive labor," partly to help meet the expense of maintaining prisons, was associated with incarceration. However, despite the proliferation of penitentiaries beginning early in the nineteenth century, the number of those confined within them remained very small.[43]

The prisoner exemption in the Thirteenth Amendment originated in Thomas Jefferson's proposed Land Ordinance of 1784, which would have barred slavery in all the new nation's territories. From there, it migrated to the Northwest Ordinance of 1787, which limited the prohibition of slavery to territories north of the Ohio River. Scholars have not explained precisely why Jefferson chose to include this language. The four states—Vermont, Pennsylvania, Connecticut, and Rhode Island—that enacted constitutions or laws abolishing slavery before Jefferson composed the Land Ordinance made no mention of involuntary labor as a punishment for crime (although Vermont allowed it for debtors). Jefferson may have feared, as he explained in *Notes on the State of Virginia*, that freed slaves would become idle and resort to unlawful behavior, for which the prospect of prison labor might act as a deterrent. Also, as a devotee of Enlightenment prison reform, Jefferson felt that labor was good for the character. Forced labor would help to rehabilitate criminals and offer an alternative to less humane punishments such as branding, long-term solitary confinement, and execution.[44]

By the time the Thirteenth Amendment was ratified, the coupling of a ban on slavery with a criminal exemption had become so common as almost to qualify as "boilerplate" language. It could be found in the Wilmot Proviso, which sought to bar slavery from the territories acquired during the Mexican-American War, the congressional law of 1862 abolishing slavery in all the territories, and in nearly all the constitutions of free states that entered the Union, from Ohio in 1803 to Nevada, the last state admitted before the amendment's ratification. Thaddeus Stevens, probably the most radical member of the House of Representatives, included the same provision in his own draft of an abolition amendment.[45]

The Thirteenth Amendment clothed a radical departure in the nation's history in what a Boston newspaper called "the well settled language of a great historical document." But because of its very familiarity the wording did not undergo necessary scrutiny. The prisoner exemption was almost never discussed in the press, or at antislavery meetings and black conventions that urged ratification. Only a handful of critics sensed that it might cause problems. The language, the abolitionist journal *The Principia* charged as early as February 1864, changed the Constitution "for the worse" by appearing to acknowledge that slavery was allowable "for adequate causes." Charles Sumner insisted that while the Northwest Ordinance "performed an excellent work in its day," its wording was "entirely inapplicable to our time," since it implied that men can be "enslaved as a punishment for crime." Sumner later wrote that he had hoped to propose eliminating the clause regarding convicted criminals but failed to act because his colleagues were anxious "to get their dinner." "I regret now my forbearance," he added.[46]

The exemption did not go unnoticed among white southerners. In November 1865, former Confederate general John T. Morgan pointed out in a speech in Georgia that the Thirteenth Amendment did not prevent states from enacting laws that enabled "judicial authorities" to consign to bondage blacks convicted of crime. The southern governments established under Andrew Johnson's Reconstruction program proceeded to enact a series of laws called the Black Codes to define and circumscribe the freedom that African-Americans now enjoyed and to make it clear, as Robert M. Patton, the new governor of Alabama, put it, that "politically and socially, ours is a white man's government." The Black Code of Mississippi, quickly followed by those of other states, gave blacks certain rights, such as having their marriages recognized in law, but also imposed all sorts of disabilities, including limiting their freedom of movement and barring them from following certain occupations, owning firearms, serving on juries, testifying in cases involving whites, or voting.

Despite the Thirteenth Amendment, involuntary black labor—justified by the criminal exemption—was central to these laws. They required all adult black men at the beginning of each year to sign a labor contract to work for a white employer or face prosecution for vagrancy or other vaguely defined crimes. Those convicted would be fined and, if unable to pay, forced to labor for a white employer. Florida's code authorized the sale for up to a year of a freed person who violated a labor contract. Apprenticeship laws authorized judges to provide planters with the unpaid labor of black children on the pretext that their parents were unable to support them. To be sure, vagrancy laws go back to the premodern era and were widely used throughout the country before the Civil War to punish able-bodied persons who appeared to be unwilling to work. But earlier vagrancy laws were not envisioned as the foundation for an entire labor system. Apprenticeship, too, had a venerable history. But the arrangements in the Black Codes bore little resemblance to traditional ones whereby a youth learned a trade. Certainly, all this was not what former slaves and their northern allies considered free labor. "If carried into effect," a local black leader wrote to the president, "it will be virtually returning us to slavery again." "Where is Justice?" asked a black convention in Mississippi. "Where is freedom?" [47]

Among other things, declared a New Haven newspaper, the Black Codes demonstrated "the necessity" of the second section of the Thirteenth Amendment, authorizing further congressional action to protect the freedom blacks had so recently acquired. "It was this sort of legislation," the prominent North Carolina Unionist Daniel R. Goodloe later recalled, "which caused the northern people to believe that there was no sincere purpose on the part of the southern people to acquiesce in the freedom of the former slaves." [48]

The laws also, however, revealed the dangers inherent in the prisoner exemption. As reports circulated in the North of blacks convicted of theft or vagrancy being "sold" for a term of years "at public outcry," disquiet rose in antislavery circles about "the unfortunate phraseology of the Amendment." A few members raised the issue in Congress. "Cunning rebels," one congressman complained, were using "the exceptional clause" to reduce freed persons to slavery. "God knows I wish we had that amendment before us at this time," said William Higby, a Radical Republican from California. "We deliberated months . . . and yet we did not cover the whole ground. . . . There is no good reason under heaven why a man for crime should be sold into slavery." In 1867, the *National Anti-Slavery Standard* called for the passage of a new amendment eliminating the words "except as a punishment for crime."[49]

That same year, John A. Kasson of Iowa introduced a resolution clarifying the meaning of the exemption clause. No one, he declared, supposed when the amendment was ratified "that in the very sentence abolishing slavery . . . they had also made provision for its survival under another form and through the action of the courts." The amendment's "true intent and meaning," his resolution declared, was to prohibit all forms of slavery and involuntary servitude "except in direct execution of a criminal sentence . . . under the immediate control of officers of the law" and not "sale or other disposition into slavery." Kasson's resolution passed the House by an overwhelming majority (122–25) but did not come to a vote in the Senate. Many senators felt the Civil Rights Act of 1866, which, among other things, mandated racial equality in access to the courts and in judicial punishments, rendered the resolution unnecessary. Time would prove them wrong.[50]

In the early years of Reconstruction, northerners spoke frequently of punishment for crime, but generally in relation to penalties for ex-Confederates. The Thirteenth Amendment was not the only Reconstruction measure that envisioned a criminal conviction as grounds for the denial of widely recognized rights. The exemption was repeated three times in the Civil Rights Act of 1866. Thaddeus Stevens did get the language removed from the 1866 bill extending the life of the

Freedmen's Bureau. "I know that men are being convicted of assault and battery and sentenced to slavery down there," he told the House. But beginning in 1867, when, under Radical Reconstruction, southern states were required by Congress to write new, egalitarian constitutions, every one included some variant of the language abolishing slavery "except as a punishment for crime." To this day, persons convicted of crimes are routinely subjected to involuntary servitude while incarcerated and to otherwise prohibited forms of discrimination—in employment, access to housing, and the right to vote—even after serving their sentences.[51]

Inadvertently, the Thirteenth Amendment had created a loophole that would later allow for the widespread leasing of convict laborers to plantations, mines, and industries in the South. It also allowed their use within prison walls by private contractors, and on chain gangs building roads, clearing land, and working on other public projects. Convict leasing began as a cost-saving measure during Reconstruction but only burgeoned after white supremacist Democrats regained control of southern governments and enacted laws greatly expanding the number of crimes that constituted felonies. The prison population rose dramatically, and while the laws, on their face, had nothing to do with race, blacks comprised the overwhelming majority of those incarcerated. "They send [a man] to the penitentiary if he steals a chicken," one black leader complained. Without violating the Thirteenth Amendment, a broadside issued by Texas Republicans declared, "the courts of law are employed to re-enslave the colored race.... The plantations are worked, as of old, by slaves, under the name of convicts." To be sure, the labor of prisoners was not, strictly speaking, chattel slavery, nor was it an entire social system such as had existed before the war. But by the end of the nineteenth century, many thousands of convicts were at work throughout the South. Even today, the use of involuntary prison labor is widespread, as are private, for-profit prisons where inmates are required to labor. Courts have ruled that prison labor does not violate the Thirteenth Amendment. As late as the 1980s, the Department of Justice concluded that the amendment attaches "some of the characteristics of slavery" to prisoners, including exemption from minimum wage laws—or, indeed, the requirement for any compensation at all.[52]

❧

THERE WERE NO African-Americans in the Congress that approved the Thirteenth Amendment. Nonetheless, during the debates over the amendment's passage and ratification, blacks in the larger public sphere put forward their own vision of what abolition meant and what kind of society should emerge from the ashes of slavery. They articulated a comprehensive claim to the rights that came with freedom and sought to act upon it. Emancipated slaves in the South moved to "throw off the badge of servitude." They reunited families separated under slavery, established churches and schools, claimed the rights of free labor, pressed for civil equality and the vote, and demanded access to land. Numerous local and statewide black mass meetings and political conventions took place in the South in 1865. Embodying the rapid spread of grass-roots politicization, their demands for equality drew on the claim to being "citizens of the republic" entitled to "the blessings of equal liberty." Black newspapers in 1864 began to include the Thirteenth Amendment in their demands, but they were already looking beyond it, their attention focused on the future rights of the freed people.[53]

In the waning months of the war, the black-owned *New Orleans Tribune* developed a coherent radical program including black male suffrage, equality before the law, equal access regardless of race to public schools and transportation, and the division of plantation lands among the freed people. In the fall of 1865 it pressed for a new constitutional amendment, barring states from making "any distinction in civil rights and privileges" among citizens because of race. Many saw the Thirteenth Amendment as insufficient because it did not mention these principles. Meanwhile, northern blacks continued their long-standing campaign for civil and political rights. "We have the question of equal rights to fight," said a speaker at a black convention in Michigan in September 1865, "which we have fought for years."[54]

Nearly all the black conventions, North and South, demanded the right to vote as "an essential and inseparable element of self-government." As always, they invoked the Declaration of Independence, but even before ratification, the Thirteenth Amendment had subtly transformed blacks' attitudes toward the Constitution. To be sure, prewar black conventions had invoked the Constitution in putting forward their claim to birthright citizenship. But with the Constitution now shorn of its proslavery features, constitutional language assumed an even more prominent place in black political culture. "Next to our heavenly father," declared a statement by a black convention in Mobile in August 1865, "we revere the good old Constitution of the United States, now that it acknowledges our existence." Moreover, the amendment demonstrated that the Constitution was malleable—it encouraged people to think that it could be amended again. In September 1865, black leaders formed the National Equal Rights League, demanding "full enjoyment of our liberties," "complete enfranchisement," and a constitutional amendment prohibiting legislation "against any civilized portion of the inhabitants, native-born or naturalized, on account of race or color." Others insisted that, once ratified, the Thirteenth Amendment, via the second section, authorized Congress to take action to protect the former slaves "in all the rights of freemen." That section, a black newspaper noted, was "exceedingly distasteful to the recent rebels of the late slave states."[55]

Meanwhile, the organized abolitionist movement could not decide whether the Thirteenth Amendment marked the end of their decades-long struggle, or the beginning of a new one. When the House approved the amendment early in 1865, William Lloyd Garrison called for the American Anti-Slavery Society to dissolve. The amendment had transformed "a covenant with death" (the original Constitution) into "a covenant with life"; as a result, "my vocation, as an abolitionist," had ended. But to many abolitionists, the Thirteenth Amendment was a resting place, not the end of their movement. "No emancipation can be effectual and no freedom real," said the veteran abolitionist Henry C. Wright, "unless the Negro has the ballot and the states are prohibited from enacting laws making any distinction among their citizens on the basis of race or color"—principles that if implemented would rewrite the statute books of the northern states as well as the southern. Wendell Phillips insisted that further measures were necessary to protect the freed people against the denial of their rights by the states— otherwise they would be "ground to powder by the power of state sovereignty." [56]

When the AASS held its annual meeting in May 1865, it rejected Garrison's motion to dissolve. He resigned as president, replaced by Phillips. The organization's official weekly, the *National Anti-Slavery Standard*, was already calling for another constitutional amendment, forbidding any state to "make distinctions among its inhabitants because of their color." Now the paper appeared with a new motto on its masthead: No Reconstruction Without Negro Suffrage. Most Republicans, at this point, were unwilling to go that far. But when Congress convened in December 1865, they had reached a consensus that the Thirteenth Amendment had brought blacks within the purview of a national citizenship in which all enjoyed equality before the law, protected by the federal government. The question was, how to write these principles into the laws and Constitution and ensure that they were enforced. "A mightier work than the abolition of slavery," Frederick Douglass declared in 1865, "now looms up before the abolitionist" and, he might have added, the nation.[57]

In January 1865, as the House debated the Thirteenth Amendment and many months before the enactment of southern Black Codes, the *New York World*, the country's leading Democratic newspaper, presciently forecast that despite the abolition of slavery, states might well rely on their traditional powers to enact laws that made the condition of the freed people "intolerable." To prevent this would require "all sorts of additional amendments," the end result of which would divest the state governments of "*all* . . . of their present powers." [58]

The *World*'s language was hyperbolic. But it pointed to the problem that confronted Republican policy makers. Detailing recent discriminatory state laws, a group of Tennessee freedmen observed, "we have nowhere to look for protection, save to the United States authority."[59] But federal jurisdiction traditionally did not extend to the problem of racially biased laws and law enforcement, or private conspiracies, often accompanied by violence, to restrict blacks' opportunities, or to the right to vote. It remained uncertain how far Congress would go to change the existing legal order by establishing federal oversight of Americans' rights. One thing, however, was clear. The Thirteenth Amendment was not a final answer to the problem of freedom. It turned out to be one indispensable part of a dynamic process that continued for years and gave birth to the Fourteenth and Fifteenth Amendments, further civil rights legislation, and an unprecedented experiment in the South in interracial democracy. "Liberty has been won," Charles Sumner declared. "The battle for equality is still pending."[60]

2

TOWARD EQUALITY

The Fourteenth Amendment

O N DECEMBER 4, 1865, the Thirty-ninth Congress, one of the most consequential in American history, assembled in Washington. Over the next fifteen months its members grappled with the profound, difficult questions arising from the Civil War and the destruction of slavery—who should rule the South, how should southern states be reintegrated into the Union, what rights should the former slaves enjoy and who should enforce them? These debates took place as a bitter split over Reconstruction policy developed between President Andrew Johnson and the Republican majority in Congress, and evidence accumulated of violent outrages against the freed people and the unwillingness of the governments Johnson had established in the South to deal justly with the former slaves. This was the context in which Congress embarked on its own Reconstruction policy, central to which was the Fourteenth Amendment.

The longest amendment ever added to the Constitution, the Fourteenth, like Reconstruction more broadly, had many purposes. Its motives were idealistic, sectional, partisan, and economic. Its final language emerged from months of deliberation. The amendment was not the creation of any single individual or party faction, or of the predetermined logic of emancipation, but arose from debate, negotiation, and compromise, which continued almost until the moment of passage. It was meant to solve specific problems arising from the war; establish general principles about the rights of the freed people and of all Americans; create a uniform definition of citizenship; outline a way back into the Union for seceded states; limit the political influence of leading Confederates; contribute to the nation-building process catalyzed by the Civil War; and serve as a political platform that would enable the Republican party to retain its hold on power. Some of these aims were achieved, some were not, and some would be left to future generations to bring to fruition. But despite its palpable limitations, no change in the Constitution since the Bill of Rights has had so profound an impact on American life as the Fourteenth Amendment.

Although fighting had ceased months earlier, Congress acted as if the nation were still at war. At the session's outset, the clerks of the House and Senate, by prearrangement with leaders of the Republican majority, omitted the names of members elected under the Reconstruction plan Johnson had established in the South. Many of these senators and representatives-elect were former Confederate political and military leaders. Their election, together with the unwillingness of the Johnson governments to acknowledge the basic rights of the former slaves, Republicans took as evidence that the white South did not fully accept the results of Union victory.

Without the South being held in what many Republicans called the "grasp of war," the party would not have enjoyed the two-thirds majority in both houses of Congress necessary for the adoption of the Fourteenth Amendment. But the Republican party was divided into wings that did not always agree on the issues confronting the nation. Radicals, the most prominent of whom were Thaddeus Stevens, the party's floor leader in the House, and Senator Charles Sumner, the politician closest to the black community, saw Reconstruction as a once-in-a-lifetime opportunity to purge the republic of the legacy of slavery and guarantee that all Americans enjoyed the same rights and opportunities, secured by a powerful and beneficent national government.

For decades, those who would later become Radical Republicans had defended the unpopular causes of black suffrage and equal citizenship. Reconstruction, in their view, meant completing "the great antislavery revolution," and laying to rest what Stevens called the "political blasphemy" that the United States was and should remain a "white man's government."[1]

Equality was the Radicals' watchword—"equality in the broadest and most comprehensive democratic sense," as Senator Henry Wilson put it, although Radicals and other Republicans differed among themselves on the precise definition of equality. (Stevens felt it required the distribution of land to the former slaves, a proposal that won little support in Congress.) On a more practical level, the Radicals did not trust President Johnson or his southern governments, and insisted that the only way to guarantee the rights of black Americans, extend the Republican party into the South (where it still had no real presence), and secure the party's continued national rule was to grant black men the right to vote. Their views reverberated among the southern freedpeople, reinforcing their own demands for equal rights. "They are well aware of the existence and position of Sumner and such men," a white North Carolina minister observed of the former slaves in 1866.[2]

The Radicals enjoyed a considerable presence in Congress but they did not constitute a majority. More numerous were moderates, who included influential senators such as Lyman Trumbull, chair of the Senate Judiciary Committee, and William Pitt Fessenden of Maine. The bookish Trumbull had achieved success in Illinois politics before the war as a widely respected lawyer and a "conservative radical" who defended fugitive slaves in court while at the same time remaining aloof from the state's abolitionist movement and sometimes pandering to racial prejudice. Like other moderates, Fessenden, while strongly antislavery, considered himself a pragmatic man of affairs responding to an immediate situation, rather than a moral crusader. He clashed frequently with Sumner, whose long philosophical speeches Fessenden considered a waste of the Senate's time.

When Congress convened, moderates had not given up hope of

working with President Johnson. They were willing to keep his southern governments intact so long as guarantees of the freedpeople's
rights were put in place. They viewed black suffrage as both unpre-
dictable in its outcome (some feared the former slaves would vote as
their former owners instructed) and too unpopular in the North to
be the basis of a successful Reconstruction policy. Stevens, a longtime
believer that all free men should vote, noted in the fall of 1865 that
Republicans in his state considered the issue "heavy and premature."
Between 1865 and 1869, no fewer than eleven referendums on extending the suffrage to the minuscule black population were held in the
northern states; only two, in Iowa and Minnesota, succeeded. Could
the North, moderates asked, demand of the South what it was unwilling to do itself? The issue was clearly politically dangerous. Johnson's
deep racism, which ended up making it impossible for the moderates
to work with him, and the conduct of the governments he had established in the South, would eventually lead moderate Republicans to
embrace black suffrage—something almost none of them anticipated
in December 1865.[3]

The original constitution said almost nothing about the right to
vote, leaving regulation of the suffrage in the hands of the states.
Nonetheless, Radicals insisted that voting rights were the logical consequence of the abolition of slavery. Without "the right to share in the
governing power," in the words of George W. Julian of Indiana, "no
man is really free." The government, declared Senator Richard Yates
of Illinois, never intended "to set four million slaves free . . . and at
the same time leave them without the civil and political rights which
attach to the free citizen." Both the Constitution's clause guaranteeing
to each state a "republican form of government" and the Thirteenth
Amendment, Radicals insisted, empowered Congress to extend the
right to vote immediately. Surprisingly, an even more sweeping view
was forcefully expressed by James Gordon Bennett, the *New York
Herald*'s editor, now in a radical phase. The Thirteenth Amendment,
the *Herald* declared in January 1866, was "the greatest political revolution of modern times. . . . With this abolition of slavery all the civil

and political distinctions in the states depending on race and color are abolished; for the constitution knows no distinctions of color." By the spring Bennett would be supporting Andrew Johnson in his battle with Congress, but for the moment he agreed with the Radicals: "as the constitution now stands . . . there is nothing . . . to justify the exclusion of the blacks from the civil and political rights of the whites." Moderates, however, believed that the federal government lacked the authority to "interfere with the right of suffrage in the states." Moreover, any attempt to do so, said Senator William M. Stewart of Nevada, would be "met by the prejudices, whether just or unjust, of a large majority of the white inhabitants of the United States."[4]

There would be no difficulty in Republicans agreeing on a Reconstruction policy, Stewart observed in January 1866, "if it were not for the question of Negro suffrage in the South. . . . If this question were out of the way, we could settle everything else in two weeks." As Stewart suggested, broad grounds of agreement did exist within the party. Nearly all Republicans believed that the federal government must give substantive meaning to emancipation by defining and guaranteeing the freedpeople's personal liberty, access to the courts, and ability to compete as free laborers. "Protection of all men in their inalienable rights," declared Schuyler Colfax, the Speaker of the House, was the crucial task confronting Congress. Moreover, the breach with Johnson, which meant that legislation would have to pass over his veto, soon put a premium on party unity.[5]

Nearly everyone seemed to anticipate further changes to the Constitution. A flood of proposed amendments greeted the opening of Congress. Stevens himself offered ones to apportion representation in the House on the basis of voters instead of population (thus significantly reducing southern representation if blacks were not enfranchised); annul the Constitution's prohibition on levying duties on exports (a concession at the Constitutional Convention to southern states whose economies depended on exporting agricultural products to Europe); make all national and state laws equally applicable to all citizens without regard to race; and bar the payment of any part of the Confederate debt. By January, according to Senator Edgar Cowan of Pennsylvania, seventy amendments were "now pending." They included measures to abolish the Electoral College and have presidents elected by direct popular vote; declare the Union "indissolvable"; bar compensation to the owners of emancipated slaves; require each state to provide for the "pursuit of happiness" of all inhabitants without distinction of race; and change the nation's official name from the United States to the more unitary "America." The proliferation of amendments became a standing joke among journalists. The *New York Times* chided congressmen who had "grossly neglected the first duty of a member" by failing to introduce one. Proposals also flooded into Washington "from all quarters." A group of Iowans called for the Constitution to be amended to acknowledge "Almighty God" as "the source of all authority and power in civil governments."[6]

THE TASK OF sifting through these proposals and drafting constitutional amendments to be presented to Congress fell to the Joint Committee on Reconstruction, a fifteen-member body appointed at the beginning of the session. Over the next several months the committee not only hammered out the content and language of the Fourteenth Amendment but conducted extensive hearings (with no fewer than one hundred forty-four witnesses) on conditions in the South. Testimony before the committee revealed shocking violations of the basic rights of the former slaves and widespread hostility in the South to white wartime Unionists and northerners, reinforcing the conviction that further federal action was necessary. The committee was constructed so as to reflect the range of opinions within the Republican party. The chair, Fessenden, was a leading moderate, but Radicals were represented by Stevens and others. These categories, however, were imprecise. Several members seemed to have one foot in each camp, and in any event the committee did not always divide along ideological lines. There were also three Democratic members, but they had no influence on the deliberations. The Joint Committee's clerk kept a journal that recorded votes but not the content of debate, a disappointment to anyone seeking in its pages the reasons for changes in wording as the Fourteenth Amendment evolved.[7]

The first version of a Fourteenth Amendment to emerge from the committee was an attempt to finesse the black suffrage issue while dealing with an ironic political consequence of the abolition of slavery. Now that all blacks were free, the Constitution's Three-Fifths Clause became inoperative. In the next reapportionment allocating membership in the House of Representatives and votes in the Electoral College, all blacks would be counted as part of each state's population. The southern states would thus enjoy added representation, giving them, as one congressman put it, "an undue and unjust amount of political power in the government."[8]

Seventeen proposals to restructure congressional representation came before the Joint Committee. The simplest way of dealing with this problem, Radicals insisted, was to require the states to enfranchise black men. This would ensure that the Slave Power would no longer control southern politics. Moderates, however, believed such an amendment would never secure ratification. Another option was to base representation on voters, not total population, as Stevens had proposed. This would leave suffrage requirements in the hands of the states. It would encourage the Johnson governments to enfranchise their black populations or leave those states with reduced power in Washington (a loss of one-third of their congressmen according to one estimate). But as Representative James G. Blaine of Maine pointed out early in January 1866, western migration was skewed toward men, and thus basing representation on voters would result in a shift of power away from eastern states, which had a higher percentage of women in their populations. The proposal, Blaine warned, might also unleash an "unseemly scramble for voters," including the enfranchisement of women, which would double a state's representation in Congress.[9]

In view of these objections, the Joint Committee, after several days of deliberation, settled on an amendment basing representation on the number of inhabitants, not voters, but penalizing states that limited voting because of "race or color" by eliminating from the calculation the entire excluded population. Because of their small black populations, this would have no bearing on northern states that restricted voting to white men, although California, with a large disenfranchised Asian population, would lose one member of the House of Representatives. The proposal was an attempt, Julian later wrote, "to unite the radical and conservative wings of the party" on the issue of suffrage. Stevens presented this amendment to the House on January 22. It quickly encountered criticism, not only from Radicals such as Julian, who considered it a betrayal of the black population, but from other Republicans who pointed out a serious flaw. Through nonracial voting requirements such as literacy and property qualifications, the southern states could limit voting almost entirely to whites without incurring any reduction in representation. This would become the "obvious policy" of every southern state, a Virginia lawyer pointed out in testimony before the Joint Committee.[10]

Nonetheless, on January 31, 1866, this first version of a Fourteenth Amendment, dealing only with the question of representation, received the required two-thirds majority in the House. In the Senate, however, it encountered the formidable opposition of Charles Sumner. In a speech that lasted two full days and took up over forty fine-print columns of the *Congressional Globe*, and in a second speech a few weeks later, Sumner attacked the proposal as a "compromise of human rights" because it recognized the authority of states to limit the suffrage on the basis of race—an unacceptable concession after "a terrible war waged against us in the name of state rights." Sumner presented a petition from Frederick Douglass and other prominent blacks denouncing the amendment as an invitation to the white South to disenfranchise blacks forever. The American Anti-Slavery Society echoed their complaint, warning that "it leaves the Negro to his fate." In response to what Blaine called Sumner's "exhaustive and masterly essay" on human rights, Fessenden, for the Joint Committee, replied that the role of Congress was to enact laws, not expound philosophy. Fessenden believed blacks were not yet ready for the suffrage but that facing a loss of political power, southern states would provide education to the former slaves and enfranchise them "at no distant day." But on March 9, 1866, Sumner and four other Radicals joined Democratic senators and a handful of conservative Republicans aligned with President Johnson in voting no, preventing the amendment from securing a two-thirds majority. Stevens, always willing to take half a loaf when a full one was unavailable, was outraged. "After having received the careful examination and approbation of the committee, and . . . the united Republican vote [in the House]," he later complained, "it was slaughtered by a puerile and pedantic criticism." [11]

Even as this debate took place, Congress was considering two bills introduced in January by Senator Lyman Trumbull. One extended the life of the Freedmen's Bureau, an agency Congress had created in March 1865 to oversee the transition from slavery to freedom. Far more significant was the second bill, which became the Civil Rights Act of 1866, the first law to declare who is a citizen of the United States and specify rights all citizens are to enjoy. Before the war, "civil rights" had been a widely discussed but poorly defined concept. Now it would be given a precise legal meaning—essentially, those rights fundamental to being a free person. Congressmen had alluded to these rights during debate over the Thirteenth Amendment. Now they moved to identify exactly what they were and how they would be enforced.

The bill declared all persons born in the United States, other than "Indians not taxed" (considered members of their own tribal sovereignties, not the nation) and individuals "subject to a foreign power," to be citizens of the United States. This for the first time put into national law the principle of birthright citizenship, which, in somewhat different wording, would make its way into the Fourteenth Amendment. The Civil Rights Act, in other words, severed citizenship from race, as abolitionists had long demanded, and abrogated the *Dred Scott* decision. It applied, however, not only to blacks but to virtually everyone born in the country. It went on to enumerate for the first time the rights all citizens "of every race and color" were to enjoy: to "make and enforce" contracts, own property, testify in court, sue and be sued, and "enjoy the full and equal benefit" of laws "for the protection of persons and property." These are essentially the rights of free labor, necessary to compete in the economic marketplace. No law or "custom," the Act declared, could deprive any citizen of these basic entitlements, "except as a punishment for crime." Trumbull insisted that the measure was fully authorized by the Thirteenth Amendment—"these are rights which the first clause of the constitutional amendment meant to secure to all. . . . With the destruction of slavery necessarily follows the incidents to slavery."[12]

The Civil Rights Act, Trumbull noted, "had nothing to do with political rights," still deemed by the majority of Congress to be privileges or "franchises," not fundamental entitlements. But its language directly challenged other expressions of racial inequality. All citizens must henceforth enjoy the delineated rights in the same way as "enjoyed by white citizens." This wording represented a remarkable innovation. Up to this point, the concept of "whiteness" existed in the law as a mark of privilege (for example, in laws specifying that only white persons could vote, serve in the militia, or become naturalized citizens). Now, the civil rights of white Americans became a baseline, a standard that applied to all citizens, and freedom from legal discrimination for the first time was added to the list of citizens' rights. No longer could states enact laws like the Black Codes. "The right of American citizens," Trumbull declared, "means something," specifically "that there shall be an equality among all classes of citizens" and "all laws must be impartial."[13]

Ohio congressman John A. Bingham believed that despite the Thirteenth Amendment, Congress lacked the power to regulate the behavior of the states in this manner. He fully supported the principle of equality before the law but deemed another amendment necessary to give it constitutional authority. Bingham was one of a handful of Republicans to vote against passage. Most Republicans, however, moderates as well as Radicals, believed that the Thirteenth

Amendment, in the words of the *New York Tribune*, did "not stop" with abolition but empowered Congress and the federal courts to protect every American "in the full enjoyment of his liberties." Even Senator Stewart, one of the more conservative Republicans, affirmed "we have given him freedom, and that implies that he shall have all the civil rights necessary to the enjoyment of that freedom." [14]

The Civil Rights Act left many questions unanswered. Did the enumerated entitlements constitute the full extent of "civil rights" (a phrase that had originally been included in the text of the bill but was later removed because of its imprecision)? Black leaders pressed an expansive understanding of civil rights, insisting that from the law's egalitarian language logically flowed other rights they had long demanded, but which were not specifically mentioned—jury service, access to public schools, the equal use of transportation and public accommodations, even the right to vote and hold office.

Also uncertain was whether the measure prohibited racially biased conspiracies, violence, and exclusionary practices by private individuals and businesses as well as discriminatory state laws and judicial proceedings. The Thirteenth Amendment, under whose authority the Civil Rights Act was passed, has no "state action" clause (no language, that is, restricting its reach to the acts of state and local governments and officials). It undoubtedly applies not only to public authorities but also to private individuals who seek to hold others as slaves. The Act's section imposing criminal penalties on "any person" who violated the listed rights mentions both discriminatory laws and customs—social norms enforced informally—making it clear that Congress had in mind not only legal discrimination but also private behavior such as the widely publicized efforts of planters to restrict the employment opportunities of the freed people and force them to sign inequitable labor contracts. But most of the discussion focused on inequitable state laws. If states could enact measures like the Black Codes with impunity, one member of Congress asked, "then I demand to know, of what practical value is the amendment abolishing slavery?" It remained unclear what would happen if states enacted laws that made no mention of race but were administered in a discriminatory manner. An ex-governor of Mississippi proposed that his state make "failure to execute a contract for labor" a "penal offence." Unlike the Black Codes, he added, such a measure would have to apply to both races "to harmonize it with the Civil Rights bill, . . . though it would operate principally on the freedmen."[15]

Trumbull himself was not entirely consistent in discussing the law's reach. Generally, his focus was on excising racial discrimination from the statute book. The Act would have "no operation," he said, in states where "the laws are equal." But he also observed that not only "state officers" but "any person who shall deprive another of any right . . . in consequence of his color or race" would be subject to penalties including fines and prison terms. And the law's enforcement sections envisioned legal cases in federal court against "any officer, civil or military, or other person." Already, moreover, some congressmen were speaking of what would come to be called the doctrine of "state neglect"—that the failure of a state government adequately to protect the rights and safety of inhabitants was itself a form of action that could trigger federal intervention.[16]

All these questions would soon arise with regard to the Fourteenth Amendment, but they were discussed at greater length in connection with the Civil Rights Act. The debate became a full-fledged examination of the meaning of equality. Democrats claimed that the bill's "logical conclusion" was black suffrage, integrated public schools, interracial marriage, and complete "political" and "social" equality— a charge Republicans vociferously denied. Opponents also contended that the bill would bring about a revolutionary change in the federal system, transforming a "free republican form of government into an absolute despotism." Republicans insisted that the measure contained "no invasion of the legitimate rights of the states." Rather, said Senator Jacob Howard, it simply extended to "these men whom we have made free the ordinary rights of a freeman," including giving to "different races or colors the same civil rights." Yet since, as Howard well knew, racial distinctions had been embedded in American law, North and

South, since the founding of the republic, the Civil Rights Act represented a dramatic departure. Its provisions were not limited to the former slaves, nor to the states where slavery had previously existed. And given that the rights it enumerated had hitherto been regulated entirely by the states, it reflected a significant enhancement of federal power. Before the war, James G. Blaine later wrote, only "the wildest fancy of a distempered brain" could have envisioned an act of Congress conferring on blacks "all the civil rights pertaining to a white man."[17]

The federal government in 1866 was hardly equipped to intervene continuously in local affairs to protect the rights of citizens. The Civil Rights Act created what one historian calls a "latent national presence within all the states." It would remain latent if white southerners "accepted the new era," but would be triggered when basic rights were being violated. Ironically, the law's enforcement mechanisms were modeled on the infamous Fugitive Slave Act of 1850. Like that statute it allowed cases to be heard in federal court and envisioned the employment of the army, navy, militia, and U.S. marshals, as well as bystanders, to enforce its execution. Both laws were efforts to use federal power to secure a constitutional right and to punish public officials and private citizens who interfered. In 1850 it was the right of an owner to the return of a runaway slave; in 1866 the right of African-Americans to genuine freedom. Thus, as James Wilson put it, Congress turned "the arsenal of slavery upon itself," wielding "the weapons which slavery has placed in our hands . . . in the holy cause of liberty."[18]

On March 27, 1866, Andrew Johnson vetoed the Civil Rights Bill. Two weeks later, it became the first important statute in American history to become law over the president's objections. One newspaper described Johnson's veto message, which raised the specter of interracial marriage, black suffrage, and congressional interference with the relations of "capital and labor," as a "noble vindication of the white man." Johnson denied that blacks were qualified for American citizenship and denounced what today is called reverse discrimination: "The distinction of race and color is by the bill made to operate in favor of the colored and against the white race." Indeed, in the idea that expanding the rights of nonwhites somehow punishes the white majority, the ghost of Andrew Johnson still haunts our discussions of race. The veto and congressional override made cooperation between Congress and the president impossible, and reinforced Republican efforts to craft an amendment that would place their understanding of the consequences of the Civil War in the Constitution, safe from presidential interference and shifting congressional majorities.[19]

❧

EVEN AS THE representation amendment went down to defeat and the Civil Rights Act wended its way through Congress, the Joint Committee was working on another proposal, which after many changes in wording became Section 1, the heart of the Fourteenth Amendment. Before the civil rights measure was introduced, John A. Bingham had proposed an amendment empowering Congress to pass "all laws necessary and proper to secure to all persons . . . equal protection in their rights to life, liberty, and property." As noted above, Bingham's constitutional views were somewhat eccentric. Not only was he virtually alone among Republicans in viewing the Civil Rights Act as unconstitutional (even voting to uphold Johnson's veto), but before the war he had insisted that the Constitution already contained the principle of equal rights regardless of race. The states, however, had failed to abide by it. The remedy was an amendment empowering Congress to enforce the principle of "the absolute equality before the law of all persons."[20]

Early in February 1866, the Joint Committee approved a revised version of Bingham's amendment, authorizing Congress to enact laws to secure "all privileges and immunities of citizens" and "equal protection in the rights of life, liberty and property." Bingham noted that the language was race-neutral—the amendment's immediate purpose was to secure the rights of blacks, but it would also protect "hundreds of thousands" of loyal white southerners he claimed were also being persecuted in the South. More broadly, it embodied Bingham's long-standing commitment to equality as a cardinal principle of American government. Democrats and some Republicans objected that the proposal granted Congress the power to pass sweeping legislation on just about any subject. It would "utterly obliterate state rights and state authority over their own internal affairs," said the conservative Republican from New York Robert Hale. A different, more influential complaint came from Congressman Giles Hotchkiss of New York, who chided Bingham for not being "sufficiently radical." The proposed amendment, he pointed out, left protection of citizens' rights entirely "to the caprice of Congress." What would happen if in the future Democrats regained control and failed to make use of the power to prevent abuses by the states? It would be far better, Hotchkiss argued, explicitly to prohibit the states from discriminating against any class of citizens. Hotchkiss's argument persuaded enough members that the House, on February 28, postponed consideration of Bingham's amendment indefinitely.[21]

It would be a long and tortuous path, with numerous wording changes along the way, from the failed amendments dealing with representation and legal equality to final approval of the Fourteenth Amendment. The Joint Committee did not even meet from early March to early April, and for a time seemed to be at an impasse. One key step toward a solution was the committee's decision to unite all of its proposed constitutional changes in a single amendment rather than a series of briefer ones. This was first proposed by the social reformer Robert Dale Owen, who had served during the war as chair of the American Freedman's Inquiry Commission, the agency that originated the idea of the Freedmen's Bureau. In April 1866, Owen took it upon himself to present to Thaddeus Stevens a five-part amendment. Its key provisions barred racial discrimination in civil rights by any state or the federal government, and set July 4, 1876, as the date when racial exclusions in voting would be prohibited. Until then, such discrimination would lead to a reduction in a state's representation in the House.

According to Owen, Stevens exclaimed that this was the best

proposal he had seen, and he quickly brought it before the Joint Committee, which, after various wording changes, approved it. But the members decided to postpone sending it to the House floor until their chair, Senator Fessenden, returned from an illness. In the interim, however, Republican members of Congress from New York, Indiana, California, and several other states warned that black suffrage, even if postponed for a decade, would prove deeply unpopular among their constituents. Determined that the committee adopt something that could pass, Stevens himself moved to eliminate the suffrage provision. Owen's plan died, but the strategy of uniting numerous provisions into one amendment survived. "Not because they have any connection with each other," the *New York Times* explained, "but in order to force Congress to swallow the whole or none." Unlike the Bill of Rights, a series of separate amendments, the Fourteenth Amendment emerged as a complex take-it-or-leave-it proposition. Sections with broad support, the Joint Committee hoped, would help win approval for less popular ones.[22]

At the end of April 1866, after a somewhat disorienting series of further votes, in which language was added and eliminated from Owen's now almost unrecognizable proposal, the Joint Committee approved a five-section Fourteenth Amendment and sent it to Congress. In the Senate it underwent further changes, most significantly the addition of the current first sentence, which put into the Constitution the principle of birthright citizenship in both the nation and the individual states. The new first sentence was meant to "settle the great question of citizenship" once and for all according to Howard, who managed passage in the Senate. Howard noted that birthright citizenship was "the law of the land already," in the Civil Rights Act. But of course a law can be repealed. "We wanted to put this question . . . ," he continued, "beyond the legislative power, beyond the reach of [those] who would pull the whole system up by the roots and destroy it." The rest of the first section remained intact. It prohibited states from abridging the privileges or immunities of citizens, depriving any "person"—a more expansive category that included aliens—of life, liberty, or property without due process of law, and denying any person the equal protection of the laws. "I can hardly believe," Stevens proclaimed, "that any person can be found who will not admit that every one of these provisions is just."[23]

·························· ❧ ··························

THE LAST-MINUTE ADDITION of a definition of American citizenship constitutionalized the principle that virtually every person born in the country is a citizen, regardless of race, national origin, or the political affiliation or legal status of one's parents. Today, the United States stands almost alone among industrialized nations in this; most countries, including every one in Europe, limit automatic access to citizenship in some way, making it dependent not simply on place of birth but on ethnicity, culture, religion, or extra requirements for children of noncitizen parents.

Adopted as part of the effort to purge the United States of the legacy of slavery, birthright citizenship, with which the Fourteenth Amendment begins, remains an eloquent statement about the nature of American society, a powerful force for assimilation of the children of immigrants, and a repudiation of a long history of racism. To be sure, this principle did not prevent subsequent egregious violations of citizens' constitutional rights, not only for African-Americans in the age of Jim Crow but also for other groups, including Japanese-Americans interned during World War II. Nonetheless, putting birthright citizenship into the Constitution represented a dramatic repudiation of the powerful tradition of equating citizenship with whiteness, a doctrine built into the naturalization process from the outset and constitutionalized by the Supreme Court in *Dred Scott*. Free black communities had long lived in a kind of legal limbo, their status as Americans constantly open to question. Some of the nation's most prominent political leaders, from Thomas Jefferson to Abraham Lincoln, had spoken of blacks as permanent aliens whose destiny lay in being "colonized" outside the United States. The first sentence of the Fourteenth Amendment also marked a radical change in the role of black women within American society. As slaves, they gave birth to property; now their children were citizens of the nation, rather than economic assets of white southerners.

The citizenship language seemed clear enough, but as one historian has noted, it was not "fully coherent," and its egalitarianism had limits. The specification of both national and state citizenship (to prevent states from denying local recognition to American citizens) was confusing and opened the door to later court decisions weakening the former while strengthening the latter—even though, as a Republican newspaper wrote in advocating ratification, "if there is one lesson written in bloody letters by the war, it is that the national citizenship must be paramount to that of the state." The status of the population that had lived longest on the land area of the United States remained unclear. Unlike the Civil Rights Act, the amendment did not explicitly exclude Native Americans, leading James R. Doolittle of Wisconsin, one of the few Republicans who still supported Andrew Johnson's Reconstruction policy, to charge that it would grant citizenship to "the wild Indians." But the amendment's requirement that citizens be "subject to the jurisdiction" of the United States was meant to leave out those living within Indian "nations." (It also, Howard noted, denied citizenship to the American-born children of foreign diplomats.) This language failed to clarify the status of Indians not residing on reservations. Unlike blacks, moreover, most Indians did not want national citizenship if it meant dissolving tribal sovereignty and making their land available to encroachment by whites. Not until 1924 did Congress extend birthright national citizenship to Native Americans, acknowledging them as members of the polity but at the same time dealing a severe blow to the idea of Indian sovereignty.

The Amendment's provision for birthright citizenship regardless of race seemed to require a revision of the naturalization laws which, beginning in 1790, had limited the process of becoming an American citizen from abroad to "white" immigrants. In 1870, Congress would amend these laws to enable black immigrants to become citizens. But even though members of Congress made it clear that birthright citizenship extended to "children begotten of Chinese parents," the bar to persons born in Asia becoming naturalized citizens remained in place until well into the twentieth century. Thus, a stark division was written into American law between immigrants from Asia, ineligible for citizenship, and their American-born, and therefore citizen, children.[24]

The remainder of the first section also made profound changes in the American legal system. The Civil Rights Act had listed specific rights that could not be denied to citizens by the states. The second sentence of the Fourteenth Amendment is couched in the language of general principles—privileges, immunities, due process, equal protection. "These words were chosen with care," George S. Boutwell, a member of a three-man subcommittee that gave final form to the amendment, later told the Senate. Most of this language appeared in the original Constitution. Bingham, with whom Section 1 originated, intentionally couched a radical transformation of the Constitution in familiar terms. "I did imitate the framers," he said; "every word . . . is today in the Constitution of our country." This was not entirely correct, but every word did have a history in either law or popular usage, although all were also subject to multiple interpretations, a process that has been going on since the amendment's ratification.[25]

Whether familiar or not, none of the language of Section 1 was self-explanatory. Even before Congress met in December 1865, Senator Lot Morrill of Maine wondered if "the words civil rights, immunities, privileges" possessed such definite meaning as to be "practicable" or whether Congress needed to "specify" their precise import. What, more than one congressman wondered during debate on the amendment, were the "privileges or immunities" of citizens? "I do not understand" that provision, complained Senator Reverdy Johnson, a Democrat from Maryland.

The prewar effort to interpret the original Constitution's mention of the "privileges and immunities" of citizens most widely cited during Reconstruction had come in an 1823 circuit court decision handed down by Justice Bushrod Washington (nephew of the first president).

The case involved a mundane matter—a law that barred people from out of state from harvesting oysters in the waters off New Jersey. It would be "more tedious than difficult" to enumerate the privileges and immunities of citizens, Washington wrote. He proceeded, nonetheless, to provide a list including protection by the government, enjoyment of life and liberty, the ability to acquire property and go to court, and even the right "to pursue and obtain happiness and safety . . . to which may be added, the elective franchise," as "regulated" by each state. Washington described these as "fundamental rights"—like Jefferson's "unalienable" rights in the Declaration of Independence, they preceded the formation of government and could not be abridged by law. (They did not, he ruled, extend to the right of people from other states to fish in New Jersey's waters.) Most of these rights, with the notable exception of the right to vote, had been included in the Civil Rights Act of 1866.[26]

The debates in Congress on the Fourteenth Amendment (which for grammatical reasons used privileges "or," not "and" immunities) did little to clarify the matter. Moreover, the issues of citizenship, rights, and federal authority had been "so elaborately and ably discussed" with regard to the Civil Rights Act, in the words of Senator Luke P. Poland of Vermont, that there was nothing more to add. More time was spent on other sections. The only detailed discussion of citizens' "privileges or immunities" was offered by Jacob Howard when he presented the amendment to the Senate. He did not seem to relish the challenge, fearing it "would be a somewhat barren discussion." Howard quoted Justice Washington's opinion, adding that Washington's list did not represent the "entire extent" of the entitlements protected by the Constitution. "To these," he said, "should be added the personal rights guaranteed and secured by the first eight amendments . . . a bill of rights in the Constitution. . . . The great object of the first section of the amendment is, therefore, to restrain the power of the states and compel them at all times to respect these great fundamental guarantees."[27]

Howard's mention of the Bill of Rights highlighted the dramatic change in the federal system brought about by the Reconstruction amendments. The Bill of Rights had been designed to restrict the actions of Congress, not the states. Chief Justice John Marshall stated this unequivocally in the case of *Barron v. Baltimore* (1833): "these amendments demanded security against the apprehended encroachments of the general government—not against those of the local governments." In legal terminology, Howard was describing the "incorporation" of the Bill of Rights—that is, requiring states to abide by its provisions—a process that has been going on for much of the twentieth century and into the twenty-first.

John A. Bingham also explicitly stated that privileges and immunities included the liberties enumerated in the Bill of Rights, many of which the state governments established by Andrew Johnson were flagrantly violating in the case of blacks, including the right to trial by "an impartial jury" and the right to bear arms. Before the war, Bingham had been one of the few who believed that the states were in fact bound by those amendments. But states had violated them with impunity, and in too many cases they had become "a mere dead letter." The Fourteenth Amendment, he declared, would "remedy this defect of the Constitution," and "arm the Congress of the United States . . . with the power to enforce the bill of rights." Thus, the Privileges or Immunities Clause of the Fourteenth Amendment applied not only to racial discrimination but to any state actions that deprived citizens of essential rights such as freedom of speech and the press, which many Republicans pointed out had long been abridged in the South. Before the war, for example, southern states adopted laws making criticism of slavery a crime without violating the First Amendment since these were state laws and not acts of Congress.[28]

On more than a dozen occasions in 1866, and many times subsequently, Bingham described the Privileges or Immunities Clause as encompassing the Bill of Rights. In 1866, however, the Bill of Rights had not acquired the iconic status in American legal thought and political culture it would later enjoy, and only a few other members mentioned it by name. Most preferred to speak more vaguely of "inalienable rights," "fundamental rights," "natural and personal rights." These categories could well extend beyond those identified in the Bill of Rights—for example to the frequently mentioned right to enjoy the fruits of one's labor, or to protection against violence or access to education. Abolitionists had long insisted that properly interpreted, the privileges and immunities of citizens included freedom from all kinds of racial discrimination. In any event, by the mid-1870s the idea that the Fourteenth Amendment "incorporated" the Bill of Rights had become, as far as Republicans were concerned, a virtually uncontroversial minimum interpretation of the amendment's purposes.[29]

The original Constitution had referred to the privileges and immunities of citizens of the states. The Fourteenth Amendment spoke instead of "citizens of the United States and of the State within which they reside" and prohibited states from abridging "the privileges or immunities of citizens of the United States." As will be related in Chapter 4, the Supreme Court soon effectively reduced the amendment's Privileges or Immunities Clause to insignificance. As a result, when the application of the Bill of Rights to the states later took place, it was almost always under the next clause of Section 1, which barred the states from abridging the life, liberty, or property of any person without "due process of law." "Due process" suggests procedural fairness, not substantive rights. It seems to promise that the lives of blacks would no longer be subject to the whims and prejudices of state and local authorities. Over time, however, the "liberty" protected by the Due Process Clause came to include most of the provisions of the Bill of Rights, as well as additional entitlements, such as the right to privacy, not mentioned there. Yet the Due Process Clause, borrowed directly from the Fifth Amendment, was barely discussed in Congress or the press in 1866. In one respect, however, its wording is more inclusive than the amendment's language protecting privileges or immunities. The latter is limited to American citizens; due process applies to "persons," a significantly broader category. Bingham made clear that this difference in wording was not inadvertent. He wanted, he said, to ensure that this part of the amendment protected "all persons, whether citizens or strangers, within this land." [30]

The final clause of Section 1 also applied to all persons, not just citizens. It barred the states from denying to any person the "equal protection of the laws." Of course, the idea of equality was deeply embedded in American political culture. The Declaration of Independence contained the stirring words "all men are created equal," a radical pronouncement at a time when most countries were ruled by monarchs and hereditary aristocrats. The proper role of government, Andrew Jackson had asserted in 1832 in his veto of the bill rechartering the Bank of the United States, was to provide "equal protection" to all citizens. Equality, Lincoln declared at Gettysburg, was the "proposition" on which the nation was founded. Unlike privileges, immunities, and due process, however, the word "equal" is not in the original Constitution (except with regard to states having an equal number of senators, and what happens if candidates for president or vice president end up with an equal number of electoral votes). The Fourteenth Amendment for the first time elevates equality to a constitutional right of all Americans. It makes the Constitution a vehicle through which aggrieved groups and individuals who believe that they are being denied equality can take their claims to court. Like the rest of Section 1, the guarantee of equal protection is race-neutral, and this has had enormous consequences. In recent decades, the courts have used the amendment to expand the legal rights of numerous Americans other than the descendants of slaves.

"Equal protection" may not have appeared in the prewar Constitution, but it was in the air. Abolitionists, black and white, had long demanded that African-Americans be accorded the equal protection of the laws. Bingham had insisted before the war not only that free blacks were American citizens but also that "the absolute equality of all, and the equal protection of each, are principles of our Constitution." The language was also invoked in the public appeals of black gatherings in the war's immediate aftermath. "We claim, . . . as citizens," declared Virginia's black convention of August 1865, that "the laws of the Commonwealth shall give to all men equal protection." The delegates went on to claim that this could only be accomplished "by extending to us the elective franchise."[31]

Like the American Revolution, Reconstruction was a moment when the language of equality reverberated in public debate. "A true republic," said William Windom, a Republican congressman from Minnesota, "rests upon the absolute equality of rights of the whole people, high and low, rich and poor, white and black." The Fourteenth Amendment's Equal Protection Clause, said a congressman from Illinois, was "so obviously right, that one would imagine nobody could be found so hard-hearted and cruel not to recognize its simple justice." Even the conservative *New York Commercial Advertiser* spoke of "making this a land of equal laws and equal rights." Like the rest of Section 1, however, equal protection was hardly self-explanatory. In the view of Senator Howard, the key was the law's impartiality, not its substantive content: "This abolishes all class legislation in the States and does away with the injustice of subjecting one caste of persons to a code not applicable to another." Many Republicans in and out of Congress went further. James A. Garfield would later describe the Equal Protection Clause as "the chief and most valuable addition made to the Constitution" during Reconstruction. "It is a broad and comprehensive limit on the power of the state governments," he explained, which required not only that laws be "equal on their face," but that they must be administered in a nondiscriminatory manner by public officials. Much of this discussion took place in vague generalities. Equality before the law—something that barely existed for blacks before the war—was a new and elusive concept. Over time, however, the Equal Protection Clause would become the vehicle for radically expanding the rights of all Americans.[32]

Section 1 of the Fourteenth Amendment primarily has to do with "state action"—preventing state governments and officials from denying citizens their basic rights, enacting discriminatory laws, or enforcing laws in a discriminatory manner—rather than the actions of private citizens. The words "law" or "laws" appear three times in the section's crucial second sentence. But an issue that would take on greater salience as Reconstruction progressed was already being discussed—did the amendment empower Congress to act against deprivations of rights not simply by laws or public officials, but by individuals, organizations, and mobs. "Equal protection" implied that it did.

In 1863, when the *National Anti-Slavery Standard* published an article entitled "Equal Protection Under the Law," it had to do with the failure of police to protect blacks from mob assault during the New York City Draft Riots. In the context of the violence sweeping the postwar South, the word "protection" in the Fourteenth Amendment conjured up not simply unequal laws but personal safety. Much congressional discussion in 1866, and much testimony before the Joint Committee, dealt with intimidation of the freed people and white Unionists by private parties. Garfield spoke of the need to ensure that the rights of citizens were "no longer left to the caprice of mobs."[33]

Was American citizenship little more than a formal status, or did it come with substantive rights—the "privileges or immunities" mentioned in the second sentence? If so, could such rights be abrogated by the actions of private citizens? Later in Reconstruction, Congress would determine that, under the Fourteenth Amendment, it had the authority to outlaw private practices that interfered with the promise of equal citizenship, including victimization by racially motivated violence and exclusion from hotels, transport, and other public venues. But, as we will see, the Supreme Court would apply a rigid understanding of state action to weaken dramatically the amendment's impact.

Future jurists would devote a great deal of energy to interpreting the individual clauses of Section 1. In 1866, however, most congressmen referred to them as a set of principles that should be viewed as a whole and reinforce one another. And despite controversy over the precise meaning of its language, the first section of the Fourteenth Amendment fundamentally transformed Americans' relationship to their government. The amendment asserted federal authority to create a new, uniform definition of citizenship and announced that being a citizen—or, in some cases, simply residing in the country—carried with it rights that could not be abridged. It proclaimed that everyone in the United States was to enjoy a modicum of equality, ultimately protected by the national government. The Fourteenth Amendment was a crucial step in transforming, in the words of the Republican editor George William Curtis, a government "for white men" into one "for mankind."[34]

❧

AS ONE HISTORIAN has written, the Fourteenth Amendment's first section set in motion a process whereby rights became attributes of a national citizenship rather than a welter of local statutes, traditional practices, and common law traditions, all of them grounded in inequality.[35] The commitment to equal rights, however, had its limits, as became clear in the amendment's second section. Here, the Joint Committee produced a long, almost incomprehensible attempt to solve the problems the original, failed representation amendment had sought to address—the enhanced political power of the South because of emancipation, and the relationship between voting requirements and a state's representation in Congress. Instead of the original proposal to penalize states that denied citizens the right to vote because of race, it substituted a reduction in representation when "adult male inhabitants" were disenfranchised for any reason other than rebellion or "other crime." The new wording answered the objection that the original language enabled states to disenfranchise most blacks without penalty through ostensibly nonracial literacy and property qualifications. It also avoided the "scramble" for voters some feared might ensue as states sought to increase their power in the House by enfranchising women. Now it made no difference to a state's representation if it allowed women to vote or not.

The original Constitution said nothing about gender, although it used the pronoun "he" some thirty times in describing federal officials, including the president. The Bill of Rights made no distinction between the civil liberties of men and women. The Fourteenth Amendment's citizenship, Privileges or Immunities, Due Process, and

Equal Protection clauses applied to all Americans and could plausibly be employed to combat gender discrimination along with other inequities. But with the second section and its penalty for states that restricted the voting rights of men but not women, the amendment for the first time introduced a gender distinction into the Constitution.

Debates over the Reconstruction amendments inevitably raised the question of the rights of women. The era's women's movement, which had grown out of abolitionism and employed that crusade's egalitarian language, sought to "bury the black man and the woman in the citizen." For women this meant erasing the common law tradition of coverture, whereby a married woman's legal identity was subsumed in that of her husband. Women should enjoy the same civil and political rights as men. Even before the Fourteenth Amendment was debated in Congress, deep divisions emerged within the abolitionist and feminist movements over whether the goal of black (male) suffrage should take precedence over the right to vote for all. Was Reconstruction, as Frederick Douglass, Wendell Phillips, and others—many of them longtime advocates of woman suffrage—claimed, "the Negro's hour?" Or was it, as Susan B. Anthony, Elizabeth Cady Stanton, and other feminists maintained, a rare hour of constitutional change which, if squandered, would set back the cause of women's rights for decades? "If that word 'male' be inserted," Stanton warned, "it will take us a century at least to get it out."[36] (If anything, Stanton was too optimistic. A century and a half after she wrote, the Constitution still does not include an Equal Rights Amendment banning discrimination based on sex.)

Having led the massive petition drive for the Thirteenth Amendment, the Women's Loyal National League in December 1865 launched a new campaign demanding that Congress prohibit the states from denying the right to vote "on the ground of sex." Already Stanton was demonstrating a penchant for using racially charged language, which she would employ more and more prominently during the next few years. Women, she insisted, should not "stand aside and see Sambo walk into the kingdom first." Black men were every bit as sexist as white, she argued, and once enfranchised would be "an added power to hold us at bay." The African-American poet, novelist, and journalist Frances Ellen Watkins Harper, who would soon strike out on a two-year speaking tour of the South during which she addressed numerous gatherings of freed women, called on white women to disassociate themselves from racism and work with blacks for the advancement of all. "We are all bound up together in one great bundle of humanity," she proclaimed, "and society cannot trample on the weakest and feeblest of its members without receiving the curse in its own soul." Harper sat on the platform with Stanton, Anthony, and others in May 1866 at the founding meeting of the American Equal Rights Association, established to press for voting rights for black men and all women. Phillips and Douglass implored the group to postpone woman suffrage. A historic opportunity to extend the suffrage to black men presented itself, while votes for women, they maintained, had no chance of approval by Congress or the states.[37]

The insertion of the word "male" into the Fourteenth Amendment resulted from a complex series of compromises relating to political power in Washington and the states' authority to regulate the right to vote. The status of women barely figured in these calculations. Debates over the Thirteenth Amendment and Civil Rights Act had already made clear that most Republican members of Congress did not see emancipation and the principle of legal equality as erasing the patriarchal rights of men, including black men, within their families. The very language used by supporters of black male suffrage associated the right to vote with martial prowess and "manhood." The ballot would be a reward for military service and a weapon with which black men could defend themselves and their families. This formulation did not seem to leave much room for votes for women. Petitions for woman suffrage came before the Joint Committee on Reconstruction during its deliberations, and the issue was occasionally debated in Congress. A handful of members supported the idea. Most did not. Richard Yates, a Radical Republican, insisted that to "thrust woman into the arena of political strife" would be "destructive of her womanly qualities." "The head of the family does the voting for the family," added John M. Broomall, another Radical.[38]

Even Charles Sumner, long an advocate of female suffrage, felt that 1866 was not "a proper time for the consideration of that question." Votes for women was "the great question of the future but for the present must be put aside." Sumner dutifully presented women's petitions to the Senate, but as his nemesis Fessenden coyly put it, the Massachusetts senator's exhaustive speeches on voting and natural rights "carefully avoided that part of the question." Sumner later related that in seeking a substitute for Section 2 he "wrote over nineteen pages of foolscap to get rid of the word 'male' and yet keep 'Negro suffrage' as a party measure intact but it could not be done." In the end, he came up with a proposal essentially the same as the final version, reducing a state's representation in Congress if it barred any male citizens from voting. Some of his colleagues thought it odd that Sumner's plan recognized the very principle he had "pronounced so infamous"—the right of states to limit the suffrage. Sumner replied that nonracial qualifications based on property or education (and presumably sex) were acceptable, "*but not color....* There must be only one rule for the two colors." The split between feminists and their erstwhile allies would soon play out in even starker form over the Fifteenth Amendment.[39]

If the first section of the Fourteenth Amendment marked "a sea change in American constitutionalism" by binding the rights of individuals to the power of the national state, the second, by leaving voting requirements in the hands of the states, illustrated that Republicans were unwilling to break completely with the traditions of federalism or to abolish the deeply rooted tradition of state and local "police" powers. But their federalism now envisioned an unprecedented degree of national authority to intervene in local affairs. While Section 2 did not enfranchise black men, for the first time it mandated a penalty for denying them the right to vote, something almost every state did before the Civil War. And in Section 3, the Fourteenth Amendment sought to ensure that, even without black suffrage, state governments in the South would be so constituted as to make federal intervention rare or unnecessary. That section, as it came from the Joint Committee, barred former Confederates from voting in national elections until 1870. But the Senate, reluctant to disenfranchise large numbers of white southerners, substituted a ban on officeholding by pre–Civil War officials who had gone on to support the Confederacy.

Many observers, Thaddeus Stevens among them, considered the revised Section 3 too lenient. But in some ways it was meant to have a deeper impact than the original version regarding voting by ex-Confederates. For it reached directly into the states to reshape their governments. It had more to do with who would exercise political power in the South than with punishing treason. Lawmakers had been flooded with complaints that "nearly every officer in all the southern states are decidedly rebels." The actions of southern governments, especially their enactment of the Black Codes and unwillingness or inability to suppress anti-black violence, had convinced Congress that they could not be trusted to put the egalitarian principles of Section 1 into effect. Section 3 was meant to prevent the rebirth of what Republicans called the Slave Power and help bring into being "a Union of truly democratic states."

The key issue was how to ensure that state governments would respect equality of rights. Congress, as James Wilson declared during debates on the Civil Rights Bill, was not "making a general criminal code for the states." If state authorities actually protected the rights of all then civil rights "could be left to the states." But if necessary, "we must do our duty by supplying the protection which the states deny." Republicans did not dismantle the federal system, but they did try to ensure that within that system, states would act responsibly. This could more readily be accomplished by the threat of federal action coupled with the establishment of what Republicans considered "loyal" governments in the South than by constant national intervention in local affairs. Section 3, one Republican member declared, sent a message that white southerners "must raise up a different class of politicians," men with "some regard for the principles that are contained in the Declaration of Independence."

Federalism endured, but a deeply modified federalism, which recognized the primacy of national citizenship and saw the states, not the national government, as most likely to infringe on Americans' fundamental rights. This point can be appreciated simply by comparing the first words of the Bill of Rights ("Congress shall make no law") with the beginning of the final sentence of each Reconstruction amendment ("Congress shall have the power"). The first constrains the federal government; the second, as Bingham explained, authorizes it to combat "the abuses of state power." Section 5 of the Fourteenth, empowering Congress to enact enforcement legislation, ensured that the process of defining Americans' rights would not end with ratification. Republicans assumed that this task would mostly fall to Congress. There were only sporadic references during the debates to the judiciary protecting Fourteenth Amendment rights, although very soon the federal courts would assert the power to pass judgment on congressional enforcement legislation.[40]

Modern discussion of the Fourteenth Amendment focuses almost exclusively on Section 1, both because of its far-reaching provisions and because virtually no jurisprudence has arisen from the rest of the amendment. Section 2—the automatic reduction of representation if states disenfranchised significant numbers of male voters—has never been implemented, even when post-Reconstruction southern governments took the right to vote away from blacks. Section 3 has long since faded into history. Section 4, also long forgotten, dealt with contentious financial issues that arose from the war. It guaranteed payment of the national debt and prohibited states or the federal government from paying any part of the Confederate debt, or providing compensation to former owners for the loss of their slave property. Democrats denounced the section as an effort to "change the Constitution for the benefit of the bond-holders." The *New York Herald* called Section 4 "the great secret strength of this constitutional amendment," as it aligned the country's major financial interests with ratification. (Section 4 recently attracted attention because of fears that congressional failure to raise the national government's debt limit would lead to a default on federal bonds, violating this part of the Fourteenth Amendment.)

Finally, like the Thirteenth, the Fourteenth Amendment ended with a section empowering Congress to enforce its provisions "by appropriate legislation." It would be up to Congress to interpret the amendment's open-ended language, determine the precise nature of the rights it protected, and, if necessary, take action to ensure that the states abided by its provisions. This "express grant of power to the Congress," Bingham told the House, was "absolutely central to American nationality."[41]

Although unable to prevent the amendment's passage, Democrats railed against it as a violation of two norms of American political life— white supremacy and the traditional power of the states to define and regulate the rights of their inhabitants. Months before passage, after a violent racist harangue against the Civil Rights Bill by Senator Garrett Davis of Kentucky, a Republican senator remarked, "it only comes back to this, that a nigger is a nigger." To which Davis responded, "that is the whole of it." Democratic members of Congress repeatedly identified American nationality with "the Caucasian race," insisted that the government "was made for white men," and objected to extending the "advantages" of American citizenship to "the Negroes, the coolies, and the Indians." William Niblack of Indiana eulogized Chief Justice Taney as "learned, distinguished, and incorruptible," and insisted that *Dred Scott* had been correctly decided. With equal persistence, Democrats contended that the amendment would destroy traditions of local self-rule and "invest all power in the national government."[42]

Democratic opposition to the amendment was predictable. The widespread disappointment voiced by Republicans was not. Many members of Congress seemed as anxious to point out what the amendment failed to accomplish as what it did. When he brought the amendment to the House floor, Thaddeus Stevens, whose radical convictions were always joined with a sense of political pragmatism, candidly explained why he supported passage: "It falls far short of my wishes, but . . . I believe it is all that can be obtained in the present state of public opinion. . . . I will take all I can get in the cause of

humanity and leave it to be perfected by better men in better times."
Shortly before final passage, Stevens again expressed disappointment,
in an eloquent statement of his political creed:[43]

> In my youth, in my manhood, in my old age, I had fondly
> dreamed that when any fortunate chance should have broken
> up for awhile the foundation of our institutions, and released
> us from obligations the most tyrannical that ever man imposed
> in the name of freedom, that the intelligent, pure and just men
> of this republic . . . would have so remodeled all our institutions
> as to have freed them from every vestige of human oppression,
> of inequality of rights, of the recognized degradation of the
> poor, and the superior caste of the rich. . . . This bright dream
> has vanished, "like the baseless fabric of a vision." I find that we
> shall be obliged to be content with patching up the worst por-
> tions of the ancient edifice, and leaving it, in many of its parts,
> to be swept through by . . . the storms of despotism. Do you
> inquire why . . . I accept so imperfect a proposition? I answer,
> because I live among men and not among angels.

"One Congress," said a Republican senator, "cannot bring about the
millennium." But a remarkable number of Republicans, Radical and
moderate, joined Stevens in expressing disappointment and promising more battles to come. A national guarantee of manhood suffrage,
said Garfield, was indispensable; "I profoundly regret, that we have
not been enabled to . . . engrave it upon our institutions." Yet he voted
for passage: "I am willing . . . when I cannot get all I wish to take what
I can get." When Howard presented the amendment to the Senate
he announced that he too would have preferred to "secure suffrage to
the colored race to some extent at least," but the states, and not only
in the South, were not yet ready for "so fundamental a change." Section 2, which might encourage southern states to extend the right to
vote to black men, was "the best that the committee could do." As for
Sumner, who said almost nothing during the final debates, the only

praise he could muster was that the amendment was "an installment, not a finality."[44]

Because it failed to include black male suffrage, abolitionists condemned the amendment. Wendell Phillips called it "a fatal and total surrender" and called for states to refuse ratification. Black activists expressed severe disappointment—they embraced the affirmation of birthright citizenship but insisted that with that status should come the vote, officeholding, jury service, and other rights. The amendment "does not go far enough," complained the *New Orleans Tribune*. While Massachusetts quickly ratified, the two black members of its legislature—one of whom, Edwin G. Walker, was the son of the famed abolitionist David Walker—were among the handful of members who voted no.[45]

On May 10, 1866, after only a few days of debate, the House approved the Fourteenth Amendment as it had emerged from the Joint Committee. On June 8, after adding the definition of citizenship to Section 1 and changing the temporary disenfranchisement of leading Confederates to barring them from office, the Senate approved it. Five days later, the House agreed to the Senate version. No Democrat voted in favor and no Republican against. Most northern states quickly voted to ratify, but to become part of the Constitution, some southern approvals would be necessary. One came almost immediately when Tennessee, now governed by anti-Johnson Republicans, ratified. In response, Congress agreed to seat the state's representatives and senators. But Republicans were split as to whether ratification by the other southern states would automatically restore them to their normal status within the Union.

The issue soon became moot, for in the ensuing months every other southern state, encouraged by President Johnson, rejected the amendment by overwhelming margins. (Louisiana's governor urged his legislature to ratify, but the lawmakers unanimously rebuffed him. "A governor without a single supporter in the legislature is without precedent in the political annals of the country," commented a local newspaper.) If Radical Republicans saw the amendment as disappointingly weak, white southerners deemed it an unwarranted, indeed outrageous, interference in their states' internal affairs. Southern objections focused both on practical political matters—loss of representation because of denying blacks the right to vote, the bar to office-holding by "the best portion of our citizens"—and on broader fears for the future of white supremacy. Opponents charged that Congress might well feel authorized to use the amendment to give "Negroes political and social equality with the whites." To accept such a fate by agreeing to ratify, a southern newspaper wrote, would be a form of "self-degradation." [46]

The Fourteenth Amendment had many objectives and served many purposes. Along with its genuinely idealistic aims, it was a plan for securing key results of the Civil War in the Constitution so that when the southern states were restored to full participation in the Union these could not be undone. It was also a political document, meant to serve as a campaign platform for the congressional elections of 1866. "Doubtless," declared the *Wisconsin State Register*, the amendment did not "meet the views of a large portion of our party.... Still, this amendment furnishes a common ground on which all ought to be able to stand. Let us go to the people with it." And the fall election of 1866 became the closest thing American politics has seen to a referendum on a constitutional amendment. Seldom, said the *New York Times*, had a political campaign been conducted "with so exclusive reference to a single issue." [47] Republicans swept to an emphatic victory in all the northern states.

Coupled with the continued intransigence of President Johnson (who broke with political tradition in the fall of 1866 to campaign actively for congressional candidates opposed to the Fourteenth Amendment) and the categorical rejection of the amendment in the South, the outcome of the fall elections spelled the end of Johnson's plan of Reconstruction. Moderate Republicans now concluded that the only way to ensure "loyal government" in the South, secure equal rights for the former slaves, and bring about the amendment's ratification was to "hurl from power," as Trumbull put it, the Johnson governments and enfranchise black men. Considering the hesitation among Republicans only a few months earlier, the rapid emergence in the second session of the Thirty-ninth Congress of a consensus in favor of black suffrage is remarkable. Beginning in December 1866, Congress enfranchised black men in Washington, D.C., and the western territories, and made black suffrage a requirement for the admission of Nebraska and Colorado as states. Early in March 1867, over Johnson's veto, Republicans launched the experiment in interracial democracy known as Radical Reconstruction. The Reconstruction Act of 1867 placed the ex-Confederate states, other than Tennessee, under temporary military rule. It required that new governments be elected by black and white male voters (with the exception of Confederate leaders barred from officeholding by the Fourteenth Amendment). The southern states were obligated to adopt new constitutions incorporating the right to vote regardless of race. And they were required to ratify the Fourteenth Amendment.[48]

Over the course of the next two years, Radical Reconstruction would be put into operation. The new southern governments adopted constitutions that attempted to create the framework for democratic, egalitarian societies. These documents built upon and extended the language of the Fourteenth Amendment. Georgia copied the wording of Section 1 into its state constitution. Texas barred the state government from depriving any citizen of "any right, privilege, or immunity . . . on account of race." North Carolina's constitution began with a quotation from the Declaration of Independence but added "enjoyment of the fruits of their own labor" to the inalienable rights of man. Louisiana's declared that all citizens "shall enjoy the same civil, political, and public rights and privileges." All the new constitutions prohibited voting restrictions based on race, and established state-supported public-school systems for white and black students (a public education system had existed before the war only in North Carolina and there only for white students). In case the future administration of law in the South did not live up to these principles, Congress also broadly expanded the right to remove cases from state to federal courts. Federal supervision of Americans' rights would not end when the southern states were restored to the Union.[49]

In July 1868, Secretary of State William H. Seward announced that the amendment had been ratified. His tally included approval by seven southern states that had first rejected the amendment and then, after new biracial governments were put in place, reversed themselves and approved it. Here, indeed, is a profound irony. The framers of the Fourteenth Amendment studiously avoided including black suffrage among its provisions. But without the votes of black men in southern elections and legislatures, the amendment could never have become part of the Constitution.[50]

Considering its centrality today to American constitutional law and legal culture, it is remarkable how little elation greeted the Fourteenth Amendment. Unlike the Thirteenth, there was no jubilation when Congress approved it. Unlike the Fifteenth, its ratification did not inspire celebratory parades throughout the country. The amendment, as we have seen, was a compromise that seemed fully to satisfy no one. Nonetheless, contemporaries recognized it as a far-reaching transformation in the legal and political system. It involved "such fundamental changes in the principle of government," wrote the *New York Journal of Commerce*, that it could "be regarded only as the commencement of a revolution in American affairs." Over time, the Fourteenth Amendment would lead many Americans to view the federal government as the ultimate protector of their rights and to expand the definition of those rights far beyond anything known before the Civil War, or anticipated by the Thirty-ninth Congress. But the rights revolution launched by the war and emancipation was not yet complete. The very ambiguity of the language of Section 1 left it uncertain how radical a shift had taken place in the relative powers of the state and federal governments and what specific rights and entitlements were now being guaranteed by national authority. The answers would be worked out over time, and would depend on the future balance of political power.

Then there was the vexed question of black suffrage, now operative in the South under the 1867 Reconstruction Act, but not in the rest of the country. This issue, declared the influential *Springfield Republican*, "is not to be got rid of." Because the amendment ignored it, the paper continued, it could not be regarded as a "final settlement" to the problem of Reconstruction. The Constitution would have to be amended one more time, to deal with the right to vote.[51]

3

THE RIGHT TO VOTE

The Fifteenth Amendment

T HE ADVENT of Radical Reconstruction in 1867 and with
it the right to vote for African-American men in the South
inspired a wave of political mobilization without precedent in
the region's history. Freedmen and freedwomen flocked to organized
meetings and impromptu gatherings. They heard speakers, including
itinerant black lecturers, agents of the Freedmen's Bureau, and Republican party organizers, discuss immediate issues such as the results of
northern elections and congressional deliberations, and broader subjects: the trajectory of American history, the "superiority" of democratic institutions, the "individual benefits of citizenship." Many such
meetings were guarded by armed black sentinels. "At least one half
of the black male population . . . have guns of all kinds," reported a
white resident of Mississippi, noting that blacks claimed that the Civil
Rights Act gave them the right to bear arms "regardless of the state
law in opposition." Throughout the South, white employers complained that black laborers abandoned their work without permission
to attend campaign rallies and meetings of newly established political
clubs. "They say now they just begin to feel their freedom and equal
rights with the white man," one Alabama overseer observed.[1]

With the Fourteenth Amendment on its way to final approval, the language of the rewritten Constitution took on increased prominence in black political discourse. "We had men of the most influence and intelligence among our people to speak to them," one black organizer related, "and to tell them what the constitution meant." What it meant, more than anything else, was equality, expansively defined. "We claim exactly the same rights, privileges and immunities as are enjoyed by white men—we ask nothing more, and will be content with nothing less," declared the address of the Colored Mass Convention that met in Mobile in April 1867. The participants' broad understanding of these privileges and immunities went beyond the traditional framework of civil and political rights to include full and equal access to all public institutions and accommodations. Black speakers insisted they did not demand "social equality" in private interactions. But equal public rights were essential to equal citizenship: "So long as a park or a street is a *public* park or street, the entire public has the right to use it; so long as a car or a steamboat is a public conveyance, it must carry all who come to it." The invocation of constitutional language persisted throughout Reconstruction. During Mississippi's violent electoral campaign of 1875, when white "rifle clubs" sought to prevent freedmen from voting, one black resident wrote to the state's governor, "Did not the 14th Article . . . say that no person shall be deprived of life nor property without due process of law? It said all persons have equal protection of the laws but I say we colored men don't get it at all. . . . Is that right, or is it not? No sir, it is wrong."[2]

The former slaves, a northern correspondent wrote in 1873, self-consciously viewed themselves as individuals "newly invested with all the rights of an American citizen." And central to their conception of rights was the suffrage. As the historian Anne C. Bailey has put it, they saw the right to vote as "the heart and soul of their freedom." Black leaders claimed the suffrage, in the words of John Mercer Langston, president of the National Equal Rights League, as "an essential and inseparable part of self-government, and therefore natural and inalienable." More than simply a way of influencing government and securing protection for their interests and rights, blacks viewed the suffrage, W. E. B. Du Bois would later write, as part of a larger aspiration—to be treated as an equal, "a co-worker in the kingdom of culture." And partly thanks to the black mobilization, congressional Republicans recognized that, as Massachusetts congressman George S. Boutwell put it, "it is impossible, . . . whatever may be the wishes, or the hopes, or the prejudices of any portion of the people of the country, for us to escape this issue as a Congress and a party."[3]

With the passage and implementation of the Reconstruction Act of 1867, the large majority of the country's black men enjoyed the right to vote. But many still did not—mainly the tens of thousands in the border states that had never left the Union and therefore were not subject to Reconstruction and in Tennessee, which had avoided the requirements of the Reconstruction Act by ratifying the Fourteenth Amendment in 1866. There was also a smaller number of disenfranchised blacks in the North. The regional disparity seemed increasingly indefensible. Indeed, wrote the *Boston Advertiser*, "the present state of the laws with regard to the elective franchise" was "absurd to the last degree." In the South, the nation, "with its mighty war power," required black suffrage. Could the northern and border states logically refuse to grant their own black populations the right now enjoyed in the South? In addition, even as southern states drew up new constitutions guaranteeing black male suffrage, fears persisted that these provisions might be altered in the future. An amendment guaranteeing black voting rights throughout the nation would, it seemed, solve these problems. More and more Republicans, in addition, now viewed the suffrage (at least for men) as an indispensable element of freedom, a natural right akin to those enumerated in the Declaration of Independence.[4]

The issue of black voting, however, remained fraught with political danger, a problem dramatically illustrated in the state elections of 1867, when northern Democrats made dramatic gains. Their victory in the pivotal state of Ohio was widely attributed to Republicans' unsuccessful attempt to establish black suffrage there via a referendum.

The party's leaders, Speaker of the House Schuyler Colfax concluded, had been too far "ahead of the people." That same year voters in Connecticut, Kansas, and Minnesota turned down black suffrage proposals, and, in Kansas, also rejected extending the vote to women. To be sure, the results, with respect to black voting rights, were far closer than in similar referendums before the Civil War. A considerable majority of Republicans voted yes, but enough joined Democrats in opposition to defeat these measures.[5]

The Republican dilemma was strikingly articulated in an exchange between Senators Henry Wilson of Massachusetts and Samuel C. Pomeroy of Kansas early in 1869. Refuting Democrats' charge that efforts to extend black suffrage to the entire nation were motivated by the prospect of partisan advantage, Wilson insisted that the struggle for racial equality cost the party far more votes than it might gain. "There is not today a square mile in the United States," he declared, "where the advocacy of the equal rights and privileges of those colored men has not been in the past and is not now unpopular." Yet Pomeroy countered that "adherence to principle" was the Republican party's raison d'être. Were it to abandon "the cause of the rights of man, of the rights of the colored men, . . . I apprehend that the party itself would not be worth preserving."[6]

"The *Negro* question," wrote former Pennsylvania congressman Henry D. Moore at the end of 1867, required "common sense. . . . We cannot overcome the prejudices of a lifetime at once." The northern people, he warned, would support black suffrage in the South to keep "rebels and traitors" out of office, but not in their own states. The party's position, Moore advised Elihu B. Washburne, an Illinois congressman and close advisor of Ulysses S. Grant, should be that black voting was necessary in the South to secure the results of the Civil War, but that it belonged to the people of each northern state to decide the question for themselves.

This was precisely the stance adopted by the Republican convention that nominated Grant for president in May 1868. The platform strongly endorsed the Reconstruction policy of Congress, includ-

"Scene in the House on the Passage of the Proposition to Amend the Constitution."
Approval of the Thirteenth Amendment by the House of Representatives on January 31, 1865, set off a
wild celebration on the floor and in the galleries. "The scene," wrote one northern correspondent, "was
entirely without precedent in all our national history."

(Library of Congress)

John A. Bingham of Ohio, chief author of
Section One of the Fourteenth Amendment.
(Library of Congress)

James M. Ashley of Ohio, who introduced
the Thirteenth Amendment in the House of
Representatives in December 1863.
(Hulton Archive/Getty Images)

Charles Sumner of Massachusetts, the
leading congressional advocate of equality for black Americans and author of the
bill that, after his death, became the Civil
Rights Act of 1875. The Supreme Court
declared it unconstitutional in 1883.
(New York Public Library)

Thaddeus Stevens of Pennsylvania, floor leader
of House Republicans and outspoken Radical.
(Library of Congress)

"The Reconstruction Policy of Congress, as Illustrated in California." Democrats appealed forthrightly to racism in opposing the expansion of citizenship and political rights to include African-Americans. This cartoon from the election campaign of 1867 portrays Republican candidate for governor George C. Gorham's support for black male suffrage as opening the door to voting by Chinese and Native Americans. On the bottom left, Brother Jonathan, a traditional symbol of the United States, places his hand over a ballot box and admonishes Gorham, "Young Man! read the history of your Country, and learn that this ballot box was dedicated to the white race alone." The three figures supported by Gorham speak in highly exaggerated dialect. On the right, a monkey is brought forward to join the voters.

(Library of Congress)

"Electioneering at the South." With the coming of black male suffrage, a wave of political mobilization swept over the South. Women as well as men took part in these grassroots gatherings. *(Library of Congress)*

A rare photograph of an election campaign in Baton Rouge, Louisiana, probably in 1868. The brass band is promoting a Republican candidate for the state senate. Black and white Louisianians observe the scene; on the right, a man holds an American flag. *(Andrew D. Lytle Collection, Mss. 1254-C-042, Louisiana and Lower Mississippi Valley Collection, LSU Libraries, Baton Rouge, La.)*

THE RESULT OF THE FIFTEENTH AMENDMENT,
And the Rise and Progress of the African Race in America and its final Accomplishment, and Celebration on May 19th A.D. 1870.

"The Result of the Fifteenth Amendment." The ratification of the Fifteenth Amendment in 1870 inspired celebrations throughout the country. This lithograph depicts the largest such event, in Baltimore, where tens of thousands of African-Americans took part. At the center, uniformed black Zouaves march down Monument Street carrying rifles, while a biracial crowd looks on. Around the central image are scenes of black life: slave labor at upper left, black Civil War soldiers at upper right, and at the bottom a schoolroom and a church scene with the motto "the day of Jubilee has come." The individuals pictured are, on the left Radical Republicans Thaddeus Stevens, Henry Winter Davis, and Charles Sumner; on the right black abolitionists Martin R. Delany and Frederick Douglass, and the first black U. S. Senator, Hiram Revels. At the top, from left to right, are Abraham Lincoln, Maryland Republican jurist Hugh Lennox Bond, John Brown, Vice President Schuyler Colfax, and Ulysses S. Grant.

(Library of Congress)

"Uncle Sam's Thanksgiving Dinner." An engraving by Thomas Nast, published shortly before the ratification of the Fifteenth Amendment, illustrates the new conception of nationhood implemented in the second founding. Whites, blacks, Asian-Americans, Native Americans, men, and women enjoy a harmonious feast, with "universal suffrage" as its centerpiece. Portraits of Abraham Lincoln, George Washington, and Ulysses S. Grant adorn the wall. At the upper right is a painting of Castle Garden, New York, where European newcomers landed before the opening of Ellis Island, and on the lower left the motto, "come one come all," indicating that the ideal of equality applied to immigrants as well as persons born in the United States.

(Library of Congress)

"The Judiciary Committee of the House of Representatives Receiving a Deputation of Female Suffragists." Women activists deeply resented the inclusion of the word "male" in the Fourteenth Amendment and the failure of the Fifteenth to extend the right to vote to women. The group pictured here, pressing the committee to enfranchise women, includes Elizabeth Cady Stanton, seated just to the right of the speaker, and Susan B. Anthony, at the table on the extreme right. Addressing the committee is Victoria Woodhull, a prominent radical feminist.
(Library of Congress)

Rodolphe Desdunes, a leader of the Citizens' Committee, which challenged the constitutionality of Louisiana's Separate Car Act of 1890 that required railroads to segregate black and white passengers. The committee fought the case of *Plessy v. Ferguson* all the way to the Supreme Court, where the law was upheld.
(Amistad Research Center, New Orleans, La.)

Justice John Marshall Harlan, principled dissenter in the *Civil Rights Cases*, *Plessy v. Ferguson*, and other Supreme Court decisions that severely limited the scope of the second founding.
(Library of Congress)

BELOW: "Fourteenth Amendment." This cartoon from 1902 chides Congress for failing to implement Section Two of the Fourteenth Amendment. After the southern states disenfranchised nearly all black men, they should have suffered a significant reduction in their members of the House of Representatives, but this penalty was never enforced.
(Library of Congress)

Don't wake him up!

CONGRESS

LAW ENFORCEMENT

14TH AMENDMENT 2ND SECTION

ing extending the right to vote to "all loyal men in the South." But it simultaneously sought to reassure uneasy northerners that Congress would not tamper with their states' voting requirements, declaring that "the question of suffrage in all the loyal states properly belongs to the people of those states." Some congressional Radicals, including Charles Sumner and Richard Yates, had argued that as a consequence of the Thirteenth and Fourteenth Amendments, Congress possessed the power to enact legislation requiring all the states to enfranchise blacks. Yates later claimed that the suffrage plank was inserted in the platform to "exclude" that possibility. In any event, Radicals and black leaders were furious at what they considered rank hypocrisy. The platform was "tame and cowardly," complained Thaddeus Stevens. "We are not now merely expounding a government," he declared, "we are making a nation.... When you attempt to depart from [universal suffrage] you cease to be men and become tyrants, deserving the execration of the human race." In August 1868, Stevens died at the age of seventy-six, depriving Radical Republicans in Congress of perhaps their foremost leader.[7]

The future of black suffrage became a major issue in the campaign of 1868, which witnessed some of the most overt appeals to racism in American political history. While pronouncing the questions of slavery and secession "settled for all time to come," the Democratic platform assailed Republicans for forcing "Negro supremacy" upon the South and promised to return to the ex-Confederate states "the regulation of the elective franchise." The Democratic candidate for vice president, Francis Preston Blair Jr., a member of one of the country's most prominent political families (his father had been a close advisor of Andrew Jackson and his brother Montgomery served in Lincoln's cabinet), promised that Reconstruction would be overthrown and southern whites authorized to create new state governments. His letter accepting the nomination charged that Republicans had put the South under the rule of "an alien race of semi-barbarous men." Horatio Seymour, the presidential candidate, eschewed such inflammatory language, but Blair set the tone for the Democratic campaign.

"All men are not equal," announced the *New York World*, the party's leading newspaper. "Races differ, and color is the sign-post to the difference," indicating, among other things, whether or not people possessed the capacity to cast an intelligent vote.[8]

In the summer of 1868, a large convention of blacks from the northern and border states gathered in Baltimore to complain that in their states, black men were "systematically deprived of suffrage, the first, the crowning right of citizenship." Content with emphasizing Grant's military accomplishments and warning that Democratic victory would set off another civil war, however, Republicans said little about black suffrage during the campaign. Fear about its unpopularity was not the only reason. Another, James G. Blaine later claimed, was that the platform plank on the subject was "so obviously unfair and unmanly . . . that the Republicans became heartily ashamed of it long before the political canvass had closed." Grant's electoral victory gave a strong impetus to the movement to enfranchise black men throughout the nation. Voters in Iowa and Minnesota approved black suffrage referendums, suggesting that Republicans could weather popular racism, while Grant's unexpectedly narrow margin of victory (300,000 votes in a total of three million) made clear the political value of safeguarding black voting in the South and extending it northward, especially into the border states, three of which Seymour carried. Three days after Grant's victory, the influential *Philadelphia Press* called for a constitutional amendment to guarantee all black men the right to vote.[9]

As soon as the next session of Congress assembled in December, Senator Aaron H. Cragin of New Hampshire introduced an amendment prohibiting the states from denying the right to vote to any adult male citizen, except for "participation in rebellion, or other crime." That same day, William D. Kelley of Pennsylvania presented to the House a proposal barring states from denying the right to vote because of race or color. Many other versions of a Fifteenth Amendment quickly followed, "no two alike, and containing widely variant principles," said one Republican newspaper, along with weeks of debate and numerous votes, in which both houses did not hesitate to change their minds. But essentially, Republicans had to choose between the approaches outlined by Cragin and Kelley at the outset—an amendment establishing a uniform national standard that enfranchised virtually all adult male citizens, or a "negative" one barring the use of race or other criteria to limit the right to vote but otherwise leaving qualifications in the hands of the states. The first possibility represents a road not taken that would have barred the methods used by southern states in the late nineteenth century to disenfranchise their black populations as well as most state voter suppresion measures today.[10]

The long, complex debates, which consumed hundreds of pages of the *Congressional Globe*, ranged over the entire ground of citizens' rights and the requirements of democratic government. Members were aware that this was the first time that voting rights had received sustained discussion at the national level. Initially focused on blacks, the debate quickly expanded to consider the right to vote more generally. For many members, the traditional idea that the suffrage was "conventional" and subject to restriction was incompatible with the democratic spirit of the age. "The irresistible tendency of modern civilization," declared Senator Pomeroy, "is in the direction of the extension of the right of suffrage. . . . The day when a few men did the voting and governing for the many has gone by." "Suffrage," said Edmund G. Ross of Kansas (a moderate whose vote in the Senate had helped acquit Andrew Johnson in his impeachment trial a few months earlier), "is one of those natural rights . . . inherent and guaranteed by the spirit if not by the letter of the Constitution. . . . It is basic to protecting all other rights." Referring to the emancipated slave, he continued, "there is not a single argument in favor of his liberation from physical servitude which does not apply with equal force in favor of his enfranchisement."[11]

The debates also revealed that Republicans differed sharply among themselves as to what restrictions on the right to vote were legitimate and how far the principle of equality actually reached. Radicals favored an amendment that created a single set of voting requirements for the entire nation, a reflection of their strong sense of nationalism born of the Civil War. The right to vote should be "uniform throughout the land," declared Thomas Jenckes of Rhode Island. State control of voting qualifications, claimed Senator Oliver P. Morton of Indiana, was a relic of state sovereignty, the frame of mind that had produced secession. "The whole fallacy," said Morton, "lies in denying our nationality. I assert that we are one people and not thirty-seven different peoples; that we are one nation, and as such we have provided for ourselves a national Constitution." In January 1869, a National Convention of the Colored Men of America assembled in Washington to press the case for a voting rights amendment. Many such gatherings had been held before and after the Civil War, but now, for the first time, the nearly two hundred delegates included numerous black political leaders and officeholders from the South. The call for the convention grounded the demand for the right to vote squarely on the national citizenship recently "declared by the [Fourteenth] Amendment"; henceforth, "no state should be "permitted to withhold from citizens, on account of color merely, the rights of citizens." Americans' liberties, the delegates resolved, "can never be safe or uniform while the states are acknowledged to be the only power to regulate the suffrage."[12]

"Our object is to secure universal suffrage to all adult male citizens of this country," declared George S. Boutwell of Massachusetts. Boutwell sought to revive the idea of achieving this by statute on the grounds that voting was one of the "privileges or immunities" of citizenship guaranteed in Section 1 of the Fourteenth Amendment. This argument failed to explain why Section 2 of the same amendment appeared to acknowledge the right of states to limit the right to vote, while imposing a political penalty for doing so. One reason a constitutional amendment was necessary, declared William Higby of California, was to resolve "the difficulty, confusion, and misconception that have grown out of the apparent conflict between the first and second sections of the fourteenth article," and to ensure that citizenship, and with it the right to vote, "will rest where it should, at the foundation of the government."[13]

"Many people who have opposed Negro suffrage," the New York *Journal of Commerce* noted as Congress debated, now favored it "as part of what is vaguely called 'the great revolution' through which we are supposed to be going." Reflecting the rapid evolution of rights consciousness during Reconstruction, even conservative Republicans, such as Senator William M. Stewart of Nevada, had by this time become convinced that extension of the suffrage to black men was the "logical result" of the destruction of slavery. "We cannot stop short of this," Stewart declared. "It is the only measure that will really abolish slavery [and] guarantee that each man shall have a right to protect his own liberty."[14] But the tradition of state control of voting requirements was deeply entrenched, and many northern states, while willing to see black men enfranchised, did not wish to surrender that power. Indeed, in a reversal of the historic pattern, expanding the right to vote to include blacks now generated less controversy than tampering with other kinds of restrictions.

Debate over the status of Chinese-Americans helped to shape the Fifteenth Amendment. In California, Nevada, and Oregon, all of which limited voting to white men, opponents focused not on the consequences of enfranchising blacks, but on the amendment's possible future impact on the Chinese population. This numbered around 50,000, most of them contract laborers in mines, on railroads, and in low-wage urban jobs. Western members of Congress gave voice to the region's strong anti-Chinese prejudices. "They are and continue to be," said Republican senator George H. Williams of Oregon, "the ignorant and besotted devotees of absolutism in politics and the blind disciples of paganism in religion." Williams warned that even an amendment limited to barring voting qualifications based on "race" or "color" might be construed in the future to apply to the Chinese, opening the door to voting rights. Henry W. Corbett, the junior senator from Oregon, distinguished sharply between the justice of extending the vote to blacks, a policy "blessed" by "the Great Ruler of the universe," and doing the same for the Chinese, "a different race entirely." Nevada's Republican congressman, Thomas Fitch, announced that there were not "ten American citizens" on the Pacific coast "who favor Chinese suffrage."[15]

If the debates demonstrated the limits of western Republicans' egalitarianism when it came to the Chinese, they also exposed prejudice in the East against other immigrants, especially Irish Catholics. Given the increasing size of the "criminal classes" in the nation's large cities, the *Cincinnati Gazette* observed, it might become necessary "to restrict the suffrage" to property owners. The *Springfield Republican* agreed that high rates of taxation in urban centers demonstrated the danger of allowing impoverished immigrants to elect officials whose spendthrift policies undermined "citizens' rights of property." Rhode Island subjected its mostly Irish immigrant population to a property qualification for voting not applied to native-born citizens. Massachusetts and Connecticut used literacy tests to curtail immigrant voting. Senator James W. Patterson of New Hampshire opposed any language that would prohibit educational qualifications. To deny the right to vote "on account of race or color or want of property," he maintained, "is doing violence to the civilization of our age." But to "guard" the suffrage against "the incoming floods of ignorance and barbarism," to throw it open to "the emissaries of arbitrary power, the minions of despotism" (a thinly veiled reference to Roman Catholics), would put liberty itself in danger. Not all Republicans shared Patterson's prejudices. Simon Cameron of Pennysvlania favored an amendment broad enough to cover "everybody; the Negro, the Irishman, the German, the Frenchman." He even added "the Chinaman" to his list, proclaiming, "I welcome every man, whatever may be the country from which he comes." But nativism helped to undermine prospects for an "affirmative" amendment. One further complication was that the constitutions of Missouri, West Virginia, and Tennessee barred certain ex-Confederates from casting ballots. A "positive" amendment would restore their right to vote.[16]

THE REPUBLICAN PARTY'S internal disunity regarding who, precisely, should have the right to vote helps explain the Fifteenth Amendment's tortured trajectory to passage in early 1869. As one Republican newspaper explained, "a positive provision would take the whole question of suffrage out of the jurisdiction of the states," and require "national supervision of registration and voting. . . . We doubt whether any one seriously contemplates so vast a change in our system." Since, as another newspaper declared, "there are not half a dozen states" that would approve a positive amendment, language guaranteeing the right to vote to all adult male citizens never won approval in either house. Debate focused instead on which qualifications were illegitimate. The most far-reaching language came from Henry Wilson, whose version of the Fifteenth Amendment barred discrimination in voting rights based on race, color, place of birth, property, education, or religious creed. This, countered his Senate colleague Jacob M. Howard, was entirely too sweeping: "it contemplates a complete revolution in state constitutions." Howard preferred an amendment limited to black men. The debate did not precisely map factional divisions within the party. Senator John Sherman of Ohio, a leading moderate, supported the Radicals' idea of removing from the states "all power to exclude any portion of male citizens" from voting. The party, Sherman added, was "about to lay the foundation for a political creed [and] the broadest and safest and best foundation for it is universal suffrage." He added that he would leave to the states the authority to decide whether women should vote.[17]

Many Republicans, however, feared that an amendment that struck down nonracial voting requirements in the northern states could not achieve ratification. There was also disagreement about whether to include the right to hold office in the amendment. Some feared that this would undermine prospects for ratification. Others insisted that officeholding was a logical consequence of suffrage and did not need to be mentioned explicitly. State restrictions on officeholding, the *Chicago Tribune* argued, were superfluous in any event. "If the people of any state want to elect a Negro, or Chinaman, or a Japanese, an Irishman, a German, a Protestant, a Catholic, a Mormon, a Jew, or an infidel, they will find a way to do it." Proposals also circulated to change the way presidential electors were chosen, or do away with the Electoral College entirely. These, unfortunately, got nowhere.[18]

Debate on the amendment became so divisive that it took up several long sessions, including one that lasted all night and proved singularly "unprofitable." In February 1869, the Senate approved Wilson's proposed amendment with its extensive list of prohibited grounds for disenfranchisement. The House, however, insisted on a narrower version confined to race but also mentioning the right to hold public office. The Senate backtracked and approved the House version, whereupon the House, in what Blaine would later call a "capricious change of opinion," voted for a broader amendment, barring nativity, property, and educational requirements. With time running out in the session of Congress, the language adopted by the two houses went to a conference committee, which further confused matters by approving the Senate's "negative" version limited to race, and dropping mention of the right to hold office, which both houses had approved.[19]

As the amendment's fate hung in the balance, a surprising intervention by Wendell Phillips helped tip the scales in favor of narrower language. In an article in the *National Anti-Slavery Standard*, Phillips urged "prudence" upon members of Congress: "for the first time in our lives we beseech them to be a little more *politicians* and a little less reformers." An amendment limited to black voting, Phillips insisted, was "all the ground that people are ready to occupy." It would demonstrate "utter lack of common sense" to include mention of "nationality, education, creed, etc." Phillips's intervention persuaded enough Radicals to go along with the conference committee's proposal to ensure passage in the Senate. "Your voice," Boutwell informed Phillips after the measure had been approved, "saved the Fifteenth Amendment."[20]

Nonetheless, some senators were irate at the conference committee's conduct in eliminating provisions both houses had approved—"unparliamentary and almost unprecedented," said Pomeroy. But with adjournment nearing, there was no alternative but to accept the committee's language. Seven Republican senators, however, abstained, among them Charles Sumner. The young Georges Clemenceau, reporting on American events for a Paris newspaper, blamed the "timidity" of the final version on "the prejudices still rife in the very heart of the Republican party." He failed to mention that these prejudices were not directed at blacks. The adoption of a weaker version, restricted to eliminating racial barriers to voting, stemmed not from a limited commitment to black rights but to opposition to equality for others, especially immigrants from China and Ireland, and the conviction that a "simple and direct" amendment was most likely to win ratification.[21]

Congress was hardly unaware that the Fifteenth Amendment's purpose might be circumvented. Several members warned that the amendment could be rendered void via poll taxes, literacy tests, and other ostensibly nonracial requirements that in the South primarily affected blacks. Even though everyone assumed that, in accordance with the Fourteenth Amendment, this would result in a reduction of southern representation in Congress, it was an "almost fatal defect," declared Samuel Shellabarger of Ohio. "The body of this race, made ignorant and destitute by our wrong, may substantially all now be excluded from the elective franchise under a qualification of intelligence or property." Without violating the wording of the amendment, warned Senator Willard Warner, representing reconstructed Alabama, nine-tenths of the black population could be disenfranchised by literacy or property qualifications.[22]

The Fifteenth Amendment, Henry Adams wrote shortly after its approval by Congress, was "more remarkable for what it does not than for what it does contain." Unlike the Fourteenth, with its universalist language, the Fifteenth did not expand the rights of citizenship for all Americans, but brought blacks into an otherwise unchanged electoral system. It left untouched, Senator Oliver P. Morton complained, "all the existing irregularities and incongruities in suffrage" other than those explicitly directed at blacks. It implemented what many referred to as "impartial" suffrage (voting requirements that applied equally to whites and blacks), not "universal" or even "manhood" suffrage (which would have guaranteed the right of virtually all men to vote). By focusing entirely on voting rights and race, the amendment did not explicitly state that suffrage carried with it officeholding, and left the door open to state suffrage laws that, while on their face racially unbiased, disenfranchised the majority of black voters.[23]

John A. Bingham, the key author of the Fourteenth Amendment, considered the Fifteenth far too weak. Without violating it, he charged, "an aristocracy of property may be established; an aristocracy of intellect may be established; an aristocracy of sect may be established." Many Republicans who voted for the amendment did so without enthusiasm. The final version was "the weakest one that can be put before the country," complained Warner, "unworthy of the great opportunity now presented to us." "I am not responsible for this half-way proposition," declared Henry Wilson. "I simply take it at this late hour as the best I can get." He expressed regret at the failure of his own version, which "covered the white man" as well as blacks. The amendment, said Morton, fell "far short" of what was desirable. He was "surprised," he added, that affirmative language establishing a national right to vote had been rejected by the conference committee. Yet there were precedents for constitutional provisions establishing a right by forbidding some action rather than stating it in positive language, among them the First and Fourteenth Amendments. Subsequent amendments relating to voting, including those enfranchising women and eighteen-year-olds and abolishing the poll tax in federal elections, would be framed in the same manner.[24]

A majority of Republicans were convinced that "shorn of everything foreign to its original purpose," the Fifteenth Amendment was much more likely to win ratification by the required number of states. Regarding nonracial means of disenfranchising blacks, "my own conviction," Boutwell asserted, "is that no such qualification will ever be imposed." Howard agreed, pointing out that limitations on the suffrage could not be implemented without operating "with equal severity" on whites as well as blacks. Time would reveal that these were disastrous miscalculations, which failed to anticipate the proliferation of disenfranchisement laws that, while ostensibly nonracial, were administered in a flagrantly biased manner. This was how the southern states would eliminate the black vote a generation after Reconstruction. Republican leaders also did not expect that the South's political leaders would not mind—or might even welcome—the fact that significant numbers of poorer whites would lose the right to vote because of such laws.[25]

Despite Congress's adoption of the weakest wording proposed, Democrats and a handful of conservative Republicans denounced the Fifteenth Amendment as "the most revolutionary measure" in the nation's history, the crowning act of a Republican conspiracy to replace a confederation of sovereign states with a consolidated despotism. Without the ability to determine voting qualifications, they insisted, the states could no longer be said to be self-governing. Senator James Dixon of Connecticut condemned the amendment for undermining "the whole foundation and principle of the government." As in previous debates, however, arguments based on concern for balance within the federal system coexisted with flagrant invocations of racism. One Democratic congressman described blacks as "a subject, inferior, ignorant, and idolatrous race." Another offered numerous reasons why blacks must be considered unequal to whites and unfit for the suffrage, including that they had never produced significant inventions. ("I wonder how many inventors there are here in this body tonight," Morton responded.) George Vickers of Maryland explained to the Senate that mankind was divided into five races: "the red man, the yellow man, the white man, the black man, and the brown man." Color, he declared, was the "mark" of inferiority, and whites should have the power to exclude other races from the ballot box. Democrats charged that political equality would lead inexorably to "social" equality and racial intermarriage.[26]

On March 4, 1869, less than two weeks after Congress approved the Fifteenth Amendment, Ulysses S. Grant was inaugurated as the nation's eighteenth president. His brief inaugural address ended with a plea for ratification, less as a matter of abstract justice than as a way of settling "the question of suffrage" and ensuring that it did not continue to "agitate" the public mind. As with the Fourteenth Amendment, the biracial governments in the South, elected in large measure by black voters, proved crucial to ratification. The six southern states that had completed the Reconstruction process quickly ratified, and Congress required Virginia, Mississippi, Texas, and Georgia, still excluded from representation in Washington, to do so as a condition of readmission. For the first three of these states, it added the requirement that they never alter their constitutions to abridge the right to vote or hold office, or to deny citizens access to education (provisions that, while never enforced, illustrated how Republicans in Congress, like the former slaves, by now considered these rights essential to citizenship). The eleventh former Confederate state, Tennessee, rejected the amendment in 1869; it would ratify it in 1997.[27]

Unlike the Thirteenth and Fourteenth Amendments, ratification proved more problematic in the northern and border states than the South. Rhode Island delayed its approval until 1870 for fear of the impact on the state's requirement that naturalized citizens own $134 in real estate in order to vote. "Rhode Island," said Wendell Phillips, "hesitates to ratify on account of these four letters; r–a–c–e," which might be interpreted as applying to the Irish. California and Oregon rejected the amendment because of the apprehension that it might in the future enfranchise Chinese residents even though at this point nearly all of them, having been born abroad and ineligible for naturalization, were not American citizens. Also refusing to ratify were Kentucky, Maryland, and Delaware, where the amendment's impact on expanding blacks' eligibility to vote would be greatest. New York ratified and then, after Democrats gained a majority in the legislature, rescinded its approval, an action the federal government refused to recognize as valid. On March 30, 1870, Secretary of State Hamilton Fish certified that three-quarters of the states had approved the Fifteenth Amendment. On that date, the laws and constitutional provisions of seventeen of the thirty-seven states, all in the North or along the sectional border, that limited voting to white men were swept away.[28]

❧

LIKE ITS TWO PREDECESSORS, the Fifteenth Amendment marked a radical change in the political system. It moved the nation into "uncharted terrain," since voting rights—like the existence of slavery and the rights of citizenship—had always been a matter for the states to determine. Despite its limitations, it expanded the right to vote to include tens of thousands of previously disenfranchised black men and seemed to guarantee that if and when Democrats regained power in the South, black male suffrage there would remain secure. Without the Fifteenth Amendment, many states in the North and West might have gone on limiting the suffrage to whites. And the amendment would soon be understood to carry with it the right to hold office.

In 1870, the amendment affected only a small number of persons outside the former slave states. But its national scope would become critically important in the twentieth century as the Great Migration brought millions of blacks to the North and West, giving them and their allies crucial political leverage during the civil rights era. Yet because of the way it was written, the amendment's purpose could too easily be circumvented by biased voter registration and criminal justice systems. The *Boston Commonwealth* assured its readers that if any state attempted to "make invidious and unjust discriminations" in voting rights, Congress and the Supreme Court would undoubtedly "remedy the wrong." Unfortunately, in the 1890s and early twentieth century both would acquiesce when southern states used nonracial requirements such as paying poll taxes and demonstrating the ability to "understand" provisions of state constitutions to strip black men of the right to vote.[29]

Even before then, numerous black southerners had been disenfranchised after being convicted of a felony. The belief that those guilty of serious crimes should lose the right to vote had deep roots in British and American history, and was not confined to the South. Section 2 of the Fourteenth Amendment provided that states could disenfranchise male citizens because of a criminal conviction without paying a representation penalty. The 1867 Reconstruction Act stated that all male citizens could vote in elections to choose delegates to southern constitutional conventions, except ex-Confederates barred from office by the Fourteenth Amendment and "such as may be disenfranchised for participation in the rebellion or for felony at common law." (Noting that the Johnson governments were convicting blacks of "a thousand and one trivial offenses," Thaddeus Stevens had tried to limit the grounds for disenfranchisement to treason, but failed.) Most proposals for a "positive" Fifteenth Amendment establishing the right of nearly all adult men to vote contained language allowing the disenfranchisement of those convicted of treason, felony, "or other infamous crime." A state had no right to deny the suffrage because of race, declared Representative Shelby Cullom of Illinois, but it "had the right to disenfranchise its felons," and most congressional Republicans seem to have agreed.[30]

In 1870, when the number of felons was quite small, no one could have anticipated the consequences of subsequent increases in incarceration. Willard Warner, who warned against the danger of nonracial tests eliminating the bulk of black voters, assured his colleagues that "the power to disenfranchise and disqualify for crime is a very limited and possibly not dangerous concession." Yet after the end of Reconstruction, southern legislatures would greatly expand the number of crimes deemed to be felonies, and blacks would find themselves caught in the justice system's web far more frequently than whites.

A truly positive Fifteenth Amendment (one that did not allow for the disenfranchisement of those convicted of crimes) might have prevented the manipulation of criminal laws after Reconstruction to disenfranchise blacks, not to mention the situation today in which millions of persons, half of them no longer in prison, cannot vote because of state felony disenfranchisement laws. Such laws make no reference to race, and thus have been deemed by the courts not to violate the Fifteenth Amendment. But because of racism inherent in our police and judicial systems, criminal laws have a disproportionate impact on black Americans. And in some states even those incarcerated for misdemeanors, or in jail awaiting trial without having been convicted of any crime, are effectively barred from voting because no provision is made for them to do so. All this would have shocked the congressmen who voted for the Fifteenth Amendment.[31]

Despite its real limitations, the Fifteenth Amendment was a remarkable achievement in the context of nineteenth-century American history. It affirmed that only a few years after the death of slavery African-Americans were now equal members of the body politic. Its ratification set off widespread celebration. The usually taciturn Grant dispatched a proclamation to Congress hailing the amendment as "a measure of grander importance than any other one act of the kind from the foundation of our free government ... the most important event that has occurred since the nation came to life." Blacks called the amendment the nation's "second birth," a "greater revolution than that of 1776." From South Carolina, Martin R. Delany, the black abolitionist now seeking a place in Reconstruction politics, reported that freedpeople were convinced that thanks to the amendment, "the Constitution had been purged of color by a Radical Congress." (Delany considered this a misconception spread by white Republicans to persuade black voters that they were under no obligation to vote for members of their own race, like Delany, for political office.) Black religious leaders saw a divine hand at work. Ratification, declared Bishop Jabez Campbell of the African Methodist Episcopal Church, represented "the final seal of God in the condemnation of American slavery."[32]

Throughout the country, black communities staged events to mark ratification. At a gathering in Jackson, James Lynch, Mississippi's black secretary of state, described the Fifteenth Amendment as not only an embodiment of the ideals of the Declaration of Independence, but also part of the worldwide spread of democracy and the spirit of nineteenth-century progress. In New York City, the "colored population ... turned out *en masse*" for a celebratory procession of seven thousand blacks down Broadway (with men and women, as in the

Constitution itself, marching separately). The largest celebration took place in Baltimore, where some ten thousand people took part in a parade of black army regiments, militia companies, trade unions, fraternal orders, and other organizations.[33]

Abolitionists hailed the amendment as the culmination of the antislavery crusade, the "most important victory" the movement had achieved. "Never was revolution more complete," declared a euphoric Frederick Douglass at a celebration in Albany. "We have all we asked, and more than we expected." "Nothing in all history," William Lloyd Garrison exulted, equaled "this wonderful, quiet, sudden transformation of four millions of human beings from the auction block to the ballot-box." Having decided not to dissolve after ratification of the Thirteenth Amendment, the American Anti-Slavery Society now deemed its work complete. Its annual meeting of May 1869, shortly after congressional approval, declared the amendment "the capstone and completion of our movement; the fulfilment of our pledge to the Negro race." It urged abolitionists to fight one last battle—for ratification—and made the unusual suggestion that Congress carve new states out of Texas (as authorized by the 1845 joint resolution annexing the Lone Star Republic) if necessary to secure ratification. Nearly a year later, after ratification, the AASS disbanded. The nation, Wendell Phillips declared triumphantly, "had constitutionally adopted the original pledge of the Society—to secure for the colored race all their rights as men and citizens." The Rev. Henry Highland Garnet, long a voice of black radicalism, sounded the one discordant note, insisting that an organization dedicated to uplifting African-Americans was still needed. But the vote to dissolve was virtually unanimous.[34]

One prominent group of reformers, however, saw little reason to celebrate. Although the amendment barred voting restrictions based on race, it did nothing to enfranchise women, causing a split in the era's feminist movement. Some women activists saw the Fifteenth Amendment as a step toward universal suffrage. But most denounced it for erecting a new barrier to women's rights. At a meeting in Washington as the amendment was being debated, the veteran black abolitionist

Robert Purvis (whose own state of Pennsylvania had disenfranchised its black population in 1837) declared that "much as he felt outraged by his proscription from the full rights of a citizen, he could wait for the door to be opened wide enough to admit all, his daughter as well as his son." Purvis's son thereupon rose to say that when he had the right to vote he would open the door to women. To which Purvis replied, "I would not trust you." Purvis knew that some black men shared their white counterparts' patriarchal outlook. A number of male delegates to the National Convention of the Colored Men of America that met in Washington in January 1869 to press for the passage of the Fifteenth Amendment objected to the presence of a female delegate, Harriet C. Johnson of Pennsylvania. After much debate, Johnson was admitted, although she does not seem to have played a part in the proceedings.[35]

Of course, through attending mass meetings, circulating petitions, and taking part in battles over access to public facilities, women had demonstrated their ability to act politically. And unlike the Fourteenth Amendment, the Fifteenth does not contain the word "male." Nothing in its language prevented a state from granting women the right to vote, a step some would in fact take later in the century. But in a country where the suffrage was the single most important emblem of political identity, feminist leaders like Susan B. Anthony considered the amendment a "humiliation," which left women "the only human beings outside of state prisons and lunatic asylums adjudged incompetent" to cast a ballot. Anthony's longtime collaborator Elizabeth Cady Stanton used ever more heated language to express her disappointment. The Fifteenth Amendment, she charged, would render "every woman inferior to every man." Stanton gave voice to a miasma of racial, ethnic, and class prejudices. The amendment, she declared, "will place the ignorant Chinaman, the Germans, who harness their wives to the plow with cows and horses, and the Southern Negroes, as rulers over our educated women." In a not very veiled allusion to the supposed danger of sexual assaults by blacks, she warned that the amendment would set "black men and all women" against one another, leading to "fearful outrages on womanhood, especially in the southern states."[36]

In 1867, Stanton and Anthony had been sharply criticized by many abolitionists for campaigning in Kansas for woman suffrage in the company of the notorious racist George Francis Train—a "crack brained harlequin and semi-lunatic," as Garrison described him. They, in turn, were furious at what they considered abandonment by male abolitionists who had previously supported votes for women. Stanton believed that the Fifteenth Amendment would at least clarify the nature of the battle over women's rights: with ratification, "it will be male versus female, the land over."[37]

Not every supporter of woman suffrage agreed with Stanton and Anthony. At a tempestuous meeting in May 1869, the American Equal Rights Association dissolved in acrimony. Frederick Douglass took Stanton to task for remarks referring to blacks as Sambos, and for complaining that black gardeners and bootblacks would get the vote before the daughters of Jefferson and Washington. "What difference is there between the daughters of Jefferson and Washington and other daughters?" he asked. Douglass urged feminists to welcome the Fifteenth Amendment. Francis Ellen Watkins Harper agreed with him in giving priority to black male suffrage, insisting it would benefit the entire race. She called on the meeting to embrace the proposed amendment and then launch a campaign for one enfranchising women, a position adopted by most, but not all, black female activists. Opponents insisted that the Fifteenth Amendment would transform American government into "an aristocracy of sex," and that it should not be ratified unless accompanied by a Sixteenth giving women the right to vote.

Observing that both positions "are perhaps right," the veteran white abolitionist and feminist Lucy Stone concluded that the women's movement should support the pending amendment. By the end of the year, Stanton, Anthony, and their followers had formed the National Woman Suffrage Association to work independently for the vote for women, while Harper, Stone, Abby Kelley, and others established the American Woman Suffrage Association, linked to the Republican party and in favor of the Fifteenth Amendment. If she failed to support black male suffrage because of the exclusion of women, declared

Kelley, who as a traveling abolitionist lecturer in the 1840s had done more than any other individual to win for women the right to speak in public, "I should think of myself as a monster of selfishness."[38]

During debates on the Fifteenth Amendment, petitions for woman suffrage flooded into Congress. One "four yards long" was delivered to the Senate in January 1869. A few Radical Republicans supported the cause. George W. Julian submitted an amendment barring discrimination in voting rights "founded on race, color, or sex." Most Republicans, however, refused to acknowledge that barring women from the suffrage contradicted their identification of voting as a fundamental right. They fell back on the supposed innate differences between the sexes (an idea many had by now abandoned concerning blacks and whites). Some invoked the principles of coverture, which consigned women to domestic life while men dominated the public arena. Votes for women, said Senator Lot Morrill, would "subvert the fundamental principles of family government, in which the husband is, by all usage and law, human and divine, the representative head." Bingham denied that a majority had the right to deny other citizens the right to vote, yet quickly added, "that is, the male citizens, for that is the meaning of the term 'the people' as used in the Constitution." John Sherman called for an amendment embracing the principle of "universal suffrage," explaining that "universal" meant denying states the power to discriminate among citizens "on account of anything except age, residence, and sex." One "powerful argument in favor" of the Fifteenth Amendment, said the *New York Times*, was that by settling the issue of voting rights, it would put an end to "agitation" for woman suffrage. With uncanny prescience, the *Springfield Republican* predicted that fifty years would pass before an amendment enfranchising women could be added to the Constitution.[39]

❧

THE RATIFICATION OF the Fifteenth Amendment marked the completion of the second founding. But constitutional provisions are not self-enforcing, nor do they automatically command universal acquiescence. It quickly became clear that for a significant number of white southerners, slavery might be dead but a commitment to white supremacy decidedly was not. From the outset of Reconstruction, violence had been endemic in the former slave states. The advent of biracial governments and the ratification of the Fourteenth and Fifteenth Amendments exacerbated the situation. In many parts of the South, the freedpeople's newly won rights, and the governments that sought to implement and protect them, came under sustained assault. The main perpetrator of the cascade of violence in the late 1860s and early 1870s was the Ku Klux Klan, which spread throughout the region after being founded in Tennessee soon after the end of the Civil War. Its campaign of assault, arson, and murder targeted a broad array of enemies, including local Republican officials and organizers, blacks who engaged in disputes with white employers, schoolteachers, interracial couples, and "scalawags," as Democrats called white southerners who allied themselves with the Republican party. Even as Klansmen claimed to be motivated by the need to protect white womanhood from black men, sexual assaults against black women became a widespread feature of their violent campaign. Especially in counties where the black and white populations were more or less equal and the balance of political power uncertain, the Klan's actions metastasized into extreme violence against anyone accused of flouting the conventions of white supremacy.[40]

Blacks understood the widespread violence as an effort to limit their freedom and deprive them of newly won rights. "What is the use of talking about equality before the law," wrote one former slave. "There is none." The public testimony by black men and women about outrages they had suffered expanded the concepts of freedom and citizenship to include a right to bodily integrity and protection against bodily harm. Victims of violence risked further retaliation by reporting such actions to officials and seeking redress in court. Letters and petitions demanding protection poured into the offices of southern governors, and when they proved unwilling or unable to act, to Congress and the president. "Life, liberty and property are unprotected among the colored race of this state," wrote a group of Kentucky blacks in 1871, requesting the passage of a national law "that will enable us to exercise the rights of citizens." That same year a black convention in Tennessee, whose state government had reverted to Democratic control, published local reports detailing the ways their rights were violated in various parts of the state, including by lack of action against perpetrators of violence. "We were pleased to have the Fifteenth Amendment passed," declared the report from Montgomery County, "but are grieved to know that there is no justice for us under it." Tennessee's government, the convention resolved, was "in violation of the Civil Rights Bill, and the amended Constitution of the United States." But even in the majority of southern states, where Republicans remained in control, governments found it difficult to suppress the violence. With local officials paralyzed, blacks increasingly looked to "the strong arm of the general government." The former slaves, a black leader in Marietta, Georgia, told the congressional committee investigating the Klan, "expect to get protection from the federal government at Washington. . . . You ask any one of my people out there, even the most ignorant of them, and they will tell you so."[41]

The widespread violence propelled the question of physical safety, and the federal government's responsibility to ensure it, to the forefront of discussions of rights and citizenship. Could constitutionally guaranteed rights be nullified by private acts of violence? Did the amendments protect blacks only against violence directly sanctioned by the state, such as an 1871 lynching conducted by members of Kentucky's militia, using weapons taken from the state armory?[42] What were the limits of the authority granted to Congress to enforce the provisions of the three Reconstruction amendments?

In 1870 and 1871, outrage over what more than one southern Republican called the Klan's "reign of terror" resulted in laws that tried to answer these questions by dramatically expanding the power of the federal government to protect citizens against acts of violence that deprived them of constitutionally guaranteed rights. Three

Enforcement Acts sought to employ federal power to remedy the breakdown of law and order. The first, a long, complex statute, became the basis of federal efforts to protect the right to vote for the next quarter century. It prescribed penalties for state officials who discriminated against voters on the basis of race; for "any person" who used force or intimidation to prevent an individual from voting; and for two or more persons going about in disguise (as Klansmen often did) to prevent the "free exercise" of any right "granted or secured" by the Constitution. It authorized federal marshals to arrest offenders against citizens' constitutional rights, and gave jurisdiction in such cases to the federal courts (where jurors had to take an oath that they had never supported the Confederacy). It also reenacted the Civil Rights Act of 1866, which among other things had made "security of person and property" a right of American citizenship, and extended that law's protections to all "persons," not just citizens, a considerable expansion of its reach. Senator John Pool of North Carolina, the law's sponsor, made clear that his purpose was to go beyond punishing actions by the states. To enforce the Fourteenth and Fifteenth Amendments, he declared, it was necessary to act against individuals as well as public officials. "If we do not possess that right," he added, "the danger to the liberty of the citizen is great indeed in many parts of this Union."

The second Enforcement Act, directed primarily at Democratic practices in the North, focused on combating irregularities in voting in large cities. The third, entitled an Act to Enforce the Fourteenth Amendment but popularly known as the Ku Klux Klan Act of 1871, made conspiracies to deprive citizens of the right to vote, serve on juries, or enjoy equal protection of the laws federal crimes, which could be prosecuted in federal courts, and authorized the president temporarily to suspend the writ of habeas corpus and use the armed forces to suppress such conspiracies. It gave the national government jurisdiction over crimes that had previously been entirely within the purview of state and local law enforcement.[43]

The Ku Klux Klan Act explicitly declared failure to provide protection against violence "a denial by such state of the equal protection of the laws," thus inserting the concept of state neglect into national legislation. Even if the Fourteenth Amendment was directed only against actions by the states, John Coburn of Indiana declared, "a systematic failure to make arrests, to put on trial, to convict, or to punish offenders against the rights of a great class of citizens" was itself a violation of the equal protection of the laws. If a state by inaction could allow the rights of citizens to be "trampled upon without color of law," another congressman asked, "of what avail is the Constitution to its citizens?" Inaction, whether intentional or not, said Senator Frederick T. Frelinghuysen of New Jersey, triggered "the constitutional right of the general government to see to it that the fundamental rights of citizens of the United States are protected."[44]

Black and white members of Congress from the South offered a sweeping defense of these laws, resting their outlook on "the broad plane of right" as well as specific constitutional provisions. They expressed impatience with what Hiram Revels of Mississippi, a free-born minister and educator and the first African-American member of the U.S. Senate, called "legal technicalities," such as the distinction between public and private acts interfering with the exercise of constitutional rights. "Tell me nothing of a constitution," declared Joseph H. Rainey, a black congressman from South Carolina whose father, a successful barber, had purchased the family's freedom in the 1840s, "which fails to shelter beneath its rightful power the people of a country." By the people who needed protection, Rainey made clear, he meant not only blacks but also white Republicans in the South. If the Constitution, he added, was unable to "afford security to life, liberty, and property," it should be "set aside."[45]

The Enforcement Acts brought the enhancement of federal power spawned by the Civil War to the outer limits of the constitutional revolution. The states had always had exclusive jurisdiction over murder and assault. Could the federal government, James A. Garfield asked, prosecute citizens for such crimes? "This," he declared, "would virtually abolish the administration of justice" by the states. To which the Civil War general Benjamin F. Butler, now representing Massachusetts in the House, replied, "If the federal government cannot pass laws to protect the rights, liberty, and lives of citizens of the United States in the states, why were guarantees of those fundamental rights put in the Constitution at all?" [46]

Democrats railed against these laws as unprecedented intrusions on local and state authority, "the crowning act" of governmental "centralization." Some Republicans, while deeming the laws authorized by the constitutional amendments, or by what Garfield called "the general power vested in Congress to punish the violators of its laws," drew back from provisions allowing for the suspension of normal judicial procedures. A few rejected the entire idea of federal enforcement. In the debate over the Ku Klux Klan Act, Carl Schurz, representing Missouri in the Senate, said that preserving intact the tradition of local self-government was even more important than "the high duty to protect the citizens of the republic in their rights." Lyman Trumbull complained that the Ku Klux Klan Act would "change the character of the government." The Fourteenth Amendment, he insisted, protected only the rights derived from national citizenship, not those that emanated from citizenship in a state (a distinction, as we will see in the next chapter, shortly to be invoked by the Supreme Court in the *Slaughterhouse* decision). Schurz and Trumbull were already drifting away from the party. In 1872 they would join other Republicans disaffected from the Grant administration and weary of Reconstruction in forming the Liberal Republican movement. Only three Republican senators joined them in opposing the Ku Klux Klan Act. But other members of Congress expressed reservations. Henry L. Dawes of Massachusetts said he was reluctant to vote for the law, but the alternative was to "abandon the attempt to secure to the American citizen these rights, given to him by the Constitution." [47]

Republicans understood that military force was sometimes crucial to blacks' ability to exercise their new rights without violent retribution. Although the army's record concerning treatment of blacks was hardly without flaws, from the earliest days of Reconstruction its presence had enabled freedpeople to try to breathe meaning into the freedom they had acquired. The use of the army in civil affairs was antithetical to democratic traditions. Nonetheless, in 1871 and 1872 President Grant used the powers granted to him by the Enforcement Acts to crush the Ku Klux Klan. Federal marshals arrested Klansmen in numerous parts of the South. In North Carolina, the army, which had stood by for two years without acting, effectively suppressed the organization. The president suspended the writ of habeas corpus in nine South Carolina counties wracked by violence. Troops arrested hundreds of Klansmen, and the group's leaders fled the state. Some sought refuge in Canada, following in the footsteps, ironically, of fugitive slaves before the Civil War. A series of widely publicized trials followed. Overall, between 1871 and 1873, federal prosecutors brought nearly 2,500 criminal cases under the Enforcement Acts, mostly for conspiracy to hinder voting or to deprive a person of equal protection of the laws because of race. They did not charge defendants with murder or assault, to avoid the question of whether the federal government could punish violations of state law.[48]

Using the federal judicial process to put down violence was not easy. The Department of Justice, only established in 1870, was understaffed. The trials overwhelmed the federal courts. Many defendants were leading members of their communities, and local whites proved reluctant to give evidence against them. Fewer than half the cases resulted in convictions, but these, coupled with the force of massive federal action, broke the Klan's back. At the same time, as Democrats joined with Liberal Republicans in nominating the venerable antislavery editor Horace Greeley for president, national and local Democratic leaders moved to tamp down southern violence, which, they feared, alienated northern voters. August Belmont, the prominent Democratic financier, warned that the party would never return to national power unless it convinced the public that "we intend to accept . . . the *Constitution as it stands.*" In 1872, in an abrupt repudiation of Democrats' previous doctrines, the national platform announced the party's opposition to the "reopening of the questions settled by the thirteenth, fourteenth and fifteenth amendments." That year's election in the South was the most peaceful of the entire Reconstruction period. Nationally, Greeley's campaign proved a disaster; Grant was reelected by one of the largest margins in the nineteenth century.[49]

※

WITH THE RATIFICATION of the Fifteenth Amendment, Georges Clemenceau reported to his French readers, "the emancipating revolution is now ended." Yet even in the celebratory speeches and editorials, ominous signs appeared. When Congress approved the amendment, Greeley's *New York Tribune* had hailed it for making "our practice conform to our principles," but added that it would "take the everlasting Negro question forever out of national politics." Greeley's quixotic campaign for president failed, but it revealed that at least some prominent Republicans now responded sympathetically to white southerners' complaints that Reconstruction had unwisely excluded the "natural leaders" of society from political power, leading to corruption and misgovernment. One lesson from the suppression of the Klan, a white teacher in a southern black school noted in 1872, was that only "the strong arm of power . . . maintains [blacks] in these blood-bought privileges." Yet many Republicans were convinced that federal intervention must come to an end. "The great struggle between freedom and slavery in this country," James A. Garfield declared, was over, with freedom triumphant. "The Fifteenth Amendment," he added, "confers upon the African race the care of its own destiny. It places their fortunes in their own hands." In Garfield's comment— echoed by many Republican leaders—lay a premonition of the later northern retreat from Reconstruction.[50]

Soon after the ratification of the Fifteenth Amendment, Senator Justin Morrill of Vermont expressed the hope that the Reconstruction amendments "yet in the gristle, may harden into the very bones of the Constitution."[51] Morrill's metaphor may have been inelegant, but it reflected the hope of many Americans that the principles of the second founding would over time win such widespread acceptance as to become fundamental to Americans' understanding of their legal and constitutional order. But beginning in the early 1870s, a new protagonist entered the debates over the meaning of the three amendments. In a series of decisions over the course of the ensuing decades, the Supreme Court would grapple with the question of how far the constitutional system and the rights of citizens had been transformed. Its answers would spell disaster for black Americans and for the Reconstruction dream of a democratic society of equals.

4

JUSTICE AND JURISPRUDENCE

I N 1885, a group of African-Americans in Baltimore banded together to challenge a Maryland statute that limited the practice of law to whites. More broadly, the group hoped to secure all of blacks' "rights as citizens." Among its members were clergymen, businessmen, and lawyers, many of the latter graduates of Howard University Law School, which had been founded in 1869. The first dean, John Mercer Langston, a pre–Civil War abolitionist who in 1854 became the first African-American admitted to the Ohio bar, emphasized the duty of black lawyers to use the courts in the battle for equality. The new organization called itself the Brotherhood of Liberty.[1]

Home to the nation's largest population of free blacks before the war, Baltimore had long been a focal point of the campaign for black citizenship. The presence of Frederick Douglass (the nation's most prominent black leader in the struggle against slavery and racial inequality and a son of Maryland) at the Brotherhood's first public meeting illustrated this link with past struggles. The group's first president was the Rev. Harvey Johnson; he was soon succeeded by Everett J. Waring, a graduate of Howard Law School and, after the Brotherhood persuaded the legislature to repeal the ban on black lawyers, the first African-American admitted to practice law in Maryland. In 1890, Waring became the first black attorney to argue a case before the U.S. Supreme Court since John Rock of Massachusetts in 1865. The Brotherhood enjoyed other successes. There was not a single black teacher in the Baltimore school system when the organization was founded, but thanks to its efforts the city soon opened a school for black children staffed by black instructors.[2]

The 1880s was a transitional decade in the abandonment of Reconstruction. The "bargain of 1877" between leaders of the two major parties, which resolved the disputed election of 1876, had elevated Republican Rutherford B. Hayes to the presidency while acknowledging Democratic control of all the southern states. Yet the full imposition of the new system of white supremacy known as Jim Crow did not take place until the 1890s. In the 1880s, blacks, although in diminished numbers, continued to vote and hold office, and black litigants won a surprising number of victories. The Brotherhood brought numerous cases in state and federal courts, some of them successful, challenging various forms of racial discrimination. Its strategy of relying on litigation was soon adopted by organizations elsewhere, including the National Afro-American League, the Afro-American Council, and the Citizens' Committee—the last of which fought the case of *Plessy v. Ferguson* all the way to the Supreme Court. These groups, while short-lived, laid the groundwork for the legal campaigns of the National Association for the Advancement of Colored People in the twentieth century. In 1906, Harvey Johnson, the Brotherhood's first president, would deliver the invocation at the meeting of the Niagara Movement, the NAACP's immediate forerunner, at Harper's Ferry.[3]

In one respect, however, the Brotherhood was unique. In 1889 it published *Justice and Jurisprudence* (with no author listed but probably written by Everett Waring), the first sustained critique by black Americans of Supreme Court rulings related to the Reconstruction amendments. Its message was clear—the promise of equal citizenship had been "imperilled by judicial interpretation." The author proposed an alternative reading of the amended Constitution based on a broad conception of federal enforcement power and a rejection of the sharp distinction, inherited from before the Civil War, between civil, political, and social rights, a distinction the courts had anxiously adopted. A new jurisprudence was required, it insisted, "in keeping with the sociological and industrial progress" reflected in the destruction of slavery and the Reconstruction amendments.[4]

With the conclusion of the second founding came the battle over its meaning. Congress enacted laws to enforce the new amendments, and state and federal courts interpreted them. By the turn of the century, according to one judge, the Fourteenth Amendment was being "appealed to . . . almost daily" for all sorts of rights claims. Ultimately, it fell to the Supreme Court to construe the constitutional amendments. To be sure, between 1873 and the end of the century, while the Supreme Court decided over one hundred fifty cases arising from the Reconstruction amendments, only twenty or so had to do with their application to black Americans, far fewer than those involving corporations challenging regulation by the states. Nonetheless, over time, the Court played a crucial role in the long retreat from the ideals of Reconstruction. The process was gradual and the outcome never total, and each decision involved its own laws, facts, and legal precedents. Recent scholars have attributed the retreat not simply to judicial racism but also to the persistence of federalism—fear among the justices that too great an expansion of nationally enforceable rights would undermine the legitimate powers of the states. For African-Americans, however, the practical consequences were the same. The broad conception of constitutional rights with which blacks attempted to imbue the abolition of slavery proved tragically insecure.[5]

A series of interconnected questions arising from the second founding cried out for resolution. How substantially had the amendments altered the federal system? Did the Thirteenth Amendment prohibit only chattel bondage or extend to the "badges and incidents" of slavery, and what exactly were these? What did key provisions of the Fourteenth, including the "privileges or immunities" of citizens and the "equal protection of the laws" mean, and did this language apply only to blacks or to all Americans? Did that amendment protect African-Americans against violation of their rights by private individuals and businesses or only by state laws and the actions of public officials? Did it encompass what blacks called "public rights," such as equal treatment by transportation companies and public accommodations? What impact, if any, did the promise of equality have on the status of women? Did the Fifteenth Amendment's prohibition of disenfranchisement "on account of race" prohibit laws, race-neutral on their face but clearly intended to limit African-Americans' right to vote? Did that amendment authorize Congress to criminalize private actions that interfered with the ability to cast a ballot? On all of these issues, the Supreme Court engaged in what the *New York Times* called "a long process of definition," not completed until the turn of the century.[6] Even though alternative understandings were readily available, in almost every instance, the Court chose to restrict the scope of the second founding.

The Thirteenth Amendment almost immediately fell into disuse. Chief Justice Salmon P. Chase invoked it in 1867 in a circuit case to overturn a Maryland law allowing courts to apprentice black children to white employers without the consent of their parents.[7] This, he declared, constituted an unconstitutional form of involuntary servitude. But very little jurisprudence followed. The Court consistently rejected claims that various forms of racial inequality amounted to "badges and incidents of slavery" against which Congress could legislate under the abolition amendment.

In interpreting the Fourteenth Amendment, the Court reduced the "privileges or immunities" guaranteed to citizens to virtual insignificance, and drew a sharp line between civil and "social" rights, overturning efforts to ban racial discrimination by private businesses as violations of the guarantee of equal protection of the laws. The Court elevated the "state action" doctrine into a shibboleth and severely restricted federal protection of rights unless states passed overtly discriminatory laws. It eventually concluded that segregation legally enforced by a state did not violate the equal rights of black

Americans. The justices insisted that the amendment had not significantly altered the balance of power between states and the nation,
and proved unreceptive to claims that a state's inaction in the face
of violence or other expressions of racial inequality provided justification for federal intervention. Federalism, however, had its limits.
Increasingly, the Court construed the Fourteenth Amendment as a
vehicle for protecting corporate rights rather than those of the former slaves, striking down state regulations of working conditions and
railroad rates on the grounds that they violated "freedom of contract"
protected under the Due Process Clause. The Court employed "a
state-centered approach in citizenship matters and a nation-centered
approach in affairs of business."[8]

At first, the Supreme Court adopted a more robust view of the Fifteenth Amendment, which it viewed as creating a new constitutionally guaranteed right—black male suffrage—and left the door open to
federal enforcement. But by the turn of the century this too fell by the
wayside. So long as disenfranchisement laws did not explicitly mention race, the justices refused to intervene even as the vast majority of
the South's African-American men lost the right to vote.

Twenty-four men served on the Supreme Court between 1870
and 1900. A few, including Samuel Miller, Stephen J. Field, Joseph P.
Bradley, and John Marshall Harlan, were talented jurists whose written opinions made significant contributions to the evolution of legal
doctrine. Most, it is fair to say, were mediocrities who left little impact
on the law. Most hailed from privileged backgrounds and had made
livings representing railroads and other corporations before joining
the Court. A majority of the justices were Republicans, reflecting the
party's hold on the presidency for most of these years. None, however, had served in Congress when it debated and approved the constitutional amendments, and few had significant contact with black
Americans. After the death of Chase in 1873, moreover, very few had
an organic connection to the prewar antislavery movement and the
rights-based constitutionalism it had developed. Other than Harlan,
none made protecting the rights of blacks a major priority compared

with preserving traditional federalism and defending the rights of property. By the 1890s, the Court's members included Edward D. White, a former Confederate soldier with a deep abhorrence of Reconstruction who as a young man had participated in efforts by a white paramilitary organization to overthrow Louisiana's biracial government. White would become chief justice in 1910.[9]

The anonymous author of *Justice and Jurisprudence* noted that judges, consciously or not, were likely to be "swayed by the general current of the feelings and actions" around them. And the Supreme Court was undoubtedly influenced by the breakdown of the Republican consensus in support of Reconstruction in the 1870s and the retreat that accelerated in the following decades. The justices shared the belief, articulated by Democrats and Liberal Republicans (the latter the self-styled representatives of the "best men," North and South), that the expansion of federal power had gone too far and that blacks must learn to stand on their own feet without national intervention on their behalf. These views inevitably affected interpretation of the Reconstruction amendments. As time went on, outright racism became more and more prevalent in national culture and increasingly evident in Supreme Court decisions.[10]

"The judgments of the Court," the *New York Tribune* remarked in 1880, "fix unmistakably the national doctrine and policy." Yet the Reconstruction amendments, as Senator John Sherman declared, were "the pride and boast of the Republican party," and many decisions evoked sharp disagreement not only from black spokesmen but also from Republican leaders and newspapers. As early as 1875, Oliver P. Morton charged in the Senate that the amendments were being "destroyed by construction." Thirteen years later, in his memoir *Twenty Years of Congress*, James G. Blaine, the party's 1884 presidential candidate, complained that thanks to Supreme Court decisions, the federal government had been deprived of the power to protect southern blacks against "outrages" committed by individuals and mobs. Those who voted to approve the Fourteenth Amendment, Blaine insisted, had "sincerely believed" that it gave Congress a "far greater scope" of action than "judicial inquiry and decision have left to it." The Court's narrow reading of the constitutional amendments was a choice, not something predetermined by public opinion or historical context. The justices did not simply reflect popular sentiment—they helped to create it. And most of them deliberated with little or no reflection on the actual consequences of their rulings for black Americans. Overall, the late nineteenth-century decisions constitute a sad chapter in the history of race, citizenship, and democracy in the United States.[11]

⟨❧⟩

IN THE EARLY 1870S, even as Congress pressed forward with Reconstruction legislation, cases involving the second founding began to appear on the docket of the Supreme Court. The first involved the scope of federal authority under the Civil Rights Act of 1866. *Blyew v. United States*, decided in 1872, arose from the gruesome ax murder of four members of a black family in Kentucky by two white men. Benjamin H. Bristow, the United States attorney in the state, removed the case from state to federal court because Kentucky still did not allow blacks to testify in cases involving whites. The murderers were convicted and sentenced to be executed. By a six–two vote, with Chief Justice Chase not participating, the Supreme Court overturned the convictions.

The *Blyew* decision anticipated many others in which the Court elevated a traditional view of federalism above protection of African-Americans. The majority opinion, written by Justice William Strong, an expert on patent and business law appointed by President Grant in 1870, acknowledged that the Civil Rights Act had been "intended to remedy" gross inequalities between the races in the southern states. It was clear that the two convicted men had committed a brutal murder motivated by racial animus. Yet Strong seemed most concerned with counteracting what he considered a dangerous expansion of federal power during Reconstruction. The Civil Rights Act allowed the removal to federal court of cases "affecting" persons denied equality in state courts. Strong declared that only parties to the case—the defendants and the government—were "affected," not potential black witnesses and not the murder victims and their families. "It will not be thought," Strong wrote, "that Congress intended to give to the [federal] courts jurisdiction over all causes both civil and criminal."

Justice Joseph P. Bradley, a former railroad attorney and another of Grant's appointees, issued a stinging dissent, joined by Noah Swayne, whom Lincoln had placed on the Court. The majority, Bradley declared, had adopted "a view of the law too narrow, too technical and too forgetful of the liberal objects it had in view." All blacks were "affected" by the race's inability to testify, and therefore removal to federal court was entirely proper. The decision, he warned, gave "unrestricted license and impunity to vindictive outlaws and felons . . . to slay them at will." But the real thrust of Bradley's dissent was a remarkably broad interpretation of the Thirteenth Amendment, under which the Civil Rights Act had been passed. Slavery, Bradley observed, "extended its influence in every direction, depressing and disenfranchising the slave and his race in every possible way." Abolition meant not merely "striking off the fetters" but destroying "the incidents and consequences of slavery" and guaranteeing the freedpeople "the full enjoyment of civil liberty and equality." To refuse to allow "a whole class of the community" to give evidence in court, he added, "is to brand them with the badge of slavery." The Court would never adopt Bradley's expansive vision of the Thirteenth Amendment, and a little over a decade later he himself would retreat from it in his majority opinion in the *Civil Rights Cases*.[12]

A more consequential ruling, "one of the most significant decisions that has ever emanated from that tribunal" according to one newspaper, came in 1873. It arose from a law enacted by the Reconstruction government of Louisiana creating a single slaughterhouse, downstream from New Orleans, to replace numerous ones operating in the city. The law required existing butchers, all of them white, to bring their cattle and hogs to the new site to be slaughtered. The facility was also open to blacks, who now could enter this occupation by paying the slaughterhouse's fee rather than having to start their own business. Slaughterhouse refuse, often dumped in the Mississippi River, posed a significant threat to public health, and the law was typical of numerous regulations to prevent the spread of disease enacted by states and localities after the Civil War. The butchers, however, sued on the grounds that by establishing a monopoly the state had violated their right to pursue a lawful occupation, a principle of free labor guaranteed, they claimed, by the Fourteenth Amendment as one of the "privileges or immunities" of American citizens. They also claimed that the legislature had been bribed to secure the bill's passage.

Ironies abounded in the *Slaughterhouse Cases*, which brought together a number of suits against the new law. The aggrieved parties who advanced an expansive understanding of the Fourteenth Amendment were whites, not former slaves. Their lead attorney, John A. Campbell, a former member of the Supreme Court who had voted with the majority in *Dred Scott* and subsequently served as the Confederacy's secretary of war, hoped to use the case to undermine the legitimacy of Louisiana's biracial legislature. To do so, he advanced a nationalistic interpretation of the amendment based on the supremacy of the federal government over the states.[13]

By a five–four vote, the Court upheld the Louisiana law's constitutionality. Written by Samuel J. Miller, one of Lincoln's appointees, the decision affirmed that under its traditional police power the legislature could regulate slaughtering. The case could have ended there. But Miller was inspired to offer a brief history lesson in order to "give construction" to the Thirteenth and Fourteenth Amendments, a "great duty" that the Court now "for the first time" assumed. Slavery, Miller related, had "undoubtedly" been the cause of the war; blacks had "proved themselves men" by fighting in the Union army; the Black Codes and denial of political rights had relegated them to a subordinate status; and the "one pervading purpose" of the constitutional amendments was "the freedom of the slave race" and the protection of their rights.

Yet in defining these rights, Miller narrowed the meaning of the

Fourteenth Amendment's Privileges or Immunities Clause so drastically as to make it all but meaningless. The second founding, Miller insisted, had not "radically" changed the federal system. It did not intend "to fetter and degrade the state governments by subjecting them to the control of Congress," or to make the Supreme Court a "perpetual censor" of state laws. The Fourteenth Amendment, he continued, protected only those rights that derived from national, not state, citizenship. These included the rights to use the nation's "navigable waters" and seaports, be protected on the high seas and when traveling abroad, and "peaceably assemble" to seek redress of grievances from the federal government. Everything else remained within the purview of the states.[14]

Miller insisted that the "history" that produced the Fourteenth Amendment was "fresh in the memory of us all." Yet his account certainly departed from what most congressmen in 1866 thought they were accomplishing. They believed they were establishing broad federal oversight over the states, and that the amendment's language applied to all Americans. The Fourteenth Amendment had declared all persons born in the United States citizens of both the nation and of the state in which they resided. These two types of citizenship were supposed to reinforce one another but Miller saw them as distinct, indeed almost mutually exclusive. Most Republicans believed that "privileges or immunities" involved far more significant rights than Miller mentioned. For John A. Bingham, as noted in Chapter Two, they comprised those enumerated in the Bill of Rights (which Miller failed to mention); for many others they included the rights associated with free labor, such as those protected by the Civil Rights Act of 1866. The *Slaughterhouse* decision evoked considerable criticism among Republicans in and outside Congress. Senator Timothy Howe of Wisconsin likened it to *Dred Scott*. Bristow worried that the first section of the Fourteenth Amendment, the "crowning glory" of the Constitution, was being "frittered away by judicial construction."[15]

Supporting the butchers' claims, the four dissenters in *Slaughterhouse* upheld a nationalistic understanding of citizenship and a broad definition of citizens' rights. The main dissenting opinion was written by Stephen J. Field, a Unionist Democrat from California whom Lincoln had appointed to the court. Field had not been involved in the antislavery movement and was not a supporter of Reconstruction. The rights of property were of far greater concern to him than those of the former slaves. He was alarmed by the growing antimonopoly, labor, and Granger movements in the North and West, which called on states to regulate railroad rates, establish eight hours as a legal day's work, and otherwise meddle in the economy. He hoped to see the Fourteenth Amendment interpreted as protecting corporations from such interference. In 1873, Field was in the minority, but as the focus of national politics shifted from the issues of slavery and the Civil War to the role of powerful corporations and the relations of capital and labor, his outlook would triumph in the "liberty of contract" jurisprudence of the late nineteenth century.[16]

In his *Slaughterhouse* dissent, Field offered a powerful rebuke to Miller's cramped reading of the Fourteenth Amendment. The fundamental rights of citizenship, he insisted, now derived from the nation, not the states. If the majority's interpretation were correct, the amendment had been "a vain and idle enactment, which accomplished nothing, and most unnecessarily excited Congress and the people on its passage." In another dissent, Bradley insisted that thanks to the second founding, national citizenship was now primary, state citizenship secondary, and the prewar federal system fundamentally changed. Both justices pointed out that the amendment's language about privileges or immunities encompassed "all citizens," not just blacks. Swayne, also dissenting, condemned the majority ruling as "much too narrow" and at odds with the purposes of those who framed the amendment. Before the war, the Constitution had offered "ample protection . . . against oppression" by the national government but very little against "oppression by the states." The postwar amendments marked a "new departure . . . in the constitutional history of the country," which the majority went far toward reversing. The fourth dissenter was Chief Justice Chase, perhaps the main architect of the antislavery constitutionalism that had helped produce the Fourteenth Amendment in the first place. Seriously ill, Chase did not write an opinion; he died less than a month after the ruling.[17]

A founder of the Republican party in Iowa, Miller seems to have thought that in upholding a law enacted by Louisiana's Reconstruction legislature he was contributing to the goal of protecting the civil and political rights of the freedpeople. With biracial governments in place, blacks could rely on the states to protect these rights. Indeed, some southern newspapers condemned the decision precisely because it seemed to strengthen the hand of the Reconstruction governments. Had Reconstruction succeeded, in the sense of permanently establishing a political system in the South that represented the interests and respected the rights of both blacks and whites, the decision's limits on federal oversight of the states would not have mattered much. Yet as events actually unfolded, *Slaughterhouse* unquestionably had a deleterious impact. The decision eviscerated the Privileges or Immunities Clause so effectively that it "ceased to have constitutional meaning." Many decades would pass before it again appeared in a Supreme Court decision. Gone was Bingham's belief that this clause required the states to respect the liberties enumerated in the Bill of Rights. Thus blacks and, indeed, other Americans were deprived of a potential constitutional avenue for asserting claims for expanded rights. The decision, however, according to a New Orleans newspaper, did lead to a dramatic increase in demand for "Slaughter-House Company stock."[18]

On the day after deciding *Slaughterhouse*, the Supreme Court beat back another effort to infuse the Fourteenth Amendment with broad meaning. This time the issue was whether the amendment prohibited states from discriminating on the basis of sex. Reconstruction had a mixed legacy for American women. Black and white women lacked the vote but took an active part in the era's politics. Reconstruction's egalitarian logic and broad definition of citizenship inspired many to claim new rights for themselves. To be sure, by introducing the word "male" into the Constitution, the Fourteenth

Amendment implicitly confirmed women's subordinate political status. Yet the first section makes no mention of gender, and women activists quickly claimed that its guarantees of the privileges or immunities of citizens and equal protection of the laws invalidated the numerous state laws denying women basic rights, including the right to vote.[19]

During Reconstruction, the age-old "woman question" for the first time took on a constitutional dimension. The issue came to the Supreme Court in *Bradwell v. Illinois*. Myra Bradwell, a leading advocate of women's rights, in 1868 founded the *Chicago Legal News*, a weekly publication that gained a wide readership among the state's lawyers. But when she sought to become an attorney herself, Bradwell was barred by a ruling of the Illinois Supreme Court that limited the practice of law to men. Having just decided that the right to pursue a livelihood did not come along with national citizenship, the Supreme Court had no difficulty rejecting Bradwell's appeal. The vote was eight to one—of the *Slaughterhouse* dissenters, only the ailing Chase, a supporter of woman suffrage (although he felt the era's feminists wanted it "a little too fast") dissented, although again he was unable to write an opinion.[20]

As in *Slaughterhouse*, the task of producing the brief majority opinion in *Bradwell v. Illinois* fell to Justice Miller. Bradley, whose dissent in *Slaughterhouse* had insisted that states could not interfere with the right to earn a living, issued his own concurring opinion. Why did butchers have a valid Fourteenth Amendment free labor claim but not Myra Bradwell? "Nature" and "divine ordinance," Bradley wrote, provided the answer: "The domestic sphere [is] that which properly belongs to the domain and functions of womanhood." On and on Bradley went, with a discussion that invoked the common law principle that a woman had "no legal existence" apart from her husband and insisted that "the Creator" had decreed that the "paramount destiny and mission of woman are to fulfill the noble and benign offices of wife and mother." The end of slavery had not altered these natural distinctions between the sexes. Thus discrimination between men and women was not a violation of equal protection of the laws (nor, despite the dire exploitation of slave women, could it be considered a badge of slavery).[21]

A number of newspaper accounts of the case echoed Bradley's patronizing outlook. The *Cleveland Plain Dealer* described Bradwell as "a little curly-headed woman, dark-eyed and good looking." It had not commented on the physical appearance of the New Orleans butchers. The decision, however, did not reflect the entirety of male views in the aftermath of the Civil War. The southern Reconstruction governments took steps to expand women's legal rights. South Carolina legalized divorce, which had been entirely banned in the state before the Civil War. Mississippi expanded women's property rights and allowed them to vote in local referendums on whether licenses to sell liquor should be issued. Several states throughout the country enacted laws giving married women legal title to the wages they earned. Even as the Supreme Court deliberated, Illinois itself enacted a law allowing women to practice law. Bradwell did not apply again but in 1890, on its own initiative, the state's Supreme Court ordered her admitted to the bar.[22]

The issue of woman suffrage played a prominent role in Reconstruction politics. Women now enjoyed the right to vote in Wyoming and Utah territories and pressed their claims elsewhere. Hundreds of women activists, who insisted that the citizenship clause of the Fourteenth Amendment extended the vote to all men and women, tried to cast ballots in the presidential election of 1872. Susan B. Anthony was allowed to do so in Rochester, New York, but was then arrested and fined (although the Grant administration decided not to take action when she refused to pay). In Missouri, Virginia Minor sued the local registrar when denied the right to vote. The Supreme Court decided her case, *Minor v. Happersett*, in 1875. Morrison J. Waite, who had succeeded Chase as chief justice, wrote the unanimous opinion. Women were citizens, he acknowledged, but citizenship in the United States had never carried with it the suffrage. Despite the amendments, the states retained the power to regulate voting, except that they could no longer deny it to black men. "Certainly," Waite concluded, "if the courts can consider any question settled, this is one."[23]

The New Orleans butchers had little in common with Myra Bradwell and Virginia Minor. But these cases all reflected how the second founding led inexorably to claims of new constitutional rights, invoking (and stretching) the language of the postwar amendments. The Supreme Court did not accept their arguments. But the cases offered a harbinger of far broader uses of the Fourteenth Amendment that in our own time would win judicial support. On the other hand, they also illustrated how the Court's retreat from an expansive understanding of that amendment with regard to blacks went hand in hand with narrowing its application to other aggrieved groups. They were "authoritative" rulings, wrote the *New York Evening Post*, that made clear that the Court would not interfere in matters it felt lay within the jurisdiction of the states.[24]

❧

THE FULL IMPORT for black Americans of these early decisions remained uncertain in the mid-1870s. This became evident as Congress debated Charles Sumner's Supplementary Civil Rights Bill, so named because it supplemented the economic and legal rights guaranteed in the Civil Rights Act of 1866 with a new set of entitlements. The bill proposed to guarantee equal access to a wide range of venues, from transportation and inns to "theaters, and other places of amusement," jury service, churches, and public schools, and to give federal courts exclusive enforcement power. These rights applied to "all persons," not just citizens.

The measure had serious flaws. Enforcement mechanisms were cumbersome: federal marshals could arrest violators, but the aggrieved party was essentially responsible for bringing a civil lawsuit. The church provision seemed to violate the First Amendment, and many southern Republicans who otherwise supported the bill warned that unless the reference to schools were removed, passage would result in the "immediate destruction" of their region's almost entirely segregated fledgling public education systems since white parents would withdraw their children rather than have them attend school with blacks. (The church and school provisions would be eliminated before final passage.) Nonetheless, the party's national platforms of 1872 and 1876 included support for equality in "civil, political and public rights." In his second inaugural address, in March 1873, President Grant called for passage of Sumner's bill. The idea of equal treatment in the public sphere regardless of race was certainly a forward-looking principle, and the bill challenged traditional federalism as fully as any other Reconstruction measure.[25]

As Sumner's proposal demonstrated, the definition of rights was in flux. The notion of an entitlement to pleasurable enjoyment represented a dramatic expansion of the meaning of civil rights. While the obligation of transportation companies and inns to accept customers had long existed in common law, there was no common law right to attend a theater, long considered a place of immorality. Blacks sought to replace the distinction between political, civil, and social rights with one between "public" and "private" rights—the former including not only the right to vote and equality before the law but also equal treatment in public space, the latter (for example, whom one invited to one's home) beyond the realm of legislation. They insisted that Sumner's proposal was fully authorized by the rewritten Constitution. Letters and petitions of support flooded into Sumner's office. One arrived in 1872 signed by every black member of Mississippi's biracial legislature. Sumner presented to the Senate the resolutions of black conventions and accounts of indignities suffered by those barred from theaters, hotels, and railroad cars not only in the South but also in his own state of Massachusetts. Until the bill became law, declared Frederick Douglass, African-Americans would not enjoy "full freedom." Better-off blacks—"refined ladies and gentlemen" humiliated by being denied first-class service and access to the "ladies' car" on trains—were most outspoken. (Despite the name, well-dressed men accompanying woman passengers could travel in the ladies' car, raising the specter of black men sitting in proximity to white women.) On many trains the only alternative was the "smoking car," where rowdy passengers congregated and which respectable women of both races tried to avoid. But as the widespread demonstrations against exclusion from urban streetcars demonstrated, the demand for equal treatment in public space also resonated among those who could not afford to patronize a hotel, theater, or first-class railroad car.[26]

The idea of public rights proved highly controversial. It was virtually without precedent in American law—Massachusetts had passed the nation's first public accommodations act in 1865. The Republican party was far more united regarding equality in civil and political rights than "public" ones. Fearing being accused of promoting "social equality," with its barely hidden implication of interracial sexual intimacy, early white Reconstruction governors Henry C. Warmoth of Louisiana and James L. Alcorn of Mississippi vetoed such bills. But in the early 1870s, as black political assertiveness increased, several southern states enacted such measures. They proved difficult to enforce. When P. B. S. Pinchback, Louisiana's lieutenant governor, sued a southern railroad after he and his family were denied accommodations in a sleeping car, the company's owner responded that he would be delighted to provide a separate sleeping car for blacks but connecting lines, including those in the North, would not carry it. This was one reason a national law was needed.[27]

Introduced in 1870, the Civil Rights Bill languished in committee, occasionally passing one house of Congress but not the other, until its enactment early in 1875. Its passage occurred a few months after Sumner's death and shortly after Democrats won control of the House of Representatives for the first time since before the Civil War, meaning that it would be impossible to win approval after the lame duck session of the Republican-controlled Congress expired. In the sometimes bitter congressional debates, the recent constitutional amendments took center stage. Opponents, not all of them Democrats, condemned the bill as an unwarranted exercise of federal power based on "a forced construction of the Constitution." Critics denied that the rights to serve on a jury, attend an integrated school, and be accorded equal treatment by private businesses were protected by the recent amendments, and warned of the dangerous consequences of racial mixing in hotels, restaurants, and places of amusement.[28]

The enfranchisement of black voters and the presence of African-Americans in Congress strongly affected the debate. Thomas J. Robertson, a white Republican from South Carolina, told the Senate that as someone indebted to "colored men" for his seat, he could hardly "allow them to be deprived of any right which any other American citizen on this continent enjoys." All seven of the blacks serving in the Forty-third Congress spoke on the bill, demanding national protection in the enjoyment of "equal public rights." Several related the indignities to which they were subjected traveling to the nation's capital. Joseph Rainey had been evicted from a streetcar, and Robert B. Elliott, Richard H. Cain, and James T. Rapier denied service in restaurants and inns.[29]

The *Slaughterhouse* decision added a new dimension to the debate. Several Democrats read from the majority opinion, citing its extremely restricted definition of the privileges and immunities of citizens, to argue that the rights Sumner was trying to protect remained under the authority of the states. Some Republicans explicitly rejected the Court's narrow reading of the Fourteenth Amendment. "It is one of the privileges of a citizen of the United States," said Senator Frederick T. Frelinghuysen of New Jersey, "not to be discriminated against on account of race or color." John Sherman declared he could not "distinguish" among "privileges, immunities, and rights." If the right to "travel, attend school, and go to a public inn" were not protected by the Constitution, he asked, "then what in the name of human rights are the privileges of citizens?" Given the Court's evisceration of the Privileges or Immunities Clause, some supporters shifted to the Fourteenth Amendment's guarantee of "equal protection." Supporters of the bill also rejected the idea that the amendment only prohibited overt state action. If a state allowed "inequality in rights" to be "meted out" by private citizens or corporations without punishment, argued Congressman William Lawrence of Ohio, who had voted for the Fourteenth

Amendment in 1866, that in itself was a violation. "What the state permits, . . ." he insisted, "it does in effect itself." Sumner preferred to invoke the Declaration of Independence and the Sermon on the Mount as justifications for the bill, as well as the general principle that the Constitution should be "interpreted uniformly for human rights." But he also insisted that the business enterprises that fell within the bill's purview were licensed by states or localities and thus fell within a reasonable definition of "state action" under the Fourteenth Amendment.[30]

In a long speech in January 1874, Robert B. Elliott of South Carolina directly confronted Democrats who "sought to shield themselves behind the Supreme Court." "There is not a line or word" in *Slaughterhouse*, he affirmed, that "casts a shade of a doubt" on the power of Congress to "legislate against a plain discrimination made by state laws or state customs against that very race for whose complete freedom and protection these great amendments" were adopted. Elliott's speech was widely praised. "Certainly the most extraordinary effort ever made by a Negro in this country," declared the *Louisville Courier Journal*.[31]

Shorn of its provisions regarding schools, churches, and cemeteries, the Civil Rights Act finally passed Congress on February 27, 1875, less than a week before adjournment. Not a single Democrat voted in favor. Of the senators who supported passage, twenty had served in Congress in 1866 and had voted for the Fourteenth Amendment, which they clearly felt authorized the new law.[32] It would take eight years for the Supreme Court to adjudicate the constitutional issues raised by the Civil Rights Act. Before then, its attention turned to whether the Reconstruction amendments allowed the federal government to protect blacks against acts of violence. This was literally a matter of life and death in the Reconstruction South.

✥

IN THE MID-1870S, paramilitary anti-Reconstruction violence again reared its head. Unlike the Klan's depredations in the late 1860s and early 1870s, the activities of Democratic "rifle clubs" were conducted by bands of undisguised men, a sign that perpetrators believed the northern public would no longer support armed intervention in the South. Widespread violence helped Democrats regain control of Alabama in the election of 1874 and Mississippi the following year. "I am all out of patience," wrote Benjamin H. Bristow in 1875, "with the idea that this government, after having manumitted four millions of slaves cannot by law protect them from murder and outrage." But with the economic depression that began in 1873 seriously undermining Republican support in the North, the Grant administration seemed paralyzed. The 1875 election in Mississippi demonstrated that the state government could not protect black voters, and that the federal government was unwilling to do so.

The Civil Rights Act of 1866 included "security of person and property" among the rights of American citizens. The Fourteenth Amendment spoke of "equal protection of the laws," and the Enforcement Acts of 1870–71 empowered the federal government to punish acts of violence meant to deprive Americans of constitutionally guaranteed rights. Nonetheless, even in the best of circumstances, the federal government was ill-equipped for prolonged intervention in the South. But judicial rulings made the task even more difficult.[33]

Two decisions by the Supreme Court in 1876 built on the precedent established in *Slaughterhouse* that restricted national jurisdiction over citizens' rights. The first, *United States v. Cruikshank*, arose from the Colfax Massacre of 1873, when, after a siege of a Louisiana courthouse, an armed mob of whites murdered scores of black men, many of them members of the local militia. This was the worst act of carnage in the entire Reconstruction era. Under the Enforcement Act of 1870, ninety-eight persons were indicted for conspiracy to deprive victims of their constitutional rights. Shielded by the local white community, only a handful of those indicted were arrested; they stood trial in federal court in New Orleans. Nearly all of the testimony came from black men and women. A first trial ended in a hung jury; in the second, in which Justice Bradley joined federal judge William B. Woods on the bench (until late in the century, Supreme Court justices regularly took part in circuit court cases), three defendants were convicted.

While Woods upheld the verdict, Bradley disagreed. In a long opinion, he launched into an esoteric discussion of the distinction between rights that existed independently of the Constitution and were subject to the jurisdiction of the states, and rights "given or guaranteed" by the Constitution and under the purview of the federal government. Most citizens' rights, including those protected by the Fourteenth Amendment, were examples of the former. The states also bore the responsibility for punishing "ordinary" crimes such as murder. Bradley added, however, that blacks' right to vote without racial discrimination was created by the Fifteenth Amendment and thus could be enforced by the federal government, even against acts of violence by private individuals. But the *Cruikshank* indictment, he continued, was flawed because it did not specifically charge that the conspiracy had been motivated by racial animus, as required by the Enforcement Act. Bradley acknowledged that since all the perpetrators were white and all the victims black race seemed to be somehow involved, but, he added, this "ought not to have been left to inference." Because Woods courageously refused to concur with his "learned brother," the split between the judges sent the case to the Supreme Court.

Bradley was very proud of his opinion. Fearing it would not receive the attention it deserved, he forwarded it to newspapers, congressional leaders, and federal judges, including his colleagues on the Supreme Court. But the unanimous decision in *Cruikshank* overturning the convictions was based not so much on Bradley's recondite distinction between various kinds of rights but on the idea that the postwar amendments had not significantly altered the structure of federalism, and the supposed problems with the indictment. In the opinion, Chief Justice Waite examined the rights of the victims that were said to have been violated and, following *Slaughterhouse*, concluded that most of them remained "under the protection of the states," not the federal government. Moreover, the Fourteenth Amendment, while authorizing national action when states violated basic rights, had added "nothing to the rights of one citizen against another." Murder and conspiracy remained under state, not national, jurisdiction. As to federally created rights, such as the right of black men to vote, Waite agreed with Bradley that the indictment was faulty for not alleging a racial motivation. "We may suspect that race was the cause of the hostility," he wrote, "but it is not so averred." The decision did not preclude future federal prosecutions, with better indictments, to protect blacks' right to vote. But it certainly encouraged further violence. Dozens of American citizens had been murdered in cold blood (a fact not mentioned in the chief justice's opinion), and the murderers had walked free.[34]

On the same day, March 27, 1876, in an eight–one decision in *United States v. Reese*, also written by Waite, the Court overturned the convictions of Kentucky officials who had conspired to prevent blacks from voting in a local election. In language almost identical to that he had employed in denying Virginia Minor's claim to vote, Waite insisted that the Fifteenth Amendment "does not confer the right of suffrage upon anyone." It did, however, make constitutional an "exemption from discrimination in the exercise of the elective franchise on account of race," a principle Congress could act to protect. But Waite went on to declare two sections of the Enforcement Act, under which the men had been indicted, unconstitutional because they prohibited all interference with voting, not just that motivated by race. Oddly, both decisions left the door open to future action on behalf of blacks while white Republican voters, also victims of violence, but not racial assaults, remained without national protection.[35]

Another issue that soon came before the Court involved efforts by former slave states to exclude blacks from jury service. By the time it handed down decisions in these cases in 1880, biracial Reconstruction government in the South had come to an end, and Republican control in Washington had been succeeded by a decade of divided government and political stalemate. In these rulings, the Supreme Court vindicated the right of blacks to serve on juries in the face of discriminatory state laws and the racist actions of state officials.

In *Strauder v. West Virginia* the Court invalidated the murder conviction of a black man because of a state law barring blacks from jury service. For the seven–two majority, Justice William Strong declared the law unconstitutional as a violation of the Equal Protection Clause of the Fourteenth Amendment. Strong cited *Slaughterhouse* to argue that the postwar amendments aimed to "assure to the colored race the enjoyment of all the civil rights that under the law are enjoyed by white persons and to empower the federal government to protect them"—an interpretation that went well beyond what that ruling had actually declared. The decision expanded the traditional definition of civil rights to include the right of litigants to face juries selected without the purposeful exclusion of black members. In a companion case, *Ex Parte Virginia*, the Court upheld the federal conviction of a state judge who, in the absence of a law limiting jury service to whites, had taken it upon himself systematically to exclude blacks from juries.[36]

These decisions surprised and alarmed the white South. A West Virginia newspaper charged the Court with "going back upon the principles of every decision heretofore made" about the Fourteenth Amendment. The Virginia Senate condemned the justices for "destroying every vestige of state sovereignty." But the rulings remained within the confines of "state action" and the requirement of overt racial motivation. Strong made clear that the guarantees of the Fourteenth Amendment had "reference to state action exclusively and not to any action of private individuals." He noted that a state could prescribe restrictive qualifications for jury service so long as they did not explicitly mention race: "it may confine the selection to males, to freeholders, . . . or to persons having educational qualifications." States that had openly biased laws relating to jury service took the hint and quickly repealed them. In practice, however, after the end of Reconstruction blacks remained almost entirely excluded from southern juries until well into the twentieth century.[37]

The decisions relating to juries, asserted the *New York Tribune*, exemplified the "system of constitutional interpretation" that was defining the "scope of the recent amendments." Combined with

Cruikshank and *Reese*, they established what the *Tribune* called a clear principle: "Congress may pass laws to prevent a state from discriminating between blacks and whites... [but] the constitutional amendments give it no power to undertake the suppression of illegal combinations of individuals to effect the same result." Congress did, however, possess the authority to "do something... for the protection of colored voters." In the next few years the Court tried to define that "something."[38]

Rutherford B. Hayes's letter accepting the Republican nomination in 1876 promised a return to "local self-government" in the South, a phrase everyone understood to mean white control. Five years later, Hayes left the presidency disillusioned, writing that "experience has shown that the protection and conduct of national elections cannot safely be left to the states." And in the early 1880s, under Hayes's successors, James A. Garfield and Chester A. Arthur, there was a revitalization of federal voting rights enforcement. This seems to have had an impact on the Supreme Court. Even as the justices severely limited the scope of the Fourteenth Amendment, they continued to take a broader view of the Fifteenth.[39]

In *Ex Parte Siebold* (1880) the justices upheld the conviction in federal court of Baltimore election officials who stuffed ballot boxes and destroyed votes cast by blacks in a congressional election. Writing for a seven–two majority, Bradley took the occasion to repudiate "mistaken notions" of federalism that "overlooked" the fact that "a national constitution has been adopted in this country." Federal enforcement laws, he proclaimed, were "constitutionally paramount" to the power of states to police elections. On the same day, the Court similarly refused to overturn the conviction of a Cincinnati election official who violated his legal duties under the Enforcement Acts.

The Court went further in *Ex Parte Yarbrough* (1884), upholding the conviction in federal court of eight Georgia men who assaulted a black man to prevent him from voting for a member of Congress. Previously, the Court had declared that the Fifteenth Amendment did not directly enfranchise anyone—it simply barred racial discrimination in voting qualifications. Now, for the majority, Miller wrote that the amendment did in fact create "a right to vote" for black men, which Congress possessed "the power to protect . . . from personal violence or intimidation." All these decisions involved federal elections, which the original Constitution gave Congress the power to regulate. How they affected state and local elections remained to be seen. Nonetheless, *Yarbrough* was a bold assertion of national enforcement power, and the decision was unanimous. "Federal Power at the Polls," proclaimed the Republican *New York Times*. Speaking for Democrats, the *Washington Post* complained, "Federal Officers to Control State Elections." Fraud and violence continued in southern elections, but so did the possibility of further federal enforcement legislation.[40]

By this point, the Court seemed to be acting in accordance with the distinction, earlier outlined by Bradley, between previously existing rights, subject to state jurisdiction (essentially rights covered by the Fourteenth Amendment, such as equal protection of the laws, enforceable only against discriminatory state action), and rights "conferred by the Constitution" (blacks' right to vote as created by the Fifteenth Amendment), which the federal government could protect against violations both public and private. Thus, even as it upheld federal enforcement power regarding voting, the Court, in *United States v. Harris* (1883), unanimously rejected the federal prosecution of members of a Tennessee mob that assaulted four imprisoned men, killing one. In doing so it declared unconstitutional a portion of the Ku Klux Klan Act of 1871 that outlawed private conspiracies to deprive persons of the equal protection of the laws. When it came to the Fourteenth Amendment, the state action doctrine held firm. Ironically, in this case, the victims were white, not black, and the county sheriff, R. G. Harris, along with two of his deputies, were among those indicted. But Justice William B. Woods, who had been appointed to the Court by Hayes in 1880 and wrote the decision, appears to have been unaware of these facts. Thus a mob action in which public officials participated became part of the accumulating jurisprudence barring federal prosecution of crimes committed by private individuals.[41]

Where all this left the equality of public rights claimed by African-Americans remained unclear. The Supreme Court answered this question in 1883. But a preview had been offered five years earlier in its unanimous decision in *Hall v. DeCuir*, the first case relating to the postwar amendments to come before the Court after the bargain of 1877. Louisiana's constitution of 1868 and a state law enacted a year later prohibited common carriers from discriminating among passengers on the basis of race. Josephine DeCuir, an affluent freeborn black woman, in 1872 was denied cabin accommodations and entry to the dining room on a Mississippi River steamboat and sued the captain for damages. At the trial, officials of steamboat lines testified that being required to allow blacks into the main cabin would drive away whites and ruin their business. But the mixed-race jury awarded DeCuir $1,000 in damages, and the state Supreme Court upheld the judgment.

In a brief opinion for a unanimous court, Chief Justice Waite declared the Louisiana statute an unconstitutional burden on interstate commerce, regulation of which the Constitution reserved to Congress. Unless Congress prohibited companies from enforcing a rule, it implicitly allowed them to do as they pleased. (Congress had in fact prohibited discrimination in transportation in the Civil Rights Act of 1875—something Waite failed to mention—but the incident involving Mrs. DeCuir preceded its passage.) It would be difficult, Waite went on, for steamboats to conduct business if one state required passengers to be separated by race and another prohibited the practice. Waite insisted that the decision was limited to "foreign and interstate commerce"; presumably, it would not apply to state laws relating to businesses that operated wholly within state lines. He did not explicitly endorse racial segregation. But the concurring opinion of Justice Nathan Clifford, a Democrat appointed decades earlier by James Buchanan, went further, insisting that companies were not obliged to accept passengers whose presence might "make their business less lucrative," and claiming that segregation in transportation, as well as separate schools for black and white children, promoted "the public interest." A decade later, the Brotherhood of Liberty would devote considerable attention to *DeCuir*, a case barely remembered today, identifying it as "the first of the succession of legal wounds from which the prostrate form of civil rights never rallied."[42]

DeCuir was a prelude to the Court's much more sweeping decision in the *Civil Rights Cases*, handed down in 1883. This concerned complaints arising under the Civil Rights Act of 1875 by blacks denied hotel accommodations in Kansas and Missouri, excluded from the ladies' car of a train in Tennessee, and barred from the dress circle of a theater in San Francisco and from the Grand Opera House of New York City. (The New York complainant wanted to see Victor Hugo's drama *Ruy Blas*, about a slave, played by Edwin Booth, the brother of Lincoln's assassin, disguised as a nobleman.) That only two of the cases originated in the former slave states suggested the national scope of the problem of racial exclusion. In an eight–one ruling, the Court declared most of Sumner's Civil Rights Act unconstitutional on the grounds that it sought to punish discrimination by private businesses, not the states. In doing so the Court powerfully reinforced both the state action doctrine and the sharp distinction between civil and political rights on the one hand and social rights on the other. As to public rights, the majority opinion, by Bradley, did not mention the phrase.

In 1876, Bradley had expressed uncertainty about the Act's constitutionality in a private letter to William B. Woods, then a federal judge. He wondered whether "freedom, citizenship and equality before the laws require that colored persons shall travel in the same cars, lodge in the same inns, and attend the same theatres and places of amusement as the whites." By 1883, Bradley had made up his mind. The Fourteenth Amendment, his opinion declared, empowered Congress to act against "state legislation, and state action of every kind" that impaired citizens' rights. But it did not extend to "the wrongful acts of individuals." As to the Thirteenth Amendment, which lacked a state action provision, Bradley acknowledged that this allowed Congress to legislate against the "badges and incidents of slavery." These, he asserted, included "civil rights," but not the access to public accommodation guaranteed by the (presumably misnamed) Civil Rights Act. "It would be running the slavery argument into the ground," he declared, "to make it apply to every act of discrimination," and the amended Constitution did not give Congress the authority "to adjust what may be called the social rights of men and races." Bradley did not consider the possibility that it was a form of state action for a state government to tolerate private discrimination.

Like many northerners, Bradley was losing patience with the seemingly endless debate about the rights of black citizens. Echoing Andrew Johnson's veto of the Civil Rights Act of 1866, Bradley wrote that blacks needed to stop seeking "to be the special favorite of the laws" and be satisfied with having their rights protected in the same ways as other Americans. (Other Americans, of course, had not been slaves, nor did they constantly face the kind of humiliating treatment Sumner's law was meant to end.) Bradley, moreover, found the idea of forced racial mixing distasteful. "Surely," he mused in private memorandums, "a white lady cannot be enforced by congressional enactment to admit colored persons to her ball or assembly or dinner party. . . . It can never be endured that the white shall be compelled to lodge and eat and sit with the Negro." "Enforced fellowship," Bradley warned, would convert "freedom of the blacks" into "slavery of the whites."[43]

The lone dissenter was the only one of the nine justices to have owned a slave, John Marshall Harlan of Kentucky, whom Hayes appointed in 1877. As a Republican leader in the early 1870s, Harlan expressed the hope that Sumner would drop his civil rights measure. Now he agonized for months over writing his opinion. Only after his wife placed on his desk the inkstand with which Roger B. Taney had written the *Dred Scott* decision, presumably to inspire her husband to use Taney's own pen to help erase his legacy, was Harlan able to proceed. And with his dissent, he emerged as black Americans' most steadfast friend in the federal judiciary and the Court's leading voice on behalf of racial justice in the late nineteenth and early twentieth centuries.

The Court's majority, Harlan declared, had adopted "entirely too narrow and artificial" a reading of the recent amendments. As a result, the purposes the American people "supposed they had accomplished by changes in their fundamental law" were being negated. The questions at hand were not federalism, state action, and social equality but freedom and citizenship. Harlan presented a history lesson about the Supreme Court's sorry relationship with slavery. The Court had happily upheld fugitive slave laws that punished private individuals who interfered with the constitutional right to recover runaway slaves. Why then should the hands of Congress be tied when it came to enforcing "a constitutional provision granting citizenship?" Harlan attempted to resurrect the Thirteenth Amendment as a source of enforceable rights. That amendment did more than prohibit slavery; it created a national entitlement to "universal civil and political freedom" and empowered Congress to prohibit all actions "inconsistent with the fundamental rights of American citizenship." Racial discrimination "with regard to civil rights" (which, unlike Bradley, he defined as including equal access to public transportation and accommodations), whether by state law or private parties, was indeed a "badge of servitude."

Harlan confronted head-on the state action doctrine. The idea that the Fourteenth Amendment only prohibited measures by the states was "unauthorized by its language," since its grant of citizenship had no such restriction. Moreover, "in every material sense," railroad companies, hotel keepers, and "managers of places of public amusement" should be considered "agents or instrumentalities of the state," as they were licensed and performed a public service. He also exposed the fallacy of defining the issue as social equality. Like so many others, Harlan recoiled from sexual intimacy between the races. In a case the same year he joined in a unanimous decision upholding the constitutionality of an Alabama law that punished interracial "fornication" more severely than intraracial. But the rights protected in Sumner's law, he insisted, were civil rights, not social rights, and as such subject to regulation by Congress. As to Bradley's complaint that blacks had become "the special favorite of the laws," Harlan pointed out that the rights of "the white race" had long enjoyed protection by the state and federal governments. He ended on a pessimistic note. The country, he wrote, was entering "upon an era of constitutional law when the rights of freedom and American citizenship cannot receive from the nation that efficient protection which heretofore was unhesitatingly accorded to slavery."[44]

Of all the Supreme Court decisions relating to Reconstruction, the *Civil Rights Cases* inspired the most comment among newspaper editors and the general public. Democrats, predictably, hailed the outcome. The Court, wrote the *Baltimore Sun*, had made clear "the scope and limitations" of the recent amendments in a way certain to "reestablish the reserved rights of the states." A northern newspaper summarized reports from the South about reactions to the decision: "The whites are represented as jubilant and the Negroes as perplexed and depressed." The Liberal Republican press echoed Bradley's view that blacks deserved the same legal status as white Americans, but were demanding special treatment. Blacks, wrote the *Chicago Tribune*, were no longer "wards of the government." It praised the Court for declining to place them "above the white man." The paper's news reports, however, indicated that commitment to Reconstruction had not died out. The decision, the *Tribune* noted, was "generally condemned by Republicans." The mayor of Pittsburgh lamented that the party's work of "the last twenty years" had been "undone." More than one party newspaper compared the decision to *Dred Scott*. "It seems . . . that now, as long ago," wrote the *Harrisburg Telegraph*, "freedom cannot be made safe in the United States as long as we have a Supreme Court." The *Cincinnati Commercial Gazette* wondered why the federal government was "strong enough to give all men their freedom [and] make them citizens with all that the word implies . . . and yet not strong enough to protect them in the enjoyment of those rights." Harlan received numerous letters praising his dissent, including from former president Hayes and ex–Supreme Court justice Noah H. Swayne.[45]

One historian has described the *Civil Rights* decision as "primarily" a question of federalism. Perhaps it was from the point of view of the Court, but not of black Americans. The prominent Ohio black leader John P. Green warned that the decision established a precedent for "unsettling the entire legal status of the former slave population." Frederick Douglass wrote to Harlan that his dissent "should be scattered like the leaves of autumn over the whole country." Mass protest meetings took place "from Maine to Florida." At one in Washington that brought together over two thousand persons, Douglass called the decision "a heavy calamity" that "construed the Constitution in defiant disregard of what was intended" by Congress, and left blacks "defenseless" against "vulgar and pitiless prejudice." The Court's studied distinction between state and private action, he pointed out, made no practical difference to "the insulted or outraged ... colored citizen." At the same gathering, the influential white Republican Robert G. Ingersoll offered a careful rebuttal of Bradley's opinion, insisting that the Court had seriously "undervalued" the Reconstruction amendments, which, he insisted, had been intended to create "affirmative rights" that expanded the scope of national citizenship. Invoking a phrase Harlan would employ in the following decade, Ingersoll declared, "the law became color blind." The black press condemned the decision. "It is comforting," wrote the *New York Globe*, referring to Harlan, "to find one man who has not forgotten that we had a great war and that among the many things it forever doomed was colorphobia in the Constitution." The *Cleveland Gazette* predicted that the decision would close "hundreds" of northern hotels and places of amusement to blacks. "In the South, it will make things worse in every way, if such a thing be possible." [46]

In his opinion, Bradley reminded his colleagues that only a few years earlier, in *Munn v. Illinois*, the Court had ruled that enterprises "clothed with a public interest" (in that case a grain elevator) could legitimately be regulated by the states. The states, in other words, could enact their own civil rights laws. This was hardly likely to happen in the southern and border states, now firmly under Democratic control. Democrats had already repealed Reconstruction-era civil rights measures, sometimes substituting ones allowing innkeepers, theater owners, and others to exclude any person whose presence the majority of customers might find "obnoxious." (Such a law remained on the books in Delaware until 1963.) Elsewhere, however, black activists launched a vigorous campaign for state legislation. In the decade following 1883, seventeen northern and western states adopted such laws, many of which closely followed the language of the now invalid 1875 national statute. Implementation proved difficult, and most state courts ruled that separate accommodations "of equal merit," including segregated schools, did not violate these laws. But their passage illustrated how equal public rights, once a fringe idea, had entered the Republican mainstream.[47]

In the face of the discouraging trend of Supreme Court decisions, black leaders continued to advance an alternative jurisprudence with a broad understanding of citizens' rights and the federal government's power to enforce them. One who assiduously promoted a different vision of the Reconstruction amendments was T. Thomas Fortune, the son of a Florida Reconstruction leader and editor of a series of newspapers in New York City. Fortune, who had studied law before turning to journalism, had little respect for most members of the Court, describing them as "deficient in legal acumen." The second founding, he insisted, had fundamentally changed the Constitution, creating a direct relationship between the individual citizen and the nation and empowering the latter to protect blacks in the exercise of new rights. He particularly attacked the state action/private action dichotomy. "What sort of government," Fortune asked, "is it which openly declares it has no power to protect its citizens from ruffianism, intimidation and murder?"[48]

The *Civil Rights Cases* also inspired Baltimore's Brotherhood of Liberty to publish *Justice and Jurisprudence*, its critique of Supreme Court rulings. It took until 1889 for this 600-page treatise on law, history, and philosophy to appear in print. Its language was ornate, even pretentious. But beneath the rhetoric lay a trenchant critique of the "legal fiction" that had made possible "the unconstitutional drift of the courts and public sentiment away from the Fourteenth Amendment."

The book explored the rights "public and private" that constituted the privileges and immunities of citizens of the United States, which the amendment was meant to protect. These rights included not only equal treatment in public accommodations, transport, and places of amusement, but those of free labor, broadly defined. The book assailed employment discrimination, housing segregation, exclusion of blacks from labor unions, and lack of access to education, insisting that citizenship carried with it the promise of economic opportunity. "Can a citizen," it asked, "be daily excluded from the paths of industrial progress . . . and be a citizen of the United States?" The book homed in on the Court's distinction between Fourteenth and Fifteenth amendment rights. "Why," the author wondered, "is there a constitutional power" to act against private interference with the right to vote, but not acts by an individual or business "discriminating against all other civil rights, immunities, and privileges of this race?" [49]

The *Baltimore Sun* denounced the authors of *Justice and Jurisprudence* for attempting to "dethrone public confidence" in the Supreme Court. But the book also received respectful notices and seems to have been widely circulated. One newspaper even accused Senator John James Ingalls of Kansas of plagiarizing from it in a speech on "southern outrages." "With a great deal of erudition," declared the *Philadelphia Inquirer, Justice and Jurisprudence* demonstrated that the courts had "practically overturned the constitutional amendments." The treatise, said the *Detroit Plaindealer*, was "destined to become an invaluable authority upon constitutional liberty" as well as "the race question in the future of America." Writing in the magazine *Science*, Thaddeus B. Wakeman, an attorney and political philosopher, chided the anonymous author for indulging in an "African exuberance of rhetoric." But Wakeman embraced the conclusion that Supreme Court jurisprudence regarding the Reconstruction amendments was entirely erroneous. The amendments' "plain purpose," he wrote, was to place under national jurisdiction "the whole subject" of citizens' rights. But too many rights had been lost as soon as they reached "that grave of liberty, the Supreme Court of the United States." [50]

⊱

THE YEAR 1889, however, was not an auspicious moment for the dissemination of this alternative constitutional outlook. In the same year that *Justice and Jurisprudence* appeared, Congress considered a new proposal to secure black suffrage in the South. The election of 1888 had given Republicans control of both the presidency and Congress for the first time since 1875. A Federal Elections Bill, introduced by Representative Henry Cabot Lodge of Massachusetts, passed the House in July 1890. It authorized federal courts to appoint supervisors for congressional elections and allowed these courts, not local officials, to certify the results. It did not apply to state and local elections. But it aroused fierce Democratic opposition. Early in 1891, just before Congress adjourned, the bill fell victim to Republican infighting and a southern filibuster in the Senate. (This was the first important piece of legislation supported by a majority in the House and Senate and by the president to be killed by a southern filibuster. It would not be the last.) George F. Hoar, who managed the bill in the Senate, received many letters from "Old Lincoln Republicans" praising his efforts. But with the Lodge Bill died the last significant effort in Congress for many decades to protect the constitutional rights of black Americans. When Democrats, in the wake of the election of 1892, found themselves in control of the presidency and Congress, they repealed large portions of the three enforcement acts of Reconstruction.[51]

During the 1890s, Republicans tacitly acquiesced in the southern Democratic demand that their states should be left free to regulate voting, labor relations, and the racial system without outside interference. In 1896, for the first time since the Civil War, the Republican national platform omitted a direct demand for securing blacks' voting rights, substituting a vague endorsement of the right of all citizens to cast a "free and unrestricted ballot." Two years later, in the Spanish-American War, the United States acquired an overseas empire, a development that strongly reinforced the idea that white populations had a right and duty to rule over nonwhite ones. Writing in 1902, the Columbia University political scientist John W. Burgess noted that because of the new "imperial enterprises," northerners were learning what white southerners and Europeans already knew—"that there are vast differences in political capacity between the races, and that it is the white man's mission . . . to hold the reins of political power." Burgess, his colleague William A. Dunning, and their students produced the first scholarly works on Reconstruction, which condemned black suffrage as a dire mistake. Acceptance of the reality of racial inequality, Dunning wrote, must be the foundation for any stable social order in the South. Well into the twentieth century, when members of the Supreme Court wished to offer historical background for decisions regarding the Reconstruction amendments, they would cite the works of the Dunning School, as well as *The Tragic Era*, Claude Bowers's lurid account of Reconstruction written for a popular audience in the 1920s.[52]

The emergence of the United States as an overseas imperial power raised new questions about the definition of citizenship and the scope of the rights protected by the Fourteenth Amendment. In 1898, following the plain language of that amendment, the Supreme Court affirmed that a person of Chinese origin born in the United States was a citizen by birthright, even though the naturalization laws barred his parents from citizenship. Once the United States acquired Puerto Rico, Guam, Samoa, and the Philippines, however, the demands of empire seeped into Court decisions, especially regarding whether the Constitution "followed the flag"—that is, whether residents of these islands possessed the same constitutional rights as other Americans. In the *Insular Cases* of 1901, the Court concluded that unlike territories on the North American continent, the "plenary power" of Congress over "insular" territories had few constitutional limitations. Lurking behind these decisions was the supposed "lesson" of Reconstruction—that nonwhite populations are unfit for participation in American democracy.[53]

Even apart from imperial adventures, the 1890s and early twentieth century witnessed the full implementation of what came to be called the Jim Crow system. The historian Rayford Logan described these years as the "nadir" of American race relations, with lynching widespread in the South; newspapers, magazines, and popular literature replete with images of blacks as lazy and prone to violence; belief in inborn racial difference embedded in scientific discourse; and racism rife in the labor market. Under the leadership of Chief Justices Melville W. Fuller and Edward D. White, both Democrats appointed by Grover Cleveland, the Supreme Court's retreat from Reconstruction reached high tide. Ironically, the number of Fourteenth Amendment cases on the Court's docket really took off in the 1890s, but almost all of these had to do with the "liberty" of corporations, not the former slaves and their descendants. (In the 1880s, the Court had declared corporations legal "persons" entitled to the protection of the amendment's Due Process Clause. This required a very creative reading of the text and of the congressional debates of 1866, neither of which mentioned corporations.) But the Court did have to decide whether the proliferation of southern laws requiring racial segregation in transportation and depriving black men of the right to vote violated the amended Constitution. In both instances, it determined that they did not.[54]

In 1890, Louisiana enacted a law directing railroad companies to provide "equal but separate accommodations" for white and black passengers. As the name of the group formed to challenge the Act— the Citizens' Committee to Test the Constitutionality of the Separate Car Act—suggests, blacks saw the law first and foremost as an affront to their rights as citizens. The organization was led by Louis A. Martinet, the son of a French father and slave mother and editor of the New Orleans weekly newspaper *The Crusader*, and Rodolphe Desdunes, a longtime political activist. Their involvement represented a direct link to the campaigns during Reconstruction for public rights. Also a reminder of Reconstruction was the committee's choice of a lawyer to fight the case, Albion W. Tourgée, who had helped write

North Carolina's progressive constitution of 1868, as a judge battled the Klan in the state, and in 1891 had written a newspaper column denouncing Louisiana's separate car law. Tourgée received assistance from a local railroad; many companies disliked the added expense of separate cars since there were often few or no black passengers.

The committee selected the light-skinned Homer A. Plessy to test the law. He entered a whites-only car, refused to leave when ordered to do so by the conductor, and was arrested. Tourgée thought the fact that Plessy could easily have passed for white demonstrated the absurdity of attempting to write racial classifications into law and of empowering train conductors to determine the race of passengers. His core argument, however, echoed Harlan's dissent in the *Civil Rights Cases*—the Fourteenth Amendment had created national protection for an entire array of rights, old and new, against invidious racial discrimination. He hoped the Court would take the opportunity to reconsider its narrow definition of the privileges or immunities of citizenship in the *Slaughterhouse* decision of 1873. He also insisted that the Louisiana law's purpose was not simply to separate the races but to insult and degrade blacks and that it should be struck down under the Thirteenth Amendment as a badge of slavery. Tourgée's Supreme Court brief asked the justices to stand in blacks' shoes. How would they feel if one day they woke up "with a black skin" and had to suffer the humiliation of being evicted from a railroad car?[55]

By the time the *Plessy* case reached the Supreme Court in 1896, the justices had already upheld the conviction of a railroad company for failing to abide by an 1888 Mississippi law requiring the segregation of passengers. So it was hardly a surprise when, in a seven to one ruling, it did the same for Louisiana's statute. The decision, written by Justice Henry B. Brown, a specialist in admiralty law who hailed from the social elite of Massachusetts, did not confront most of Tourgée's arguments but simply blamed blacks for being oversensitive. So long as facilities were equal, Brown insisted, separation was not "a badge of inferiority," even if the "colored race" chose "to put that construction upon it." Thus the Fourteenth Amendment's Equal Protection Clause did not apply. Nor did the Thirteenth Amendment have any bearing, for racial segregation was a "reasonable" exercise of the state's police power, not a badge of servitude.

But Brown went beyond legal arguments to raise the old bugbear of enforced "social equality" and to offer his thoughts about the immutable nature of racial "instincts" and the undesirability of "enforced commingling" of the races. The Reconstruction amendments, he declared, "could not have been intended to abolish distinctions based upon color." Brown portrayed blacks as imagining themselves being dealt with unfairly, but at the same time referred to whites as the "dominant race" and added, "if one race be inferior to the other socially, the Constitution of the United States cannot put them upon the same plane." Indeed, were white passengers forced to sit with blacks, their reputations would suffer. Whiteness, wrote Brown, was a form of "property," and the railroad could be sued for devaluing it. Plessy, however, despite his skin color, was not white and thus not entitled to "the reputation of being a white man," evidently worth more than a reputation of being black.[56]

The lone dissenter, John Marshall Harlan, wrote an opinion that would come to be recognized as a classic statement of constitutional egalitarianism. To be sure, Harlan's commitment to equality had its limits. He shared prevailing anti-Chinese prejudices; indeed, one reason he objected to the Louisiana law was that it allowed Chinese travelers, barred from citizenship by the naturalization laws, to sit in the same car with whites while excluding black citizens, some of whom might have "risked their lives for the preservation of the Union." Two years later, he would dissent from the Court's ruling that the Fourteenth Amendment's principle of birthright citizenship applied to the American-born children of Chinese immigrants.[57]

Regarding blacks, however, Harlan irrefutably took apart Brown's racist logic. "The white race," Harlan wrote, was undoubtedly "the dominant race" in wealth, power, prestige, and achievements. "But in view of the Constitution, in the eye of the law, there is in this country no superior, dominant ruling class of citizens. . . . Our Constitution is color-blind." What was at stake was not an illusory social equality but "personal liberty," and thus the Louisiana law violated not only the Fourteenth Amendment but the Thirteenth as well. The "thin disguise" of equal facilities could not obscure the fact that enforced segregation was not an innocuous separation of the races but an expression of racial dominance rooted in slavery. The law assumed that blacks were "so inferior and degraded that they cannot be allowed to sit in proximity to white citizens." "In my opinion," Harlan added, "the judgment this day rendered will, in time, prove to be quite as pernicious as the decision made by this tribunal in the *Dred Scott Case.*" Harlan correctly predicted that the decision would unleash a flood of statutes segregating every realm of southern life. In fact, segregated facilities were never "equal," and in any event the Supreme Court quickly retreated from the idea that they must be. In 1899, it allowed a Georgia school board to close its black high school for economic reasons while the high school for white students remained in operation. Even Harlan went along—indeed, he wrote the decision, which argued that the allocation of school funds was a matter for state and local authorities to determine.[58]

Thanks to the iconic status acquired by *Brown v. Board of Education*, which over half a century later overturned the "separate but equal" doctrine with regard to public education, *Plessy v. Ferguson* is today the most widely known of the Court's late nineteenth-century decisions. At the time, however, it attracted little attention, and what coverage it did receive generally treated it as a "railroad case" rather than one about citizens' rights. Harlan's dissent, however, solidified his reputation in the black community. "Nothing but profound respect and gratitude," one black newspaper commented, "can attach to Justice Harlan." White southerners by and large took a different view. When Harlan died in 1911, a Memphis newspaper commented that if his outlook had become law, "all the old doctrines of the reconstructionists . . . would have been enforced and the country would have probably passed through race war."

The following year, retired justice Henry B. Brown, author of the *Plessy* decision, published a memoir of his late colleague. Brown now acknowledged as "probably the fact" Harlan's contention that the Louisiana law originated in an illegitimate discriminatory purpose. He also admitted that while the majority opinion in the *Civil Rights Cases* of 1883 "has met with the general approval of the country," doubt still lingered "whether the spirit of the amendments was not sacrificed to the letter" and whether, as Harlan had insisted, blacks were constitutionally entitled to equal treatment "in all places affected with a public interest." By the time Brown wrote in 1912, however, Harlan's prediction that *Plessy* would unleash a wave of segregation legislation had come to pass, all constitutional under the Court's interpretation of the Fourteenth Amendment.[59]

As to the right to vote, by the early twentieth century, with the acquiescence of the Supreme Court, the Fifteenth Amendment had been essentially nullified throughout the South. Although Democrats had long used the disenfranchisement of persons convicted of a crime, gerrymandering, violence, and fraud to reduce the number and impact of black voters, the failure of the Lodge Bill was taken as a green light to eliminate black suffrage entirely. Mississippi led the way, in 1890 adopting a new constitution that required payment of a poll tax, expanded the number of crimes (down to "obtaining money or goods under false pretenses") that disqualified a person from voting, and barred prospective voters who could not read a section of the state constitution or provide a reasonable interpretation of it. The "understanding" clause left the right to vote in the hands of local registrars, generally low-level Democratic party functionaries. The Mississippi convention also called for repeal of the Fifteenth Amendment. In the meantime, to avoid directly confronting that amendment, the requirements did not explicitly mention race.[60]

By the time disenfranchisement had been completed in the early twentieth century, African-Americans' right to vote, enshrined in the Constitution in 1870, had been eliminated throughout the old Confederacy as well as in Oklahoma and Delaware. As the southern historian Francis B. Simkins later noted, disenfranchisement was justified "on a single ground: the memory of the alleged horrors of Reconstruction." The result should have triggered enforcement of Section 2 of the Fourteenth Amendment, which provided for an automatic reduction in congressional representation for states that deprived male citizens of the franchise. But no action was ever taken. Writing in 1901, former Reconstruction legislator George S. Boutwell lamented that the Fifteenth Amendment had been "defeated" and called the governments of the southern states "usurpations." The amendment's fate was an extraordinary example of constitutional nullification and an unusual event in the history of democracy. There cannot have been many instances in which millions of persons who enjoyed the right to vote suddenly had it taken away.[61]

The Supreme Court refused to invalidate state disenfranchisement measures. The first case, *Williams v. Mississippi* (1898), arose from the appeal of Henry Williams, a black man indicted and convicted of murder before all-white grand and petit juries. Since jurors were selected from Mississippi's voter rolls, which now excluded virtually all blacks, Williams challenged the voting provisions of the state constitution of 1890. The case was notable for being argued before the Court by Cornelius Jones, the first time a black attorney appeared unassisted by a white one. But the justices refused to interfere with Mississippi's disenfranchising policies.

In 1886, in *Yick Wo v. Hopkins*, the Court, invoking the Fourteenth Amendment, had unanimously overturned a conviction for violating a San Francisco ordinance concerning operating a laundry. Although the law was "fair on its face and impartial in appearance," making no mention of nationality or race, the justices concluded that it was "applied and administered" in a discriminatory manner against Chinese-run businesses ("with an evil eye and an unequal hand" was Justice Stanley Matthews's arresting language). As such, the ordinance amounted to a "practical denial by the state" of legal equality. When it came to African-Americans, however, the Court proved unwilling to look beyond the language of the law. Members of the Mississippi constitutional convention of 1890 had forthrightly announced their purpose—"to exclude the Negro," as one delegate asserted—and had succeeded. Yet the Supreme Court unanimously ruled (with Harlan strangely joining the decision) that since the Mississippi constitution did not "on its face" mention race, it did not violate the Fifteenth Amendment. Even though implementation of the voting requirements left virtually no blacks registered to vote, the Court declared, it had not been demonstrated that they had been applied in a discriminatory manner.[62]

Equally devastating to black voting rights was the 1903 decision in *Giles v. Harris*, another case argued before the Court by a black lawyer, Wilford H. Smith, a graduate of Boston University School of Law. Jackson W. Giles, president of the Alabama Negro Suffrage Association, had cast ballots from 1871 to 1901. He sued to overturn Alabama's new voting requirements, which allowed registrars to exclude those who lacked "good character" or did not understand "the duties and obligations of citizenship." His complaint argued that the state's entire registration system was racially biased. Oliver Wendell Holmes, recently appointed by Theodore Roosevelt, wrote the opinion for a six–three majority. In effect, Holmes threw up his hands and described the Supreme Court as impotent. If "the great mass of the white population intends to keep the blacks from voting," he wrote, there was nothing the justices could do unless they were prepared to have the federal courts supervise voting throughout Alabama. "Relief from a great political wrong" could only come from the "people of a state" through their elected officials, or from Congress. (Of course, the definition of the "people" of Alabama was precisely the point at issue.) Holmes would go on to a distinguished judicial career. *Giles v. Harris*, one scholar has written, "is—or should be—the most prominent stain" on his reputation.[63]

Giles v. Harris generated more newspaper coverage than any case involving blacks since the *Civil Rights Cases* decision of 1883. The Democratic press hailed the ruling as an indication that the Court would not interfere with "a sovereign state's regulation of its elections." Although Holmes had not explicitly upheld Alabama's voting requirements, newspapers North and South ran headlines suggesting that he had, among them "Supreme Court Sustains the Alabama Constitution" and "Can Stop Negro Voting." Some signs of discontent appeared in the North. "Is the Constitution non-enforceable?" asked the *Springfield Republican*. "We are brought face to face with the consideration that the Constitution may be violated with impunity."[64]

The irrepressible Giles, who lost not only his lawsuit but his job as a mail carrier, promised to continue the fight. In 1904 he brought a suit for damages, asking the Supreme Court to declare the Alabama voting provisions null and void. Again, his plea was denied. A year later, the battle to reinvigorate the Reconstruction amendments was taken up by the Niagara Movement and soon afterward the NAACP. But the road to success would be very long. For now the abrogation of Reconstruction's legal legacy continued. In *Hodges v. United States* (1906), the Court seriously weakened the Civil Rights Act of 1866, which prohibited interfering with blacks' free labor rights, overturning the conviction in federal court of three white men who violently drove eight blacks from their jobs at an Arkansas sawmill. "I cannot assent," wrote Harlan, "to an interpretation of the Constitution which denies national protection to vast numbers of our people in respect of rights derived by them from the nation."

The one positive thing that can be said of this long train of decisions is that, as Rodolphe Desdunes, a leader of the New Orleans Citizens' Committee, wrote of *Plessy*, "our people had the satisfaction of putting the American government's back to the wall," forcing it to make plain the depth of the nation's commitment to Jim Crow.[65]

EPILOGUE

THE STORY of the long battle to reinvigorate the Reconstruction amendments, culminating in decisions of the Warren Court during the Second Reconstruction of the 1950s and 1960s, has often been told.[1] Today, many of the goals of the Brotherhood of Liberty, Justice John Marshall Harlan, and others who put forward an alternative, rights-based interpretation of the amendments, have been embedded in statute law and upheld by the Supreme Court. The country has come a long way toward fulfilling the agenda of Reconstruction, although deep inequalities remain. Yet key elements of the second founding, including birthright citizenship, equal protection of the laws, and the right to vote, remain highly contested. And in a legal environment that relies so heavily on precedent, crucial decisions of the retreat from Reconstruction, with what Harlan called the Court's "narrow and artificial" understanding of the Thirteenth, Fourteenth, and Fifteenth Amendments, remain undisturbed.

With a few exceptions, such as early twentieth-century cases invalidating state laws establishing peonage, there is still very little Thirteenth Amendment jurisprudence. Nor has Congress proved willing to enact legislation under that amendment's enforcement section. In 1968, at the height of the civil rights revolution, the Court came to the verge of revitalizing the Thirteenth Amendment, then stepped back. In *Jones v. Alfred H. Mayer Co.* a 7–2 majority allowed suits for damages under the Civil Rights Act of 1866 (enacted under that amendment) for racial discrimination in the sale of homes. The majority identified such discrimination, which deprived blacks of the right to own property in the same way as whites, as a stigma that arose from slavery. But the Court has never gone on to define more broadly the "badges and incidents" of bondage. As a result, the Thirteenth Amendment remains essentially a "dead letter" whose purpose was fulfilled when chattel slavery vanished. This is unfortunate because the amendment's language lacks any reference to state action. Its latent power has almost never been invoked as a weapon against the racism that forms so powerful a legacy of American slavery.[2]

Like the Thirteenth Amendment, the Fifteenth plays only a minor role in modern constitutional law. It did provide constitutional sanction for the Voting Rights Act of 1965, which restored the suffrage to millions of black southerners, as well as the more modest voting provisions of the Civil Rights Acts of 1957 and 1964. To this day, however, the right to vote remains the subject of bitter disputation. Many states have recently enacted laws that do not explicitly mention race or ethnicity but impose suffrage requirements that seem designed to restrict the voting rights of blacks, Hispanics, and Native Americans. The Supreme Court has upheld some of these laws; others remain the subject of litigation.

The main recent Fifteenth Amendment decision came in 2013, in a case arising from Shelby County, Alabama. The Court invalidated the Voting Rights Act's requirement that certain jurisdictions with long histories of racial discrimination in voting obtain prior federal approval before changing voting rules. This provision, the majority declared, represented "a drastic departure from the basic principles of federalism" enshrined in the original Constitution. It would be unfair, the Court insisted, to suspect states and localities that had discriminated in the past of desiring to do so in the present. As anyone with a deeper understanding of American history would have predicted, Alabama immediately took the decision as a green light to enact laws meant to restrict the voting population. The state, for example, required a photo ID to vote and then closed driver's license offices—where such documents can be obtained—in counties with the highest percentage of blacks in the population. In affirming a commitment to federalism, the Shelby County decision took no note of how the second founding had altered the original federal system. Indeed, to this day, when conservative jurists discuss federalism, they almost always concentrate on the ideas of eighteenth-century framers, ignoring those of the architects of Reconstruction.[3]

As for the Fourteenth Amendment, this has undergone an astonishing expansion, although one in keeping with the widespread aspiration of 1866 to establish a broad standard of equality for the entire nation. The amendment played a crucial role in the rights revolution of the twentieth century. Incorporation—John A. Bingham's dream of requiring the states to abide by the protections of the Bill of Rights—has essentially been achieved, not all at once but individually over time. The process culminated in the 2010 decision in *McDonald v. City of Chicago*, requiring states to adhere to the Second Amendment's right to bear arms, and in *Timbs v. Indiana* (2019), incorporating the Eighth Amendment's ban on excessive fines. Contrary to Bingham's expectations, however, the application of the Bill of Rights to the states has come via the Fourteenth Amendment's Due Process Clause, not its prohibition of states impairing the privileges or immunities of American citizens, which would have been more logical. The latter language had been rendered almost meaningless in the *Slaughterhouse* decision of 1873. That decision remains "good law." In *McDonald*, Justice Samuel Alito's majority opinion explicitly stated, "we decline to disturb the *Slaughterhouse* ruling."[4]

Thanks to incorporation, the states are now required to act in accordance with the fundamental liberties enumerated in the Bill of Rights, tremendously expanding the ability of all Americans to protect their civil liberties against abridgement by state and local authorities. Yet ironically, when it comes to the status of black Americans, the Fourteenth Amendment's promise has never truly been fulfilled. Of course, the Warren Court of the 1950s and 1960s deserves tremendous credit for systematically dismantling the edifice of legal segregation. But with the exception of repudiating *Plessy v. Ferguson*, in their landmark desegregation cases the justices did not directly confront the long train of decisions that restricted national power over citizens' basic rights. Instead, they opted to work around that jurisprudence. Even at the height of the civil rights revolution, they could not bring themselves to say that for eighty years or more the Court had been wrong.[5]

While upholding legislation punishing discriminatory behavior by individuals and businesses, the Court has never repudiated the state action doctrine. In 1948, in a ruling that discriminatory covenants in housing contracts could not be enforced in court (which would make the state complicit), the justices reaffirmed the principle, "firmly embedded in our constitutional law," that the Fourteenth Amendment prohibited "only actions by the states, not merely private conduct, however discriminatory." Later, in affirming the constitutionality of the Civil Rights Act of 1964 barring discrimination by businesses of all kinds, the Court relied not on the Reconstruction amendments but on the Constitution's Interstate Commerce Clause. When Congress in 2009 enacted a federal "hate crimes" law allowing for federal prosecution of acts of violence motivated by bias related to race, gender, religion, and national origin, it too mainly based its action on the Commerce Clause. Federal courts have upheld the statute on these grounds, but the Supreme Court has yet to rule on its constitutionality. (The outlook if such a case arises is by no means clear. In 2000, in *United States v. Morrison*, the Supreme Court invoked two 1883 decisions—the *Civil Rights Cases* and *United States v. Harris*— to conclude that Congress lacks power to provide a remedy in federal courts for violence against women that is not "state-sponsored.")

The elevation of the Commerce Clause into a "charter of human rights," a way of compensating for the Supreme Court's cramped view of the Reconstruction amendments, has made the judiciary look ridiculous. Everyone knows that guaranteeing the free flow of goods was not the motivation of those who took to the streets to demand passage of the Civil Rights Act or of the members of Congress who voted for that law. Relying on the Fourteenth Amendment, however, would require repudiating a jurisprudence dating back to the 1870s.[6]

In *Morrison*, in words that echoed the *Slaughterhouse* majority, Chief Justice William Rehnquist declared that the Fourteenth Amendment was not aimed at "obliterating the framers' carefully crafted balance of power" between the states and the federal government. Rehnquist defended reliance on the decisions in the *Civil Rights Cases* and *United States v. Harris* not simply because of the "length of time they have been on the books," but because the justices who issued them "had intimate knowledge and familiarity with the events surrounding the adoption of the Fourteenth Amendment." He ignored entirely the widespread criticism at the time by people equally familiar with those events and the surrounding history.[7]

Today, even though many forms of private racial discrimination are outlawed and no state or federal law overtly discriminates against blacks or other racial minorities, a state action interpretation of the Fourteenth Amendment can be debilitating. It has been used, for example, in rulings that do not allow race to be taken into account in voluntary school desegregation programs, on the grounds that segregation today results not from laws, as in the past, but from "private choices" that produced racially homogeneous housing patterns. This sharp distinction between public and private action makes it difficult to address the numerous connections between federal, state, and local housing, zoning, transportation, and mortgage insurance policies, and the "private" decisions of banks, real estate companies, and individual home buyers, that together have produced widespread segregation in housing and education.[8]

The Fourteenth Amendment's Equal Protection Clause has followed a similar pattern—an impact expanded well beyond the initial purposes of Reconstruction, but limited in relation to African-Americans. Equal protection was the basis of the Court's landmark 1960s "one man one vote" decision requiring that legislative and congressional districts have equal populations. It was employed in the pioneering legal arguments of Pauli Murray and Ruth Bader Ginsburg that persuaded the courts, beginning in the 1970s, to apply the Fourteenth Amendment to discrimination based on gender. It underpinned a 1982 decision barring states from excluding the children of undocumented immigrants from public schools. In tandem with the

Due Process Clause, it formed the constitutional basis for the 2015 ruling requiring states to allow gay couples to marry. The Equal Protection Clause has made the Fourteenth Amendment a vehicle through which Americans of all backgrounds can claim greater rights and seek redress from various forms of discrimination.

Yet when it comes to racial justice, the Court has lately proved more sympathetic to white plaintiffs complaining of reverse discrimination because of affirmative action policies than to blacks seeking assistance in overcoming the legacies of centuries of slavery and Jim Crow. John Marshall Harlan's dictum, "our Constitution is color-blind," hurled at the majority in *Plessy* as a reminder of the egalitarian purposes of the second founding, has lately been invoked by conservative justices to challenge any consideration of race whatsoever. The Court appears to view "racial classifications," whether remedial or oppressive, not inequality, as the root of the country's race problems. This outlook, rooted more in modern-day politics than the actual history of the Reconstruction era, has helped to fuel a long retreat from race-conscious efforts to promote equality.[9] As for the Fourteenth Amendment's first sentence, establishing the principle of birthright citizenship, this has become very controversial of late because of its application to children born in the United States to undocumented immigrants. Prominent political figures have called for that portion of the amendment's outright repeal. In the runup to the 2018 midterm elections, President Donald Trump stated that he planned to issue an executive order overturning the principle. The idea that the president can unilaterally abrogate the plain words of the Constitution is alarming. One wonders which provision might be next.

Of course we live today in a legal era far different from that of the late nineteenth century. But the shadow of the retreat from Reconstruction still hangs over contemporary jurisprudence. The counter-interpretation developed in Reconstruction and its aftermath, with its more powerful assertion of the rights enshrined in the Constitution by the second founding and the power of the federal government to enforce them, however, remains available, if the political environment changes. There is no reason why the Thirteenth Amendment cannot be reinvigorated as a weapon against enduring inequalities rooted in slavery, or the Fourteenth's clause related to the privileges or immunities of citizens must remain a dead letter, why it cannot be understood to encompass rights denied by slavery and essential to full membership in American society today, such as access to an adequate education, or even the "reasonable wages" to which Lincoln said the freed slaves were entitled in the Emancipation Proclamation. Why, in the twenty-first century, should the right to vote not be considered a privilege of citizenship enjoyed by all adult Americans? There is no reason that "societal racism," cavalierly dismissed by the Supreme Court as a justification for affirmative action and school integration programs, cannot legitimately be taken into account by the courts, or why the state action doctrine must hamstring federal efforts to protect the rights of all Americans against violation by private parties. Nor is there any reason to rely on an implausible invocation of the Constitution's Commerce Clause when pursuing the goal of racial equality. The point is not that the counterinterpretation is the one true meaning of the Reconstruction amendments, but that viable alternatives exist to actual Supreme Court jurisprudence, alternatives rooted in the historical record, which would infuse the amendments with greater power.

In his second inaugural address, Abraham Lincoln identified slavery as the fundamental cause of the Civil War and implicitly challenged Americans to confront unblinkingly its legacy, to think creatively about how to fulfill the aspirations unleashed by its destruction. The three constitutional amendments formed part of the nation's response. Their checkered history reminds us that, as James Madison warned in *The Federalist*, under certain circumstances constitutional guarantees can become little more than "parchment barriers" to infringements on Americans' liberties.[10]

Rights can be gained, and rights can be taken away. A century and a half after the end of slavery, the project of equal citizenship remains unfinished. However flawed, the era that followed the Civil War can serve as an inspiration for those striving to achieve a more equal, more just society. Every day we live the complex legacy of Reconstruction and its overthrow. And because the ideals of freedom, equality, and democracy are always contested, our understanding of the Reconstruction amendments will forever be a work in progress. So long as the legacy of slavery and Jim Crow continue to plague our society, we can expect Americans to return to the nation's second founding and find there new meanings for our fractious and troubled times.

Appendix

"WHAT IS FREEDOM?": RECONSTRUCTION

1865–1877

O N THE evening of January 12, 1865, less than a month after Union forces captured Savannah, Georgia, twenty leaders of the city's black community gathered for a discussion with General William T. Sherman and Secretary of War Edwin M. Stanton. Mostly Baptist and Methodist ministers, the group included several men who within a few years would assume prominent positions during the era of Reconstruction that followed the Civil War. Ulysses S. Houston, pastor of the city's Third African Baptist Church, and James Porter, an Episcopal religious leader who had operated a secret school for black children before the war, in a few years would win election to the Georgia legislature. James D. Lynch, who had been born free in Baltimore and educated in New Hampshire, went on to serve as secretary of state of Mississippi.

The conversation revealed that the black leaders brought out of slavery a clear definition of freedom. Asked what he understood by slavery, Garrison Frazier, a Baptist minister chosen as the group's spokesman, responded that it meant one person's "receiving by irresistible power the work of another man, and not by his consent." Freedom he defined as "placing us where we could reap the fruit of our own labor, and take care of ourselves." The way to accomplish this was "to have land, and turn it and till it by our own labor." Frazier insisted that blacks possessed "sufficient intelligence" to maintain themselves in freedom and enjoy the equal protection of the laws.

Sherman's meeting with the black leaders foreshadowed some of the radical changes that would take place during the era known as Reconstruction (meaning, literally, the rebuilding of the shattered nation). In the years following the Civil War, former slaves and their white allies, North and South, would seek to redefine the meaning and boundaries of American freedom and citizenship. Previously an entitlement of whites, these would be expanded to include black Americans. The laws and Constitution would be rewritten to guarantee African-Americans, for the first time in the nation's history, recognition as citizens and equality before the law. Black men would be granted the right to vote, ushering in a period of interracial democracy throughout the South. Black schools, churches, and other institutions would flourish, laying the foundation for the modern African-American community. Many of the advances of Reconstruction would prove temporary, swept away during a campaign of violence in the South and the North's retreat from the ideal of equality. But Reconstruction laid the foundation for future struggles to extend freedom to all Americans.

All this, however, lay in the future in January 1865. Four days after the meeting, Sherman responded to the black delegation by issuing Special Field Order 15. This set aside the Sea Islands and a large area along the South Carolina and Georgia coasts for the settlement of black families on forty-acre plots of land. He also offered them broken-down mules that the army could no longer use. In Sherman's order lay the origins of the phrase "forty acres and a mule," which would reverberate across the South in the next few years. By June, some 40,000 freed slaves had been settled on "Sherman land." Among the emancipated slaves, Sherman's order raised hopes that the end of slavery would be accompanied by the economic independence that they, like other Americans, believed essential to genuine freedom.

THE MEANING OF FREEDOM

With the end of the Civil War, declared an Illinois congressman in 1865, the United States was a "new nation," for the first time "wholly free." The destruction of slavery, however, made the definition of freedom the central question on the nation's agenda. "What is freedom?" asked Congressman James A. Garfield in 1865. "Is it the bare privilege of not being chained? If this is all, then freedom is a bitter mockery, a cruel delusion." Did freedom mean simply the absence of slavery, or did it imply other rights for the former slaves, and if so, which ones: equal civil rights, the vote, ownership of property? During Reconstruction, freedom became a terrain of conflict, its substance open to different, often contradictory interpretations. Out of the conflict over the meaning of freedom arose new kinds of relations between black and white southerners, and a new definition of the rights of all Americans.

African-Americans' understanding of freedom was shaped by their experiences as slaves and their observation of the free society around them. To begin with, freedom meant escaping the numerous injustices of slavery—punishment by the lash, the separation of families, denial of access to education, the sexual exploitation of black women by their owners—and sharing in the rights and opportunities of American citizens. "If I cannot do like a white man," Henry Adams, an emancipated slave in Louisiana, told his former master in 1865, "I am not free."

Blacks relished the opportunity to demonstrate their liberation from the regulations, significant and trivial, associated with slavery. They openly held mass meetings and religious services free of white supervision, and they acquired dogs, guns, and liquor, all barred to them under slavery. No longer required to obtain a pass from their owners to travel, former slaves throughout the South left the plantations in search of better jobs, family members, or simply a taste of personal liberty. Many moved to southern towns and cities, where, it seemed, "freedom was free-er."

With slavery dead, institutions that had existed before the war, like the black family, free blacks' churches and schools, and the secret slave church, were strengthened, expanded, and freed from white supervision. The family was central to the postemancipation black community. Former slaves made remarkable efforts to locate loved ones from whom they had been separated under slavery. One northern reporter in 1865 encountered a freedman who had walked more than 600 miles from Georgia to North Carolina, searching for the wife and children from whom he had been sold away before the war. Meanwhile, widows of black soldiers successfully claimed survivors' pensions, forcing the federal government to acknowledge the validity of prewar relationships that slavery had attempted to deny.

But while Reconstruction witnessed the stabilization of family life, freedom subtly altered relationships within the family. Emancipation increased the power of black men and brought to many black families the nineteenth-century notion that men and women should inhabit separate "spheres." Immediately after the Civil War, planters complained that freedwomen had "withdrawn" from field labor and work as house servants. Many black women preferred to devote more time to their families than had been possible under slavery, and men considered it a badge of honor to see their wives remain at home. Eventually, the dire poverty of the black community would compel a far higher proportion of black women than white women to go to work for wages.

At the same time, blacks abandoned white-controlled religious institutions to create churches of their own. On the eve of the Civil War, 42,000 black Methodists worshiped in biracial South Carolina churches; by the end of Reconstruction, only 600 remained. The rise of the independent black church, with Methodists and Baptists commanding the largest followings, redrew the religious map of the South. As the major institution independent of white control, the church played a central role in the black community. A place of worship, it also housed schools, social events, and political gatherings. Black ministers came to play a major role in politics. Some 250 held public office during Reconstruction.

Another striking example of the freedpeople's quest for individual and community improvement was their desire for education. Education, declared a Mississippi freedman, was "the next best thing to liberty." The thirst for learning sprang from many sources—a desire to read the Bible, the need to prepare for the economic marketplace, and the opportunity, which arose in 1867, to take part in politics. Blacks of all ages flocked to the schools established by northern missionary societies, the Freedmen's Bureau, and groups of ex-slaves. Northern journalist Sidney Andrews, who toured the South in 1865, was impressed by how much education also took place outside of the classroom: "I had occasion very frequently to notice that porters in stores and laboring men in warehouses, and cart drivers on the streets, had spelling books with them, and were studying them during the time they were not occupied with their work." Reconstruction also witnessed the creation of the nation's first black colleges, including Fisk University in Tennessee, Hampton Institute in Virginia, and Howard University in the nation's capital.

In a society that had made political participation a core element of freedom, the right to vote inevitably became central to the former slaves' desire for empowerment and equality. As Frederick Douglass put it soon after the South's surrender in 1865, "Slavery is not abolished until the black man has the ballot." In a "monarchial government," Douglass explained, no "special" disgrace applied to those denied the right to vote. But in a democracy, "where universal suffrage is the rule," excluding any group meant branding them with "the stigma of inferiority." As soon as the Civil War ended, and in some parts of the South even earlier, free blacks and emancipated slaves claimed a place in the public sphere. They came together in conventions, parades, and petition drives to demand the right to vote and, on occasion, to organize their own "freedom ballots." Anything less than full citizenship, black spokesmen insisted, would betray the nation's democratic promise and the war's meaning.

Former slaves' ideas of freedom, like those of rural people throughout the world, were directly related to land ownership. Only land, wrote Merrimon Howard, a freedman from Mississippi, would enable "the poor class to enjoy the sweet boon of freedom." On the land they would develop independent communities free of white control. Many former slaves insisted that through their unpaid labor, they had acquired a right to the land. "The property which they hold," declared an Alabama black convention, "was nearly all earned by the sweat of *our* brows." In some parts of the South, blacks in 1865 seized property, insisting that it belonged to them. On one Tennessee plantation, former slaves claimed to be "joint heirs" to the estate and, the owner complained, took up residence "in the rooms of my house."

In its individual elements and much of its language, former slaves' definition of freedom resembled that of white Americans—self-ownership, family stability, religious liberty, political participation, and economic autonomy. But these elements combined to form a vision very much their own. For whites, freedom, no matter how defined, was a given, a birthright to be defended. For African-Americans, it was an open-ended process, a transformation of every aspect of their lives and of the society and culture that had sustained slavery in the first place. Although the freedpeople failed to achieve full freedom as they understood it, their definition did much to shape national debate during the turbulent era of Reconstruction.

Most white southerners reacted to military defeat and emancipation with dismay, not only because of the widespread devastation but also because they must now submit to northern demands. "The demoralization is complete," wrote a Georgia girl. "We are whipped, there is no doubt about it." The appalling loss of life, a disaster without parallel in the American experience, affected all classes of southerners. Nearly 260,000 men died for the Confederacy—more than one-fifth of the South's adult male white population. The wholesale destruction of work animals, farm buildings, and machinery ensured that economic revival would be slow and painful. In 1870, the value of property in the South, not counting that represented by slaves, was 30 percent lower than before the war.

Planter families faced profound changes in the war's aftermath. Many lost not only their slaves but also their life savings, which they had patriotically invested in now-worthless Confederate bonds. Some, whose slaves departed the plantation, for the first time found themselves compelled to do physical labor. General Braxton Bragg returned to his "once prosperous" Alabama home to find "*all, all* was lost, except my debts." Bragg and his wife, a woman "raised in affluence," lived for a time in a slave cabin.

Southern planters sought to implement an understanding of freedom quite different from that of the former slaves. As they struggled to accept the reality of emancipation, most planters defined black freedom in the narrowest manner. As journalist Sidney Andrews discovered late in 1865, "The whites seem wholly unable to comprehend that freedom for the negro means the same thing as freedom for them. They readily enough admit that the government has made him free, but appear to believe that they have the right to exercise the same old control." To southern leaders, freedom still meant hierarchy and mastery; it was a privilege not a right, a carefully defined legal status rather than an open-ended entitlement. Certainly, it implied neither economic autonomy nor civil and political equality. A Kentucky newspaper summed up the stance of much of the white South: the former slave was "*free*, but free only to labor."

Along with former slaves and former masters, the victorious Republican North tried to implement its own vision of freedom. Central to its definition was the antebellum principle of free labor, now further strengthened as a definition of the good society by the Union's triumph. In the free labor vision of a reconstructed South, emancipated blacks, enjoying the same opportunities for advancement as northern workers, would labor more productively than they had as slaves. At the same time, northern capital and migrants would energize the economy. The South would eventually come to resemble the "free society" of the North, complete with public schools, small towns, and independent farmers. Unified on the basis of free labor, proclaimed Carl Schurz, a refugee from the failed German revolution of 1848, who rose to become a leader of the Republican Party, America would become "a republic, greater, more populous, freer, more prosperous, and more powerful" than any in history.

With planters seeking to establish a labor system as close to slavery as possible, and former slaves demanding economic autonomy and access to land, a long period of conflict over the organization and control of labor followed on plantations throughout the South. It fell to the Freedmen's Bureau, an agency established by Congress in March 1865, to attempt to establish a working free labor system.

Under the direction of O. O. Howard, a graduate of Bowdoin College in Maine and a veteran of the Civil War, the Bureau took on responsibilities that can only be described as daunting. The Bureau was an experiment in government social policy that seems to belong more comfortably to the New Deal of the 1930s or the Great Society of the 1960s than to nineteenth-century America. Bureau agents were supposed to establish schools, provide aid to the poor and aged, settle disputes between whites and blacks and among the freedpeople, and secure for former slaves and white Unionists equal treatment before the courts. "It is not . . . in your power to fulfill one-tenth of the expectations of those who framed the Bureau," General William T. Sherman wrote to Howard. "I fear you have Hercules' task."

The Bureau lasted from 1865 to 1870. Even at its peak, there were fewer than 1,000 agents in the entire South. Nonetheless, the Bureau's achievements in some areas, notably education and health care, were striking. While the Bureau did not establish schools itself, it coordinated and helped to finance the activities of northern societies committed to black education. By 1869, nearly 3,000 schools, serving more than 150,000 pupils in the South, reported to the Bureau. Bureau agents also assumed control of hospitals established by the army during the war, and expanded the system into new communities. They provided medical care to both black and white southerners. In economic relations, however, the Bureau's activities proved far more problematic.

The idea of free labor, wrote one Bureau agent, was "the noblest principle on earth." All that was required to harmonize race relations in the South was fair wages, good working conditions, and the opportunity to improve the laborer's situation in life. But blacks wanted land of their own, not jobs on plantations. One provision of the law establishing the Bureau gave it the authority to divide abandoned and confiscated land into forty-acre plots for rental and eventual sale to the former slaves.

In the summer of 1865, however, President Andrew Johnson, who had succeeded Lincoln, ordered nearly all land in federal hands returned to its former owners. A series of confrontations followed, notably in South Carolina and Georgia, where the army forcibly evicted blacks who had settled on "Sherman land." When O. O. Howard, head of the Freedmen's Bureau, traveled to the Sea Islands to inform blacks of the new policy, he was greeted with disbelief and protest. A committee of former slaves drew up petitions to Howard and President Johnson. "We want Homesteads," they declared, "we were promised Homesteads by the government." Land, the freedmen insisted, was essential to the meaning of freedom. Without it, they declared, "we have not bettered our condition" from the days of slavery—"you will see, this is not the condition of really free men."

Because no land distribution took place, the vast majority of rural freedpeople remained poor and without property during Reconstruction. They had no alternative but to work on white-owned plantations, often for their former owners. Far from being able to rise in the social scale through hard work, black men were largely confined to farm work, unskilled labor, and service jobs, and black women to positions in private homes as cooks and maids. Their wages remained too low to allow for any accumulation. By the turn of the century, a significant number of southern African-Americans had managed to acquire small parcels of land. But the failure of land reform produced a deep sense of betrayal that survived among the former slaves and their descendants long after the end of Reconstruction. "No sir," Mary Gaffney, an elderly ex-slave, recalled in the 1930s, "we were not given a thing but freedom."

Out of the conflict on the plantations, new systems of labor emerged in the different regions of the South. The task system, under which workers were assigned daily tasks, completion of which ended their responsibilities for that day, survived in the rice kingdom of South Carolina and Georgia. Closely supervised wage labor predominated on the sugar plantations of southern Louisiana. Sharecropping came to dominate the Cotton Belt and much of the Tobacco Belt of Virginia and North Carolina.

Sharecropping initially arose as a compromise between blacks' desire for land and planters' demand for labor discipline. The system allowed each black family to rent a part of a plantation, with the crop divided between worker and owner at the end of the year. Sharecropping guaranteed the planters a stable resident labor force. Former slaves preferred it to gang labor because it offered them the prospect of working without day-to-day white supervision. But as the years went on, sharecropping became more and more oppressive. Sharecroppers' economic opportunities were severely limited by a world market in which the price of farm products suffered a prolonged decline.

The plight of the small farmer was not confined to blacks in the postwar South. Wartime devastation set in motion a train of events that permanently altered the independent way of life of white yeomen, leading to what they considered a loss of freedom. Before the war, most small farmers had concentrated on raising food for their families and grew little cotton. With much of their property destroyed, many yeomen saw their economic condition worsened by successive crop failures after the war. To obtain supplies from merchants, farmers were forced to take up the growing of cotton and pledge a part of the crop as collateral (property the creditor can seize if a debt is not paid). This system became known as the crop lien. Since interest rates were extremely high and the price of cotton fell steadily, many farmers found themselves still in debt after marketing their portion of the crop at year's end. They had no choice but to continue to plant cotton to obtain new loans. By the mid-1870s, white farmers, who cultivated only 10 percent of the South's cotton crop in 1860, were growing 40 percent, and many who had owned their land had fallen into dependency as sharecroppers, who now rented land owned by others.

Both black and white farmers found themselves caught in the sharecropping and crop-lien systems. A far higher percentage of black than white farmers in the South rented land rather than owned it. But every census from 1880 to 1940 counted more white than black sharecroppers. The workings of sharecropping and the crop-lien system are illustrated by the case of Matt Brown, a Mississippi farmer who borrowed money each year from a local merchant. He began 1892 with a debt of $226 held over from the previous year. By 1893, although he produced cotton worth $171, Brown's debt had increased to $402, because he had borrowed $33 for food, $29 for clothing, $173 for supplies, and $112 for other items. Brown never succeeded in getting out of debt. He died in 1905; the last entry under his name in the merchant's account book is a coffin.

Even as the rural South stagnated economically, southern cities experienced remarkable growth after the Civil War. As railroads penetrated the interior, they enabled merchants in market centers like Atlanta to trade directly with the North, bypassing coastal cities that had traditionally monopolized southern commerce. A new urban middle class of merchants, railroad promoters, and bankers reaped the benefits of the spread of cotton production in the postwar South.

Thus, Reconstruction brought about profound changes in the lives of southerners, black and white, rich and poor. In place of the prewar world of master, slave, and self-sufficient yeoman, the postwar South was peopled by new social classes—landowning employers, black and white sharecroppers, cotton-producing white farmers, wage-earning black laborers, and urban entrepreneurs. Each of these groups turned to Reconstruction politics in an attempt to shape to its own advantage the aftermath of emancipation.

The United States, of course, was not the only society to confront the transition from slavery to freedom. Indeed, many parallels exist between the debates during Reconstruction and struggles that followed slavery in other parts of the Western Hemisphere over the same issues of land, control of labor, and political power. In every case, former planters (or, in Haiti, where the planter class had been destroyed, the government itself) tried to encourage or require former slaves to go back to work on plantations to grow the same crops as under slavery. Planters elsewhere held the same stereotypical views of black laborers as were voiced by their counterparts in the United States—former slaves were supposedly lazy, were lacking in ambition, and thought that freedom meant an absence of labor.

For their part, former slaves throughout the hemisphere tried to carve out as much independence as possible, both in their daily lives and in their labor. They attempted to reconstruct family life by withdrawing women and children from field labor (in the West Indies, women turned to marketing their families' crops to earn income). Wherever possible, former slaves acquired land of their own and devoted more time to growing food for their families than to growing crops for the international market. In many places, the plantations either fell to pieces, as in Haiti, or continued operating with a new labor force composed of indentured servants from India and China, as in Jamaica, Trinidad, and British Guiana. Southern planters in the United States brought in a few Chinese laborers in an attempt to replace freedmen, but since the federal government opposed such efforts, the Chinese remained only a tiny proportion of the southern workforce.

But if struggles over land and labor united its postemancipation experience with that of other societies, in one respect the United States was unique. Only in the United States were former slaves, within two years of the end of slavery, granted the right to vote and, thus, given a major share of political power. Few anticipated this development when the Civil War ended. It came about as the result of one of the greatest political crises of American history—the battle between President Andrew Johnson and Congress over Reconstruction. The struggle resulted in profound changes in the nature of citizenship, the structure of constitutional authority, and the meaning of American freedom.

THE MAKING OF RADICAL RECONSTRUCTION

To Lincoln's successor, Andrew Johnson, fell the task of overseeing the restoration of the Union. Born in poverty in North Carolina, as a youth Johnson worked as a tailor's apprentice. After moving to Tennessee, he achieved success through politics. Beginning as an alderman (a town official), he rose to serve in the state legislature, Congress, and for two terms as governor of Tennessee. Johnson identified himself as the champion of his state's "honest yeomen" and a foe of large planters, whom he described as a "bloated, corrupted aristocracy." A strong defender of the Union, he became the only senator from a seceding state to remain at his post in Washington, D.C., when the Civil War began. When northern forces occupied Tennessee, Abraham Lincoln named him military governor. In 1864, Republicans nominated him to run for vice president as a symbol of the party's hope of extending its organization into the South.

In personality and outlook, Johnson proved unsuited for the responsibilities he shouldered after Lincoln's death. A lonely, stubborn man, he was intolerant of criticism and unable to compromise. He lacked Lincoln's political skills and keen sense of public opinion. A fervent believer in states' rights, Johnson insisted that since secession was illegal, the southern states had never actually left the Union or surrendered the right to govern their own affairs. Moreover, while Johnson had supported emancipation once Lincoln made it a goal of the war effort, he held deeply racist views. African-Americans, Johnson believed, had no role to play in Reconstruction.

A little over a month after Lee's surrender at Appomattox, and with Congress out of session until December, Johnson in May 1865 outlined his plan for reuniting the nation. He issued a series of proclamations that began the period of Presidential Reconstruction (1865–1867). Johnson offered a pardon (which restored political and property rights, except for slaves) to nearly all white southerners who took an oath of allegiance to the Union. He excluded Confederate leaders and wealthy planters whose prewar property had been valued at more than $20,000. This exemption suggested at first that Johnson planned a more punitive Reconstruction than Lincoln had intended. Most of those exempted, however, soon received individual pardons from the president. Johnson also appointed provisional governors and ordered them to call state conventions, elected by whites alone, that would establish loyal governments in the South. Apart from the requirement that they abolish slavery, repudiate secession, and refuse to pay the Confederate debt—all unavoidable consequences of southern defeat—he granted the new governments a free hand in managing local affairs.

At first, most northerners believed Johnson's policy deserved a chance to succeed. The conduct of the southern governments elected under his program, however, turned most of the Republican North against the president. By and large, white voters returned prominent Confederates and members of the old elite to power. Reports of violence directed against former slaves and northern visitors in the South further alarmed Republicans.

But what aroused the most opposition to Johnson's Reconstruction policy were the Black Codes, laws passed by the new southern governments that attempted to regulate the lives of the former slaves. These laws granted blacks certain rights, such as legalized marriage, ownership of property, and limited access to the courts. But they denied them the rights to testify against whites, to serve on juries or in state militias, or to vote. And in response to planters' demands that the freedpeople be required to work on the plantations, the Black Codes declared that those who failed to sign yearly labor contracts could be arrested and hired out to white landowners. Some states limited the occupations open to blacks and barred them from acquiring land, and others provided that judges could assign black children to work for their former owners without the consent of the parents. "We are not permitted to own the land whereon to build a schoolhouse or a church," complained a black convention in Mississippi. "Where is justice? Where is freedom?"

Clearly, the death of slavery did not automatically mean the birth of freedom. But the Black Codes so completely violated free labor principles that they called forth a vigorous response from the Republican North. Wars—especially civil wars—often generate hostility and bitterness. But few groups of rebels in history have been treated more leniently than the defeated Confederates. A handful of southern leaders was arrested but most were quickly released. Only one was executed—Henry Wirz, the commander of Andersonville prison, where thousands of Union prisoners of war had died. Most of the Union army was swiftly demobilized. What motivated the North's turn against Johnson's policies was not a desire to "punish" the white South, but the inability of the South's political leaders to accept the reality of emancipation. "We must see to it," announced Republican senator William Stewart of Nevada, "that the man made free by the Constitution of the United States is a freeman indeed."

When Congress assembled in December 1865, Johnson announced that with loyal governments functioning in all the southern states, the nation had been reunited. In response, Radical Republicans, who had grown increasingly disenchanted with Johnson during the summer and fall, called for the dissolution of these governments and the establishment of new ones with "rebels" excluded from power and black men guaranteed the right to vote. Radicals tended to represent constituencies in New England and the "burned-over" districts of the rural North that had been home to religious revivalism, abolitionism, and other reform movements. Although they differed on many issues, Radicals shared the conviction that Union victory created a golden opportunity to institutionalize the principle of equal rights for all, regardless of race.

The Radicals fully embraced the expanded powers of the federal government born during the Civil War. Traditions of federalism and states' rights, they insisted, must not obstruct a sweeping national effort to protect the rights of all Americans. The most prominent Radicals in Congress were Charles Sumner, a senator from Massachusetts, and Thaddeus Stevens, a lawyer and iron manufacturer who represented Pennsylvania in the House of Representatives. Before the Civil War, both had been outspoken foes of slavery and defenders of black rights. "The same national authority," declared Sumner, "that destroyed slavery must see that this other pretension [racial inequality] is not permitted to survive."

Thaddeus Stevens's most cherished aim was to confiscate the land of disloyal planters and divide it among former slaves and northern migrants to the South. "The whole fabric of southern society," he declared, "*must* be changed. Without this, this Government can never be, as it has never been, a true republic." But his plan to make "small independent landholders" of the former slaves proved too radical even for many of his Radical colleagues. Congress, to be sure, had already offered free land to settlers in the West in the Homestead Act of 1862. But this land had been in the possession of the federal government, not private individuals (although originally, of course, it had belonged to Indians). Most congressmen believed too deeply in the sanctity of property rights to be willing to take land from one group of owners and distribute it to others. Stevens's proposal failed to pass.

With the South unrepresented, Republicans enjoyed an overwhelming majority in Congress. But the party was internally divided. Most Republicans were moderates, not Radicals. Moderates believed that Johnson's plan was flawed, but they desired to work with the president to modify it. They feared that neither northern nor southern whites would accept black suffrage. Moderates and Radicals joined in refusing to seat the southerners recently elected to Congress, but moderates broke with the Radicals by leaving the Johnson governments in place.

Early in 1866, Senator Lyman Trumbull of Illinois proposed two bills, reflecting the moderates' belief that Johnson's policy required modification. The first extended the life of the Freedmen's Bureau, which had originally been established for only one year. The second, the Civil Rights Bill of 1866, was described by one congressman as "one of the most important bills ever presented to the House for its action." It defined all persons born in the United States as citizens and spelled out rights they were to enjoy without regard to race. Equality before the law was central to the measure—no longer could states enact laws like the Black Codes discriminating between white and black citizens. So were free labor values. According to the law, no state could deprive any citizen of the right to make contracts, bring lawsuits, or enjoy equal protection of one's person and property. These, said Trumbull, were the "fundamental rights belonging to every man as a free man." The bill made no mention of the right to vote for blacks. In constitutional terms, the Civil Rights Bill represented the first attempt to give concrete meaning to the Thirteenth Amendment, which had abolished slavery, to define in law the essence of freedom.

To the surprise of Congress, Johnson vetoed both bills. Both, he said, would centralize power in the national government and deprive the states of the authority to regulate their own affairs. Moreover, he argued, blacks did not deserve the rights of citizenship. By acting to secure their rights, Congress was discriminating "against the white race." The vetoes made a breach between the president and nearly the entire Republican Party inevitable. Congress failed by a single vote to muster the two-thirds majority necessary to override the veto of the Freedmen's Bureau Bill (although later in 1866, it did extend the Bureau's life to 1870). But in April 1866, the Civil Rights Bill became the first major law in American history to be passed over a presidential veto.

Congress now proceeded to adopt its own plan of Reconstruction. In June, it approved and sent to the states for ratification the Fourteenth Amendment, which placed in the Constitution the principle of birthright citizenship, except for Native Americans subject to tribal authority, and empowered the federal government to protect the rights of all Americans. The amendment prohibited the states from abridging the "privileges or immunities" of citizens or denying any person of the "equal protection of the laws." This broad language opened the door for future Congresses and the federal courts to breathe meaning into the guarantee of legal equality.

In a compromise between the radical and moderate positions on black suffrage, the amendment did not grant blacks the right to vote. But it did provide that if a state denied the vote to any group of men, that state's representation in Congress would be reduced. (This provision did not apply when states barred women from voting.) The abolition of slavery threatened to increase southern political power, since now all blacks, not merely three-fifths, as in the case of slaves, would be counted in determining a state's representation in Congress. The Fourteenth Amendment offered the leaders of the white South a choice—allow black men to vote and keep their state's full representation in the House of Representatives, or limit the vote to whites and sacrifice part of their political power.

The Fourteenth Amendment produced an intense division between the parties. Not a single Democrat in Congress voted in its favor, and only 4 of 175 Republicans were opposed. Radicals, to be sure, expressed their disappointment that the amendment did not guarantee black suffrage. (It was far from perfect, Stevens told the House, but he intended to vote for it, "because I live among men and not among angels.") Nonetheless, by writing into the Constitution the principle that equality before the law regardless of race is a fundamental right of all American citizens, the amendment made the most important change in that document since the adoption of the Bill of Rights.

The Fourteenth Amendment became the central issue of the political campaign of 1866. Johnson embarked on a speaking tour of the North, called by journalists the "swing around the circle," to urge voters to elect members of Congress committed to his own Reconstruction program. Denouncing his critics, the president made wild accusations that the Radicals were plotting to assassinate him. His behavior further undermined public support for his policies, as did riots that broke out in Memphis and New Orleans, in which white policemen and citizens killed dozens of blacks.

In the northern congressional elections that fall, Republicans opposed to Johnson's policies won a sweeping victory. Nonetheless, at the president's urging, every southern state but Tennessee refused to ratify the Fourteenth Amendment. The intransigence of Johnson and the bulk of the white South pushed moderate Republicans toward the Radicals. In March 1867, over Johnson's veto, Congress adopted the Reconstruction Act, which temporarily divided the South into five military districts and called for the creation of new state governments, with black men given the right to vote. Thus began the period of Radical Reconstruction, which lasted until 1877. But the conflict between

President Johnson and Congress did not end with the passage of the Reconstruction Act.

In March 1867, Congress adopted the Tenure of Office Act, barring the president from removing certain officeholders, including cabinet members, without the consent of the Senate. Johnson considered this an unconstitutional restriction on his authority. In February 1868, he dismissed Secretary of War Edwin M. Stanton, an ally of the Radicals. The House of Representatives responded by approving articles of impeachment—that is, it presented charges against Johnson to the Senate, which had to decide whether to remove him from office.

That spring, for the first time in American history, a president was placed on trial before the Senate for "high crimes and misdemeanors." By this point, virtually all Republicans considered Johnson a failure as president. But some moderates disliked Benjamin F. Wade, a Radical who, as temporary president of the Senate, would become president if Johnson were removed. Others feared that conviction would damage the constitutional separation of powers between Congress and the executive. Johnson's lawyers assured moderate Republicans that, if acquitted, he would stop interfering with Reconstruction policy. The final tally was 35–19 to convict Johnson, one vote short of the two-thirds necessary to remove him. Seven Republicans joined the Democrats in voting to acquit the president.

A few days after the vote, Republicans nominated Ulysses S. Grant, the Union's most prominent military hero, as their candidate for president. Grant's Democratic opponent was Horatio Seymour, the former governor of New York. Reconstruction became the central issue of the bitterly fought 1868 campaign. Republicans identified their opponents with secession and treason, a tactic known as "waving the bloody shirt." Democrats denounced Reconstruction as unconstitutional and condemned black suffrage as a violation of America's political traditions. They appealed openly to racism. Seymour's running mate, Francis P. Blair Jr., charged Republicans with placing the South under the rule of "a semi-barbarous race" who longed to "subject the white women to their unbridled lust."

Grant won the election of 1868, although by a margin—300,000 of 6 million votes cast—that many Republicans found uncomfortably slim. The result led Congress to adopt the era's third and final amendment to the Constitution. In February 1869, it approved the Fifteenth Amendment, which prohibited the federal and state governments from denying any citizen the right to vote because of race. Bitterly opposed by the Democratic Party, it was ratified in 1870.

Although the Fifteenth Amendment left the door open to suffrage restrictions not explicitly based on race—literacy tests, property qualifications, and poll taxes—and did not extend the right to vote to women, it marked the culmination of four decades of abolitionist agitation. As late as 1868, even after Congress had enfranchised black men in the South, only eight northern states allowed African-American men to vote. With the Fifteenth Amendment, the American Anti-Slavery Society disbanded, its work, its members believed, now complete. "Nothing in all history," exclaimed veteran abolitionist William Lloyd Garrison, equaled "this wonderful, quiet, sudden transformation of four millions of human beings from . . . the auction-block to the ballot-box."

The laws and amendments of Reconstruction reflected the intersection of two products of the Civil War era—a newly empowered national state and the idea of a national citizenry enjoying equality before the law. What Republican leader Carl Schurz called the "great Constitutional revolution" of Reconstruction transformed the federal system and with it, the language of freedom so central to American political culture.

The laws and amendments of Reconstruction repudiated the pre–Civil War idea that citizenship was an entitlement of whites alone. The principle of equality before the law, moreover, did not apply only to the South. The Reconstruction amendments voided many northern laws discriminating on the basis of race. As one congressman noted, the amendments expanded the liberty of whites as well as blacks, including "the millions of people of foreign birth who will flock to our shores."

The new amendments also transformed the relationship between the federal government and the states. The Bill of Rights had linked civil liberties to the autonomy of the states. Its language—"Congress shall make no law"—reflected the belief that concentrated national power posed the greatest threat to freedom. The authors of the Reconstruction amendments assumed that rights required national power to enforce them. Rather than a threat to liberty, the federal government, in Charles Sumner's words, had become "the custodian of freedom."

The Reconstruction amendments transformed the Constitution from a document primarily concerned with federal-state relations and the rights of property into a vehicle through which members of vulnerable minorities could stake a claim to freedom and seek protection against misconduct by all levels of government. In the twentieth century, many of the Supreme Court's most important decisions expanding the rights of American citizens were based on the Fourteenth Amendment, including the 1954 *Brown* ruling that outlawed school segregation and the decision in 2015 preventing states from discriminating against gay Americans in the right to marry.

Together with far-reaching congressional legislation meant to secure to former slaves access to the courts, ballot box, and public accommodations, and to protect them against violence, the Reconstruction amendments transferred much of the authority to define citizens' rights from the states to the nation. They were crucial in creating the world's first biracial democracy, in which people only a few years removed from slavery exercised significant political power. Introducing into the Constitution for the first time the words "equal protection of the law" and "the right to vote" (along with "male," to the outrage of the era's advocates of women's rights), the amendments both reflected and reinforced a new era of individual rights consciousness among Americans of all races and backgrounds. They forged a new constitutional relationship between individual Americans and the national government and created a new definition of citizenship.

Today, the legal doctrine of birthright citizenship sets the United States apart. Most countries, including every one in Europe, limit automatic access to citizenship via ethnicity, culture, or religion. Birthright citizenship remains an eloquent statement about the nature of American society and a repudiation of a long history of equating citizenship with whiteness.

So profound were these changes that the amendments are frequently seen not simply as an alteration of an existing structure but as a second founding, which created a fundamentally new document with a new definition of both the status of blacks and the rights of all Americans.

Reconstruction redrew the boundaries of American freedom. Lines of exclusion that limited the privileges of citizenship to white men had long been central to the practice of American democracy. Only in an unparalleled crisis could they have been replaced, even temporarily, by the vision of a republic of equals embracing black Americans as well as white. That the United States was a "white man's government" had been a widespread belief before the Civil War. It is not difficult to understand why Andrew Johnson, in one of his veto messages, claimed that federal protection of blacks' civil rights violated "all our experience as a people."

Another illustration of the new spirit of racial inclusiveness was the Burlingame Treaty, negotiated by Anson Burlingame, an antislavery congressman from Massachusetts before being named American envoy to China. Other treaties with China had been one-sided, securing trading and political advantages for European powers. The Burlingame Treaty reaffirmed China's national sovereignty, and provided reciprocal protection for religious freedom and against discrimination for citizens of each country emigrating or visiting the other. When Burlingame died, Mark Twain wrote a eulogy that praised him for "outgrow[ing] the narrow citizenship of a state [to] become a citizen of the world."

Reconstruction Republicans' belief in universal rights had its limits. In his remarkable "Composite Nation" speech of 1869, Frederick Douglass condemned prejudice against immigrants from China. America's destiny, he declared, was to transcend race by serving as an asylum for people from all corners of the globe. A year later, Charles Sumner moved to strike the word "white" from naturalization requirements. Senators from the western states objected. At their insistence, the naturalization law was amended to make Africans eligible to obtain citizenship when immigrating from abroad. But Asians remained ineligible. The racial boundaries of nationality had been redrawn, but not eliminated. The juxtaposition of the amended naturalization law and the Fourteenth Amendment created a significant division in the Asian-American community. Well into the twentieth century, Asian immigrants could not become citizens, but their U.S.-born children automatically did.

"The contest with the South that destroyed slavery," wrote the Philadelphia lawyer Sidney George Fisher in his diary, "has caused an immense increase in the popular passion for liberty and equality." But advocates of women's rights encountered the limits of the Reconstruction commitment to equality. Women activists saw Reconstruction as the moment to claim their own emancipation. No less than blacks, proclaimed Elizabeth Cady Stanton, women had arrived at a "transition period, from slavery to freedom." The rewriting of the Constitution, declared suffrage leader Olympia Brown, offered the opportunity to sever the blessings of freedom from sex as well as race and to "bury the black man and the woman in the citizen."

The destruction of slavery led feminists to search for ways to make the promise of free labor real for women. Every issue of the new women's rights journal, *The Agitator*, edited by Mary Livermore, who had led fund-raising efforts for aid to Union soldiers during the war, carried stories complaining of limited job opportunities and unequal pay for females who entered the labor market. Other feminists debated how to achieve "liberty for married women." Demands for liberalizing divorce laws (which generally required evidence of adultery, desertion, or extreme abuse to terminate a marriage) and for recognizing "woman's control over her own body" (including protection against domestic violence and access to what later generations would call birth control) moved to the center of many feminists' concerns. "Our rotten marriage institution," one Ohio woman wrote, "is the main obstacle in the way of woman's freedom."

In one place, women's political rights did expand during Reconstruction—not, however, in a bastion of radicalism such as Massachusetts, but in the Wyoming territory. This had less to do with the era's egalitarian impulse than with the desire to attract female immigrants to an area where men outnumbered women five to one. In 1869, Wyoming's diminutive legislature (it consisted of fewer than twenty men) extended the right to vote to women, and the bill was then signed by the governor, a federal appointee. Wyoming entered the Union in 1890, becoming the first state since New Jersey in the late eighteenth century to allow women to vote.

In general, however, talk of woman suffrage and redesigning marriage found few sympathetic male listeners. Even Radical Republicans insisted that Reconstruction was the "Negro's hour" (the hour, that is, of the black male). The Fourteenth Amendment for the first time introduced the word "male" into the Constitution, in its clause penalizing a state for denying any group of men the right to vote. The Fifteenth Amendment outlawed discrimination in voting based on race but not gender. These measures produced a bitter split both between feminists and Radical Republicans, and within feminist circles.

Some leaders, like Stanton and Susan B. Anthony, opposed the Fifteenth Amendment because it did nothing to enfranchise women. They denounced their former abolitionist allies and moved to sever the women's rights movement from its earlier moorings in the antislavery tradition. On occasion, they appealed to racial and ethnic prejudices, arguing that native-born white women deserved the vote more than non-whites and immigrants. "Patrick and Sambo and Hans and Yung Tung, who do not know the difference between a monarchy and a republic," declared Stanton, had no right to be "making laws for [feminist leader] Lucretia Mott." But other abolitionist-feminists, like Abby Kelley and Lucy Stone, insisted that despite their limitations, the Reconstruction amendments represented steps in the direction of truly universal suffrage and should be supported. The result was a split in the movement and the creation in 1869 of two hostile women's rights organizations—the National Woman Suffrage Association, led by Stanton, and the American Woman Suffrage Association, with Lucy Stone as president. They would not reunite until 1890.

Thus, even as it rejected the racial definition of freedom that had emerged in the first half of the nineteenth century, Reconstruction left the gender boundary largely intact. When women tried to use the rewritten legal code and Constitution to claim equal rights, they found the courts unreceptive. Myra Bradwell invoked the idea of free labor in challenging an Illinois rule limiting the practice of law to men, but the Supreme Court in 1873 rebuffed her claim. Free labor principles, the justices declared, did not apply to women, since "the law of the Creator" had assigned them to "the domestic sphere."

Despite their limitations, the Fourteenth and Fifteenth Amendments and the Reconstruction Act of 1867 marked a radical departure in American history. "We have cut loose from the whole dead past," wrote Timothy Howe, a Republican senator from Wisconsin, "and have cast our anchor out a hundred years" into the future. The Reconstruction Act of 1867 inaugurated America's first real experiment in interracial democracy.

RADICAL RECONSTRUCTION IN THE SOUTH

Among the former slaves, the passage of the Reconstruction Act inspired an outburst of political organization. At mass political meetings—community gatherings attended by men, women, and children—African-Americans staked their claim to equal citizenship. Blacks, declared an Alabama meeting, deserved "exactly the same rights, privileges and immunities as are enjoyed by white men. We ask for nothing more and will be content with nothing less."

These gatherings inspired direct action to remedy long-standing grievances. Hundreds took part in sit-ins that integrated horse-drawn public streetcars in cities across the South. Plantation workers organized strikes for higher wages. Speakers, male and female, fanned out across the South. Frances Ellen Watkins Harper, a black veteran of the abolitionist movement, embarked on a two-year tour, lecturing on "Literacy, Land, and Liberation." James D. Lynch, a member of the group that met with General Sherman in 1865, became known, in the words of a white contemporary, as "a great orator, fluid and graceful," who "stirred the emotions" of his listeners "as no other man could do."

Determined to exercise their new rights as citizens, thousands joined the Union League, an organization closely linked to the Republican Party, and the vast majority of eligible African-Americans registered to vote. James K. Green, a former slave in Hale County, Alabama, and a League organizer, went on to serve eight years in the Alabama legislature. In the 1880s, Green looked back on his political career. Before the war, he declared, "I was entirely ignorant; I knew nothing more than to obey my master; and there were thousands of us in the same attitude. . . . But the tocsin [warning bell] of freedom sounded and knocked at the door and we walked out like free men and shouldered the responsibilities."

By 1870, all the former Confederate states had been readmitted to the Union, and in a region where the Republican Party had not existed before the war, nearly all were under Republican control. Their new state constitutions, drafted in 1868 and 1869 by the first public bodies in American history with substantial black representation, marked a considerable improvement over those they replaced. The constitutions established the region's first state-funded systems of free public education and created new penitentiaries, orphan asylums, and homes for the insane. They guaranteed equality of civil and political rights and abolished practices of the antebellum era such as whipping as a punishment for crime, property qualifications for officeholding, and imprisonment for debt. A few states initially barred former Confederates from voting, but this policy was quickly abandoned by the new state governments.

Throughout Reconstruction, black voters provided the bulk of the Republican Party's support. But African-Americans did not control Reconstruction politics, as their opponents frequently charged. The highest offices remained almost entirely in white hands, and only in South Carolina, where blacks made up 60 percent of the population, did they form a majority of the legislature. Nonetheless, the fact that some 2,000 African-Americans occupied public offices during Reconstruction represented a fundamental shift of power in the South and a radical departure in American government.

African-Americans were represented at every level of government. Fourteen were elected to the national House of Representatives. Two blacks served in the U.S. Senate during Reconstruction, both representing Mississippi. Hiram Revels, who had been born free in North Carolina, was educated in Illinois, and served as a chaplain in the wartime Union army, in 1870 became the first black senator in American history. The second, Blanche K. Bruce, a former slave, was elected in 1875. The next African-American elected to the Senate was Edward W. Brooke of Massachusetts, who served 1967–1978.

Pinckney B. S. Pinchback of Louisiana, the Georgia-born son of a white planter and a free black woman, served briefly during the winter of 1872–1873 as America's first black governor. More than a century would pass before L. Douglas Wilder of Virginia, elected in 1989, became the second. Some 700 blacks sat in state legislatures during Reconstruction, and scores held local offices ranging from justice of the peace to sheriff, tax assessor, and policeman. The presence of black officeholders and their white allies made a real difference in southern life, ensuring that blacks accused of crimes would be tried before juries of their peers and enforcing fairness in such aspects of local government as road repair, tax assessment, and poor relief.

In South Carolina and Louisiana, homes of the South's wealthiest and best-educated free black communities, most prominent Reconstruction officeholders had never experienced slavery. In addition, a number of black Reconstruction officials, like Pennsylvania-born Jonathan J. Wright, who served on the South Carolina Supreme Court, had come from the North after the Civil War. The majority, however, were former slaves who had established their leadership in the black community by serving in the Union army, working as ministers, teachers, or skilled craftsmen, or engaging in Union League organizing. Among the most celebrated black officeholders was Robert Smalls, who had worked as a slave on the Charleston docks before the Civil War and who won national fame in 1862 by secretly guiding the *Planter*, a Confederate vessel, out of the harbor and delivering it to Union forces. Smalls became a powerful political leader on the South Carolina Sea Islands and was elected to five terms in Congress.

The new southern governments also brought to power new groups of whites. Many Reconstruction officials were northerners who for one reason or another made their homes in the South after the war. Their opponents dubbed them carpetbaggers, implying that they had packed all their belongings in a suitcase and left their homes in order to reap the spoils of office in the South. Some carpetbaggers were undoubtedly corrupt adventurers. The large majority, however, were former Union soldiers who decided to remain in the South when the war ended, before there was any prospect of going into politics. Others were investors in land and railroads who saw in the postwar South an opportunity to combine personal economic advancement with a role in helping to substitute, as one wrote, "the civilization of freedom for that of slavery." Teachers, Freedmen's Bureau officers, and others who came to the region genuinely hoping to assist the former slaves represented another large group of carpetbaggers.

Most white Republicans had been born in the South. Former Confederates reserved their greatest scorn for these scalawags, whom they considered traitors to their race and region. Some southern-born Republicans were men of stature and wealth, like James L. Alcorn, the owner of one of Mississippi's largest plantations and the state's first Republican governor.

Most scalawags, however, were non-slaveholding white farmers from the southern upcountry. Many had been wartime Unionists, and they now cooperated with the Republicans in order to prevent "rebels" from returning to power. Others hoped Reconstruction governments would help them recover from wartime economic losses by suspending the collection of debts and enacting laws protecting small property holders from losing their homes to creditors. In states like North Carolina, Tennessee, and Arkansas, Republicans initially commanded a significant minority of the white vote. Even in the Lower South, the small white Republican vote was important, because the population remained almost evenly divided between blacks (almost all of whom voted for the party of Lincoln) and whites (overwhelmingly Democratic).

In view of the daunting challenges they faced, the remarkable thing is not that Reconstruction governments in some respects failed, but how much they did accomplish. Perhaps their greatest achievement lay in establishing the South's first state-supported public schools. The new educational systems served both black and white children, although generally in schools segregated by race. Only in New Orleans were the public schools integrated during Reconstruction, and only in South Carolina did the state university admit black students (elsewhere, separate colleges were established). By the 1870s, in a region whose prewar leaders had made it illegal for slaves to learn and had done little to provide education for poorer whites, more than half the children, black and white, were attending public schools. The new governments also pioneered civil rights legislation. Their laws made it illegal for railroads, hotels, and other institutions to discriminate on the basis of race. Enforcement varied considerably from locality to locality, but Reconstruction established for the first time at the state level a standard of equal citizenship and a recognition of blacks' right to a share of public services.

Republican governments also took steps to strengthen the position of rural laborers and promote the South's economic recovery. They passed laws to ensure that agricultural laborers and sharecroppers had the first claim on harvested crops, rather than merchants to whom the landowner owed money. South Carolina created a state Land Commission, which by 1876 had settled 14,000 black families and a few poor whites on their own farms.

Rather than land distribution, however, the Reconstruction governments pinned their hopes for southern economic growth and opportunity for African-Americans and poor whites alike on regional economic development. Railroad construction, they believed, was the key to transforming the South into a society of booming factories, bustling towns, and diversified agriculture. "A free and living republic," declared a Tennessee Republican, would "spring up in the track of the railroad." Every state during Reconstruction helped to finance railroad construction, and through tax reductions and other incentives tried to attract northern manufacturers to invest in the region. The program had mixed results. Economic development in general remained weak. With abundant opportunities existing in the West, few northern investors ventured to the Reconstruction South.

To their supporters, the governments of Radical Reconstruction presented a complex pattern of disappointment and accomplishment. A revitalized southern economy failed to materialize, and most African-Americans remained locked in poverty. On the other hand, biracial democratic government, a thing unknown in American history, for the first time functioned effectively in many parts of the South. Public facilities were rebuilt and expanded, school systems established, and legal codes purged of racism. The conservative elite that had dominated southern government from colonial times to 1867 found itself excluded from political power, while poor whites, newcomers from the North, and former slaves cast ballots, sat on juries, and enacted and administered laws. "We have gone through one of the most remarkable changes in our relations to each other," declared a white South Carolina lawyer in 1871, "that has been known, perhaps, in the history of the world." It is a measure of how far change had progressed that the reaction against Reconstruction proved so extreme.

THE OVERTHROW OF
RECONSTRUCTION

The South's traditional leaders—planters, merchants, and Democratic politicians—bitterly opposed the new governments. They denounced them as corrupt, inefficient, and examples of "black supremacy." "Intelligence, virtue, and patriotism" in public life, declared a protest by prominent southern Democrats, had given way to "ignorance, stupidity, and vice." Corruption did exist during Reconstruction, but it was confined to no race, region, or party. The rapid growth of state budgets and the benefits to be gained from public aid led in some states to a scramble for influence that produced bribery, insider dealing, and a get-rich-quick atmosphere. Southern frauds, however, were dwarfed by those practiced in these years by the Whiskey Ring, which involved high officials of the Grant administration, and by New York's Tweed Ring, controlled by the Democrats, whose thefts ran into the tens of millions of dollars. The rising taxes needed to pay for schools and other new public facilities and to assist railroad development were another cause of opposition to Reconstruction. Many poor whites who had initially supported the Republican Party turned against it when it became clear that their economic situation was not improving.

The most basic reason for opposition to Reconstruction, however, was that most white southerners could not accept the idea of former slaves voting, holding office, and enjoying equality before the law. In order to restore white supremacy in southern public life and to ensure planters a disciplined, reliable labor force, they believed, Reconstruction must be overthrown. Opponents launched a campaign of violence in an effort to end Republican rule. Their actions posed a fundamental challenge both for Reconstruction governments in the South and for policymakers in Washington, D.C.

The Civil War ended in 1865, but violence remained widespread in large parts of the postwar South. In the early years of Reconstruction, violence was mostly local and unorganized. Blacks were assaulted and murdered for refusing to give way to whites on city sidewalks, using "insolent" language, challenging end-of-year contract settlements, and attempting to buy land. The violence that greeted the advent of Republican governments after 1867, however, was far more pervasive and more directly motivated by politics. In wide areas of the South, secret societies sprang up with the aim of preventing blacks from voting and destroying the organization of the Republican Party by assassinating local leaders and public officials.

The most notorious such organization was the Ku Klux Klan, which in effect served as a military arm of the Democratic Party in the South. The Klan was a terrorist organization. Led by planters, merchants, and Democratic politicians, men who liked to style themselves the South's "respectable citizens," the Klan committed some of the most brutal criminal acts in American history. In many counties, it launched what one victim called a "reign of terror" against Republican leaders, black and white.

The Klan's victims included white Republicans, among them wartime Unionists and local officeholders, teachers, and party organizers. William Luke, an Irish-born teacher in a black school, was lynched in 1870. But African-Americans—local political leaders, those who managed to acquire land, and others who in one way or another defied the norms of white supremacy—bore the brunt of the violence. In York County, South Carolina, where nearly the entire white male population joined the Klan (and women participated by sewing the robes and hoods Klansmen wore as disguises), the organization committed eleven murders and hundreds of whippings.

On occasion, violence escalated from assaults on individuals to mass terrorism and even local insurrections. In Meridian, Mississippi, in 1871, some thirty blacks were murdered in cold blood, along with a white Republican judge. The bloodiest act of violence during Reconstruction took place in Colfax, Louisiana, in 1873, where armed whites assaulted the town with a small cannon. Scores of former slaves were murdered, including fifty members of a black militia unit after they had surrendered.

Unable to suppress the Klan, the new southern governments appealed to Washington for help. In 1870 and 1871, Congress adopted three Enforcement Acts, outlawing terrorist societies and allowing the president to use the army against them. These laws continued the expansion of national authority during Reconstruction. They defined crimes that aimed to deprive citizens of their civil and political rights as federal offenses rather than violations of state law. In 1871, President Grant dispatched federal marshals, backed up by troops in some areas, to arrest hundreds of accused Klansmen. Many Klan leaders fled the South. After a series of well-publicized trials, the Klan went out of existence. In 1872, for the first time since before the Civil War, peace reigned in most of the former Confederacy.

Despite the Grant administration's effective response to Klan terrorism, the North's commitment to Reconstruction waned during the 1870s. Many Radicals, including Thaddeus Stevens, who died in 1868, had passed from the scene. Within the Republican Party, their place was taken by politicians less committed to the ideal of equal rights for blacks. Northerners increasingly felt that the South should be able to solve its own problems without constant interference from Washington. The federal government had freed the slaves, made them citizens, and given them the right to vote. Now, blacks should rely on their own resources, not demand further assistance.

In 1872, an influential group of Republicans, alienated by corruption within the Grant administration and believing that the growth of federal power during and after the war needed to be curtailed, formed their own party. It included Republican founders like Lyman Trumbull and prominent editors and journalists such as E. L. Godkin of the *Nation*. Calling themselves Liberal Republicans, they nominated Horace Greeley, editor of the *New York Tribune*, for president.

The Liberals' alienation from the Grant administration initially had little to do with Reconstruction. They claimed that corrupt politicians had come to power in the North by manipulating the votes of immigrants and workingmen, while men of talent and education like themselves had been pushed aside. Democratic criticisms of Reconstruction, however, found a receptive audience among the Liberals. As in the North, they became convinced, the "best men" of the South had been excluded from power while "ignorant" voters controlled politics, producing corruption and misgovernment. Power in the South should be returned to the region's "natural leaders." During the campaign of 1872, Greeley repeatedly called on Americans to "clasp hands across the bloody chasm" by putting the Civil War and Reconstruction behind them.

Greeley had spent most of his career, first as a Whig and then as a Republican, denouncing the Democratic Party. But with the Republican split presenting an opportunity to repair their political fortunes, Democratic leaders endorsed Greeley as their candidate. Many rank-and-file Democrats, unable to bring themselves to vote for Greeley, stayed at home on election day. As a result, Greeley suffered a devastating defeat by Grant, whose margin of more than 700,000 popular votes was the largest in a nineteenth-century presidential contest. But Greeley's campaign placed on the northern agenda the one issue on which the Liberal reformers and the Democrats could agree—a new policy toward the South.

The Liberal attack on Reconstruction, which continued after 1872, contributed to a resurgence of racism in the North. Journalist James S. Pike, a leading Greeley supporter, in 1874 published *The Prostrate State*, an influential account of a visit to South Carolina. The book depicted a state engulfed by political corruption and under the control of "a mass of black barbarism." The South's problems, Pike insisted, arose from "Negro government." The solution was to restore leading whites to political power. Newspapers that had long supported Reconstruction now began to condemn black participation in southern government. Engravings depicting the former slaves as heroic Civil War veterans, upstanding citizens, or victims of violence were increasingly replaced by caricatures presenting them as little more than unbridled animals. Resurgent racism offered blacks' alleged incapacity as a convenient explanation for the "failure" of Reconstruction.

Other factors also weakened northern support for Reconstruction. In 1873, the country plunged into a severe economic depression. Distracted by economic problems, Republicans were in no mood to devote further attention to the South. The depression dealt the South a severe blow and further weakened the prospect that Republicans could revitalize the region's economy. Democrats made substantial gains throughout the nation in the elections of 1874. For the first time since the Civil War, their party took control of the House of Representatives. Before the new Congress met, the old one enacted a final piece of Reconstruction legislation, the Civil Rights Act of 1875. This outlawed racial discrimination in places of public accommodation like hotels and theaters. But it was clear that the northern public was retreating from Reconstruction.

The Supreme Court whittled away at the guarantees of black rights Congress had adopted. In the *Slaughterhouse Cases* (1873), white butchers excluded from a state-sponsored monopoly in Louisiana went to court, claiming that their right to pursue a livelihood, a privilege of American citizenship guaranteed by the Fourteenth Amendment, had been violated. The justices rejected their claim, ruling that the amendment had not altered traditional federalism. Most of the rights of citizens, it declared, remained under state control. Three years later, in *United States v. Cruikshank*, the Court gutted the Enforcement Acts by throwing out the convictions of some of those responsible for the Colfax Massacre of 1873.

By the mid-1870s, Reconstruction was clearly on the defensive. Democrats had already regained control of states with substantial white voting majorities such as Tennessee, North Carolina, and Texas. The victorious Democrats called themselves Redeemers, since they claimed to have "redeemed" the white South from corruption, misgovernment, and northern and black control.

In those states where Reconstruction governments survived, violence again erupted. This time, the Grant administration showed no desire to intervene. In contrast to the Klan's activities—conducted at night by disguised men—the violence of 1875 and 1876 took place in broad daylight, as if to underscore Democrats' conviction that they had nothing to fear from Washington. In Mississippi, in 1875, white rifle clubs drilled in public and openly assaulted and murdered Republicans. When Governor Adelbert Ames, a Maine-born Union general, frantically appealed to the federal government for assistance, President Grant responded that the northern public was "tired out" by southern problems. On election day, armed Democrats destroyed ballot boxes and drove former slaves from the polls. The result was a Democratic landslide and the end of Reconstruction in Mississippi. "A revolution has taken place," wrote Ames, "and a race are disfranchised—they are to be returned to . . . an era of second slavery."

Similar events took place in South Carolina in 1876. Democrats nominated for governor former Confederate general Wade Hampton. Hampton promised to respect the rights of all citizens of the state, but his supporters, inspired by Democratic tactics in Mississippi, launched a wave of intimidation. Democrats intended to carry the election, one planter told a black official, "if we have to wade in blood knee-deep."

Events in South Carolina directly affected the outcome of the presidential campaign of 1876. To succeed Grant, the Republicans nominated Governor Rutherford B. Hayes of Ohio. Democrats chose as his opponent New York's governor, Samuel J. Tilden. By this time, only South Carolina, Florida, and Louisiana remained under Republican control in the South. The election turned out to be so close that whoever captured these states—which both parties claimed to have carried—would become the next president.

Unable to resolve the impasse on its own, Congress in January 1877 appointed a fifteen-member Electoral Commission, composed of senators, representatives, and Supreme Court justices. Republicans enjoyed an 8–7 majority on the commission, and to no one's surprise, the members decided by that margin that Hayes had carried the disputed southern states and had been elected president. Even as the commission deliberated, however, behind-the-scenes negotiations took place between leaders of the two parties. Hayes's representatives agreed to recognize Democratic control of the entire South and to avoid further intervention in local affairs. They also pledged that Hayes would place a southerner in the cabinet position of postmaster general and that he would work for federal aid to the Texas and Pacific railroad, a transcontinental line projected to follow a southern route. For their part, Democrats promised not to dispute Hayes's right to office and to respect the civil and political rights of blacks.

Thus was concluded the Bargain of 1877. Not all of its parts were fulfilled. But Hayes became president, and he did appoint David M. Key of Tennessee as postmaster general. Hayes quickly ordered federal troops to stop guarding the state houses in Louisiana and South Carolina, allowing Democratic claimants to become governor. (Contrary to legend, Hayes did not remove the last soldiers from the South—he simply ordered them to return to their barracks.) But the Texas and Pacific never did get its land grant. Of far more significance, the triumphant southern Democrats failed to live up to their pledge to recognize blacks as equal citizens.

As a historical process—the nation's adjustment to the destruction of slavery—Reconstruction continued well after 1877. Blacks continued to vote and, in some states, hold office into the 1890s. But as a distinct era of national history—when Republicans controlled much of the South, blacks exercised significant political power, and the federal government accepted the responsibility for protecting the fundamental rights of all American citizens—Reconstruction had come to an end. Despite its limitations, Reconstruction was a remarkable chapter in the story of American freedom. Nearly a century would pass before the nation again tried to bring equal rights to the descendants of slaves. The civil rights era of the 1950s and 1960s would sometimes be called the Second Reconstruction.

Even while it lasted, however, Reconstruction revealed some of the tensions inherent in nineteenth-century discussions of freedom. The policy of granting black men the vote while denying them the benefits of land ownership strengthened the idea that the free citizen could be a poor, dependent laborer. Reconstruction placed on the national agenda a problem that would dominate political discussion for the next half-century—how, in a modern society, to define the economic essence of freedom.

ACKNOWLEDGMENTS

N O BOOK of history can be written without building on the work of earlier scholars, and *The Second Founding* is no exception. My greatest debt is to the fraternity of historians who have preceded me in studying the origins, ratification, and interpretation of the Thirteenth, Fourteenth, and Fifteenth Amendments, and who have illuminated the era of the Civil War and Reconstruction that gave birth to the constitutional revolution.

I do wish, however, to thank a number of individuals who responded to inquiries about specific aspects of this project, shared ideas and sources, and in other ways offered assistance. Brendan Gillis, David Konig, Alan Taylor, and Peter Onuf shared ideas about Thomas Jefferson and the origins of the Thirteenth Amendment's notorious prisoner exemption. Gabrielle Foreman of the Colored Conventions Project at the University of Delaware directed me to little-known gatherings that shed light on African-Americans' ideas about the Constitution, and Leslie Rowland located relevant documents in the files of the Freedmen and Southern Society Project at the University of Maryland. In conversations dating back many years Akhil Amar, Laura Edwards, Randall Kennedy, Kate Masur, and Amy Dru Stanley shared their own thinking related to the issues discussed in this book. I have learned enormously from all of them.

I am particularly indebted to three outstanding scholars—Martha S. Jones, Michael Klarman, and Christopher Schmidt, who generously read the entire manuscript and offered invaluable suggestions.

Thanks, too, to participants in conferences during the past few years, whose incisive comments on my presentations helped me clarify my thoughts: the Thirteenth Amendment Symposium (Columbia Law School); Salmon P. Chase Lecture and Symposium (Georgetown Center for the Constitution); The Many Fourteenth Amendments (University of Miami); Symposium on the Fifteenth Amendment (University of the South); Lincoln's Unfinished Work (Clemson University); the White House Counsel's Office Retreat (Camp David); and the Second and Tenth Circuit Judicial Conferences.

As always, I thank my literary agent and all-around advisor and advocate Sandra Dijkstra and her staff, and the team at W. W. Norton & Company, especially Steve Forman, an insightful and supportive editor, and his colleague Lily Gellman.

My greatest debt is to my wife, Lynn Garafola, a writer and editor extraordinaire, who took time from her own writing projects to read the manuscript and who offered counsel and support in numerous other ways.

New York City
NOVEMBER 2018

NOTES

ABBREVIATIONS USED IN NOTES

AJLH	*American Journal of Legal History*
CG	*Congressional Globe*
CR	*Congressional Record*
CLR	*Columbia Law Review*
GJLP	*Georgetown Journal of Law and Public Policy*
HL	Houghton Library, Harvard University
JAH	*Journal of American History*
JCWE	*Journal of the Civil War Era*
JSCH	*Journal of Supreme Court History*
LC	Library of Congress
LHR	*Law and History Review*
NAS	*National Anti-Slavery Standard*
YLJ	*Yale Law Journal*

PREFACE

1. *CG*, 41st Congress, 2nd Session, 3607.

2. Eric Foner, *Reconstruction: America's Unfinished Revolution 1863–1877* (New York, 2014 ed.). For a collection of essays surveying current scholarship on Reconstruction, see John David Smith, ed., *Interpreting American History: Reconstruction* (Kent, 2016).

3. John David Smith, ed., *The Dunning School: Historians, Race, and the Meaning of Reconstruction* (Lexington, 2013).

4. John W. Burgess, *Reconstruction and the Constitution 1866–1876* (New York, 1902), 217; Claude G. Bowers, *The Tragic Era: The Revolution After Lincoln* (Cambridge, 1929).

5. Marilyn Lake and Henry Reynolds, *Drawing the Global Colour Line: White Men's Countries and the International Challenge of Racial Equality* (New York, 2008), 6–10, 50–65.

6. Jason Morgan Ward, "Causes Lost and Found: Remembering and Refighting Reconstruction in the Roosevelt Era," in Carole Emberton and Bruce E. Baker, eds., *Remembering Reconstruction: Struggles Over the Meaning of America's Most Turbulent Era* (Baton Rouge, 2017), 37–39; Gunnar Myrdal, *An American Dilemma: The Negro Problem and Modern Democracy* (New York, 1944), 446.

7. Eric Foner, "The Supreme Court and the History of Reconstruction—and Vice Versa," *CLR*, 112 (November 2012), 1585–1608; David M. O'Brien, *Justice Robert H. Jackson's Unpublished Opinion in Brown v. Board: Conflict, Compromise, and Constitutional Interpretation* (Lawrence, 2017), 124.

8. W. E. B. Du Bois, *Black Reconstruction in America* (New York, 1935).

9. George S. Boutwell, *Reminiscences of Sixty Years in Public Affairs* (2 vols.: New York, 1902), 2:42.

10. David E. Kyvig, ed., *Unintended Consequences of Constitutional Amendments* (Athens, 2000).

11. *CG*, 39th Congress, 1st Session, 2466–67; Barry Friedman, "Reconstructing Reconstruction: Some Problems for Originalists (And for Everybody Else, Too)," *University of Pennsylvania Journal of Constitutional Law*, 11 (July 2009), 1707. See also Jamal Greene, "Fourteenth Amendment Originalism," *Maryland Law Review*, 71 (2012), 979–84.

12. Faye E. Dudden, *Fighting Chance: The Struggle over Woman Suffrage and Black Suffrage in Reconstruction America* (New York, 2011), 51.

13. Elizabeth Cady Stanton, *Eighty Years and More (1815–1897)* (New York, 1898), 241; Elizabeth Beaumont, *The Civic Constitution: Civic Visions and Struggles in the Path Toward Constitutional Democracy* (New York, 2014), xv–xvi, 2–4; Laura F. Edwards, *A Legal History of the Civil War and Reconstruction: A*

Nation of Rights (New York, 2015), 6; Hendrik Hartog, "The Constitution of Aspiration and 'The Rights that Belong to Us All,'" *JAH*, 74 (December 1987), 354; Catherine A. Jones, "Women, Gender, and the Boundaries of Reconstruction," *JCWE*, 8 (March 2018), 116.

14. *CG*, 41st Congress, 2nd Session, 3607; Foner, *Reconstruction*, 232.
15. David W. Blight, *Frederick Douglass: Prophet of Freedom* (New York, 2018), 743.
16. Michael Vorenberg, *Final Freedom: The Civil War, the Abolition of Slavery, and the Thirteenth Amendment* (New York, 2001), 60; *Philadelphia North American and United States Gazette*, June 8, 1866.

INTRODUCTION

1. Michael J. Klarman, *The Framers' Coup: The Making of the United States Constitution* (New York, 2016), 261.
2. Sean Wilentz, *No Property in Man: Slavery and Antislavery at the Nation's Founding* (Cambridge, 2018), 162–63; "Interview: Linda Colley," *British Academy Review*, 28 (Summer 2016), 26. I borrow the observation about "We the People" from a talk by James Sidbury at "The Future of the African-American Past," a conference held in Washington, D.C., in May 2016.
3. Benedict R. Anderson, *Imagined Communities: Reflections on the Origin and Spread of Nationalism* (London, 1983); J. Hector St. John de Crèvecoeur, *Letters from an American Farmer*, ed. Alfred E. Stone (New York, 1981), 69.
4. Carrie Hyde, *Civic Longing: The Speculative Origins of U.S. Citizenship* (Cambridge, 2018), 10; Rogers M. Smith, *Civic Ideals: Conflicting Visions of Citizenship in U.S. History* (New Haven, 1997), 115–25; Eric Mathiesen, *The Loyal Republic: Traitors, Slaves, and the Remaking of Citizenship in Civil War America* (Chapel Hill, 2018), 13–14; *CG*, 40th Congress, 3rd Session, Appendix, 95–96; William J. Novak, "The Legal Transformation of Citizenship in Nineteenth-Century America," in Meg Jacobs, William J. Novak, and Julian E. Zelizer, eds., *The Democratic Experiment: New Directions in American Political History* (Princeton, 2003), 110.
5. *CG*, 40th Congress, 3rd Session, Appendix, 95–96; William M. Wiecek, "Emancipation and Civil Status: The American Experience, 1865–1915," in Alexander Tsesis, ed., *The Promises of Liberty: The History and Contemporary Relevance of the Thirteenth Amendment* (New York, 2010), 79–83; Smith, *Civic Ideals*, 180; Paul Finkelman, "Prelude to the Fourteenth Amendment: Black Legal Rights in the Antebellum North," *Rutgers Law Journal*, 17 (Spring/Summer 1986), 415–82; James H. Kettner, *The Development of American Citizenship, 1608–1870* (Chapel Hill, 1978), 311–23.

6. Nathan Perl-Rosenthal, *Citizen Sailors: Becoming American in the Age of Revolution* (Cambridge, 2015), 188–90; Smith, *Civic Ideals*, 175–77, 255–58.

7. Eric Foner, "The Meaning of Freedom in the Age of Emancipation," *JAH*, 81 (September 1994), 443; Noah Webster, *A Dictionary of the English Language* (2 vols.: London, 1852); Laura E. Free, *Suffrage Reconstructed: Gender, Race, and Voting Rights in the Civil War Era* (Ithaca, 2015), 11.

8. J. R. Pole, *The Pursuit of Equality in American History* (rev. ed.: Berkeley, 1993), 38; Linda K. Kerber, "The Meanings of Citizenship," *JAH*, 84 (December 1997), 834–40; Linda A. Tvrdy, "Constitutional Rights in a Common Law World: The Reconstruction of North Carolina Legal Culture, 1865–1874" (Ph.D. diss., Columbia University, 2013); *CG*, 38th Congress, 1st Session, 1488; Novak, "Legal Transformation," 88–97; Laura F. Edwards, *The People and Their Peace: Legal Culture and the Transformation of Inequality in the Post-Revolutionary South* (Chapel Hill, 2009), 5–13.

9. James Oakes, "Natural Rights, Citizenship Rights, States' Rights, and Black Rights: Another Look at Lincoln and Race," in Eric Foner, ed., *Our Lincoln: New Perspectives on Lincoln and His World* (New York, 2008), 110–14; Laura F. Edwards, "The Reconstruction of Rights: The Fourteenth Amendment and Popular Conceptions of Governance," *JSCH*, 41 (November 2016), 313.

10. Eric Foner, *Free Soil, Free Labor, Free Men: The Ideology of the Republican Party Before the Civil War* (New York, 1995 ed.), 290–95; *New York Times*, November 8, 1860.

11. Heather Cox Richardson, "North and West of Reconstruction: Studies in Political Economy," in Thomas J. Brown, ed., *Reconstructions: New Perspectives on the Postbellum United States* (New York, 2006), 69; Kate Masur, "'The People's Welfare,' Police Powers, and the Rights of Free People of African Descent," *AJLH*, 57 (June 2017), 238–42; Laura F. Edwards, "Reconstruction and the History of Governance," in Gregory P. Downs and Kate Masur, eds., *The World the Civil War Made* (Chapel Hill, 2015), 22–45; William J. Novak, *The People's Welfare: Law and Regulation in Nineteenth-Century America* (Chapel Hill, 1996).

12. Philip S. Foner, ed., *The Life and Writings of Frederick Douglass* (5 vols.: New York, 1950–75), 4: 199; *New York World*, April 5, 1872; Downs and Masur, *World the Civil War Made*, 3–15.

13. Smith, *Civic Ideals*, 247; Randy E. Barnett, "Whence Comes Section One? The Abolitionist Origins of the Fourteenth Amendment," *Journal of Legal Analysis*, 3 (Spring 2011), 165–69; *Liberator*, July 14, 1854; Michael Kammen, *A Machine That Would Go of Itself: The Constitution in American Culture* (New York, 1986), 101; Mark E. Brandon, *Free in the World: American Slavery and Constitutional Failure* (Princeton, 1998), 52–57; C. Peter Ripley et al., eds., *The Black Abolitionist Papers* (5 vols.: Chapel Hill, 1985–92), 2: 202; Freder-

ick Douglass, *The Constitution of the United States: Is It Pro-Slavery or Anti-Slavery* (Halifax, 1860), 12; *Frederick Douglass' Paper*, December 7, 1855.

14. Foner, *Free Soil*, 73–102; James Oakes, *Freedom National: The Destruction of Slavery in the United States, 1861–1865* (New York, 2012), 1–48; James Oakes, *The Scorpion's Sting: Antislavery and the Coming of the Civil War* (New York, 2014).

15. Foner, *Free Soil*, 83; Roy P. Basler, ed., *The Collected Works of Abraham Lincoln* (8 vols.: New Brunswick, 1953–55), 3: 522–50; Elizabeth Beaumont, *The Civic Constitution: Civic Visions and Struggles in the Path Toward Constitutional Democracy* (New York, 2014), 120–22.

16. Larry Ceplair, ed., *The Public Years of Sarah and Angelina Grimké: Selected Writings 1835–1839* (New York, 1989), 194–95; William Yates, *Rights of Colored Men to Suffrage, Citizenship and Trial by Jury* (Philadelphia, 1838); Manisha Sinha, *The Slave's Cause: A History of Abolition* (New Haven, 2016), 462; *The Constitution of the American Anti-Slavery Society: with the Declaration of the National Anti-Slavery Convention at Philadelphia, 1833* (New York, 1838), 7. Martha S. Jones discusses Yates and his treatise in *Birthright Citizens: A History of Race and Rights in Antebellum America* (New York, 2018), 1–8.

17. *Liberator*, December 29, 1832; *Proceedings of the New England Anti-slavery Convention: held in Boston, May 24, 25, 26, 1836* (Boston, 1836), 17; Foner, *Free Soil*, 281–84; Gerard N. Magliocca, *American Founding Son: John Bingham and the Invention of the Fourteenth Amendment* (New York, 2013), 56.

18. Jones, *Birthright Citizens*; Donald G. Nieman, "The Language of Liberation: African Americans and Equalitarian Constitutionalism, 1830–1950," in Nieman, ed., *The Constitution, Law, and American Life: Critical Aspects of the Nineteenth-Century Experience* (Athens, 1992), 69; Martin R. Delany, *The Condition, Elevation, and Destiny of the Colored People of the United States* (Philadelphia, 1852), 48; *Colored American*, May 9, 1840; *Minutes of the National Convention of Colored Citizens; Held at Buffalo* (New York, 1843), 17.

19. Ripley, *Black Abolitionist Papers*, 4: 230, 252; Elizabeth Stordeur Pryor, *Colored Travelers: Mobility and the Fight for Citizenship before the Civil War* (Chapel Hill, 2016), 1–4; Andrew K. Diemer, *The Politics of Black Citizenship: Free African Americans in the Mid-Atlantic Borderland, 1817–1863* (Athens, 2016), 6–7.

20. Eric Slauter, *The State as a Work of Art: The Cultural Origins of the Constitution* (Chicago, 2009), 173–74; Harold M. Hyman and William M. Wiecek, *Equal Justice Under Law: Constitutional Development 1835–1875* (New York, 1982), 400; Eric Foner, "Rights and the Constitution in Black Life During the Civil War and Reconstruction," *JAH*, 74 (December 1987), 213; Philip S. Foner and George E. Walker, eds., *The Proceedings of the Black State Conventions, 1840–1865* (2 vols.: Philadelphia, 1979), 1: 172.

21. Paul Finkelman, *Supreme Injustice: Slavery in the Nation's Highest Court*

(Cambridge, 2018), 52; Smith, *Civic Ideals*, 265–68; Robert J. Cottrol, *The Long, Lingering Shadow: Slavery, Race, and Law in the American Hemisphere* (Athens, 2013), 80–81.

22. *Anglo-African Magazine* (May 1859), 144–50; Richard L. Aynes, "Unintended Consequences of the Fourteenth Amendment," in David E. Kyvig, ed., *Unintended Consequences of Constitutional Amendments* (Athens, 2000), 113.

23. James M. McPherson, *The Struggle for Equality: Abolitionists and the Negro in the Civil War and Reconstruction* (Princeton, 1964), 221; William G. Shade, " 'Revolutions May Go Backwards': The American Civil War and the Problem of Political Development," *Social Science Quarterly*, 55 (December 1974), 760; James M. McPherson, ed., *The Negro's Civil War* (New York, 1965), 251–52.

24. Michael Vorenberg, "Citizenship and the Thirteenth Amendment: Understanding the Deafening Silence," in Tsesis, *Promises of Liberty*, 70; Jones, *Birthright Citizens*, 148; Earl M. Maltz, *Civil Rights, the Constitution, and Congress, 1863–1869* (Lawrence, 1990), 7–8.

25. *Christian Recorder*, July 9, 1864; Christian G. Samito, *Becoming American Under Fire: Irish Americans, African Americans, and the Politics of Citizenship During the Civil War Era* (Ithaca, 2009), 170–71; Foner, *Reconstruction*, 62–65; McPherson, *Negro's Civil War*, 250–54.

26. *CG*, 40th Congress, 3rd Session, Appendix, 294; Charles Sumner to John Bright, May 27, 1867, John Bright Papers, British Library; Foner, *Reconstruction*, 24.

27. Foner, *Douglass*, 3: 394–401; *New York Times*, January 17, 1864; *Journal of Commerce* in *NAS*, May 7, 1864.

28. Foner, *Reconstruction*, 40–66.

29. Colin Kidd, "The Grail of Original Meaning: Uses of the Past in American Constitutional Theory," *Transactions of the Royal Historical Society*, 6 ser., 26 (2016), 177–78; *Thomas Paine: Collected Writings* (New York, 1995), 574; Eric Foner, *The Fiery Trial: Abraham Lincoln and American Slavery* (New York, 2010), 171–72, 242; Kammen, *A Machine*, 112.

30. Foner, *Reconstruction*, 232; David Donald, *Charles Sumner and the Rights of Man* (New York, 1970), 352; Gideon Welles, "A Defense of Andrew Johnson's Administration," manuscript, 1868, Gideon Welles Papers, Huntington Library.

31. E. L. Godkin, "The Constitution and Its Defects," *North American Review*, 99 (July 1864), 120.

32. Wendell Phillips to Charles Sumner, March 24, 1866, Charles Sumner Papers, HL.

Chapter 1: What Is Freedom?

1. Roy P. Basler, ed., *The Collected Works of Abraham Lincoln* (8 vols.: New Brunswick, 1953–55), 8: 333; *Chicago Daily Tribune*, May 15, 1858.

2. *New York Times*, December 17, 1864; Gregory P. Downs, *After Appomattox: Military Occupation and the Ends of War* (Cambridge, 2015), 41; Charles Fairman, *Reconstruction and Reunion 1864–88, Part One* (New York, 1971), 1156.

3. Manisha Sinha, *The Slave's Cause: A History of Abolition* (New Haven, 2016), 587; Michael Vorenberg, *Final Freedom: The Civil War, the Abolition of Slavery, and the Thirteenth Amendment* (New York, 2001), 18–22.

4. Basler, *Collected Works*, 2: 492; Eric Foner, *The Fiery Trial: Abraham Lincoln and American Slavery* (New York, 2010).

5. Basler, *Collected Works*, 2: 461; 3: 181; James Oakes, *The Scorpion's Sting: Antislavery and the Coming of the Civil War* (New York, 2014), 16–17.

6. Ira Berlin, *Many Thousands Gone: The First Two Centuries of Slavery in North America* (New York, 1998), 8; Moses I. Finley, *Ancient Slavery and Modern Ideology* (New York, 1980), 79–80; R. L. Meek et al., eds., *The Glasgow Edition of the Works and Correspondence of Adam Smith* (8 vols.: New York, 1976–83), 5: 173; Eric Foner, "Lincoln and Colonization," in Foner, ed., *Our Lincoln: New Perspectives on Lincoln and His World* (New York, 2008), 135–66.

7. Rebecca J. Scott, "Paper Thin: Freedom and Re-enslavement in the Diaspora of the Haitian Revolution," *LHR*, 29 (November 2011), 1061–87.

8. Foner, *Fiery Trial*, 171–220.

9. Ibid., 230–38.

10. Ibid., 240–47; Philip S. Foner, ed., *The Life and Writings of Frederick Douglass* (5 vols.: New York, 1950–75), 3: 394.

11. Basler, *Collected Works*, 6: 28–29.

12. James Oakes, "Making Freedom National: Salmon P. Chase and the Abolition of Slavery," *GJLP*, 13 (Summer 2015), 407; Basler, *Collected Works*, 7: 1–2, 36–54; Foner, *Fiery Trial*, 305–06, 315; *Wisconsin State Register*, April 16, 1864.

13. *CG*, 38th Congress, 1st Session, 19, 1199; *The Miscellaneous Writings of Francis Lieber* (2 vols.: Philadelphia, 1881), 2: 177–79.

14. Faye E. Dudden, *Fighting Chance: The Struggle Over Woman Suffrage and Black Suffrage in Reconstruction America* (New York, 2011), 51–61; Elizabeth Beaumont, *The Civic Constitution: Civic Visions and Struggles in the Path Toward Constitutional Democracy* (New York, 2014), 157; James M. McPherson, "In Pursuit of Constitutional Abolitionism," in Alexander Tsesis, ed., *The Promises of Liberty: The History and Contemporary Relevance of the Thirteenth Amendment* (New York, 2010), 29; *NAS*, February 6, March 19, May 28, 1864; Sinha, *Slave's Cause*, 587.

15. David Donald, *Charles Sumner and the Rights of Man* (New York, 1970), 147–51; *NAS*, January 9, 1864; *CG*, 38th Congress, 1st Session, 521, 1482.

16. Ibid., 39th Congress, 1st Session, 1118.

17. Ibid., 38th Congress, 1st Session, 1314, 1488.

18. Ibid., 38th Congress, 1st Session, 523, 1320–21.

19. *New York Herald*, January 12, 1866; *Chicago Tribune*, November 14, 1864.

20. The first eight amendments, the core of the Bill of Rights, were almost universally understood to protect civil liberties against violation by the federal government; the Ninth and Tenth reserved other, unspecified, rights and powers to the states and the people; the Eleventh restricted federal judicial power. The Twelfth revised how votes were cast by presidential electors and did not affect the balance of power between the state and national governments.

21. Harold M. Hyman and William M. Wiecek, *Equal Justice Under Law: Constitutional Development 1835–1875* (New York, 1982), 386–87; James G. Blaine, *Twenty Years of Congress* (2 vols.: Norwich, 1884), 1: 539.

22. Stephen Sawyer and William J. Novak, "Emancipation and the Creation of Modern Liberal States in America and France," *JCWE*, 3 (December 2016), 471.

23. Foner, *Fiery Trial*, 292–93; *CG*, 38th Congress, 1st Session, 1364–66, 1484, 2941, 2987.

24. Ibid., 38th Congress, 1st Session, 2615, 2981, 2986, 2991.

25. Ibid., 38th Congress, 1st Session, 1864, 2995; *New York Herald*, February 6, April 9, 1864.

26. Isaac N. Arnold to Abraham Lincoln, December 4, 1863, Abraham Lincoln Papers, LC; Foner, *Fiery Trial*, 298–99; *NAS*, July 9, 1864; *New York Times*, February 13, June 13, 1864.

27. Vorenberg, *Final Freedom*, 94; *NAS*, November 5, 1864; Foner, *Fiery Trial*, 312–13.

28. *New York Times*, January 12, 1865; *CG*, 38th Congress, 2nd Session, 122, 260; Leonard L. Richards, *Who Freed the Slaves? The Fight Over the Thirteenth Amendment* (Chicago, 2015), 204–15.

29. *CG*, 38th Congress, 2nd Session, 531; *Chicago Tribune*, February 1, 1865; *Boston Daily Advertiser*, February 1, 4, 1865; "George W. Julian's Journal—the Assassination of Lincoln," *Indiana Magazine of History*, 11 (December 1915), 327; *New York Tribune*, February 1, 1865; *New York Herald*, February 1, 1865; *New York Times*, February 1, 1865.

30. Basler, *Collected Works*, 8: 254; David E. Kyvig, *Explicit and Authentic Acts: Amending the U.S. Constitution, 1776–1995* (Lawrence, 1996), 162.

31. Foner, *Fiery Trial*, 316; Eric Foner, *Reconstruction: America's Unfinished Revolution 1863–1877* (New York, 2014 ed.), 176–77; Bruce Ackerman, *We the People: Transformations* (Cambridge, 1998), 139.

32. M. Audley Couper to Francis P. Corbin, July 28, 1866, Francis P. Corbin Papers, New York Public Library; Samuel L. M. Barlow to Montgomery Blair, November 13, 1865, Samuel L. M. Barlow Papers, Huntington Library; Ackerman, *We the People*, 143; Richards, *Who Freed the Slaves?*, 239.

33. *New York Times*, December 20, 1865; Mitch Kachun, *Festivals of Freedom:*

Memory and Meaning in African American Emancipation Celebrations, 1808–1915 (Amherst, 2003), 117–20, 176, 183, 258–60; William H. Wiggins Jr., *O Freedom! Afro-American Emancipation Celebrations* (Knoxville, 1987), 20.

34. *Memoirs of Cornelius Cole* (New York, 1908), 220; Guyora Binder, "Did the Slaves Author the Thirteenth Amendment? An Essay in Redemptive History," *Yale Journal of Law and the Humanities*, 5 (Summer 1993), 471–506; *CG*, 38th Congress, 1st Session, 1203, 1324; 2nd Session, 202.

35. Ibid., 38th Congress, 1st Session, 1465, 2960–62.

36. Ibid., 38th Congress, 1st Session, 1313, 1439–40, 2989.

37. Jacobus tenBroek, "Thirteenth Amendment to the Constitution of the United States: Consummation to Abolition and Key to the Fourteenth Amendment," *California Law Review*, 39 (June 1951), 180–81; *CG*, 38th Congress, 1st Session, 1324, 1424, 2990; 2nd Session, 202; Michael Vorenberg, "Citizenship and the Thirteenth Amendment: Understanding the Deafening Silence," in Tsesis, *Promises of Liberty*, 58–61.

38. Lea S. VanderVelde, "The Labor Vision of the Thirteenth Amendment," *University of Pennsylvania Law Review*, 138 (December 1989), 437–504; Basler, *Collected Works*, 8: 332–33; *CG*, 37th Congress, 2nd Session, Appendix, 322; 38th Congress, 1st Session, 2989–90.

39. Ibid., 38th Congress, 1st Session, 2990.

40. Stacey L. Smith, *Freedom's Frontier: California and the Struggle Over Unfree Labor, Emancipation, and Reconstruction* (Chapel Hill, 2013), 3–5, 206–17; Stacey L. Smith, "Emancipating Peons, Excluding Coolies," in Gregory P. Downs and Kate Masur, eds., *The World the Civil War Made* (Chapel Hill, 2015), 46–74.

41. Laura F. Edwards, *A Legal History of the Civil War and Reconstruction: A Nation of Rights* (New York, 2015), 124–27; Thavolia Glymph, "'I'm a Radical Black Girl': Black Women Unionists and the Politics of Civil War History," *JCWE*, 8 (September 2018), 364–66; Foner, *Reconstruction*, 85–88, 290–91; Catherine A. Jones, "Women, Gender, and the Boundaries of Reconstruction," *JCWE*, 8 (March 2018), 113.

42. *CG*, 38th Congress, 2nd Session, 193.

43. Roger Ekirch, *Bound for America: The Transportation of British Convicts to the Colonies, 1718–1775* (New York, 1987), 22–27, 236–37; Rebecca M. McLennan, *The Crisis of Imprisonment: Protest, Politics, and the Making of the American Penal State, 1776–1941* (New York, 2008), 53–55, 63–66; Matthew J. Mancini, *One Dies, Get Another: Convict Leasing in the American South, 1866–1928* (Columbia, 1996), 1–14; Alex Lichtenstein, *Twice the Work of Free Labor: The Political Economy of Convict Labor in the New South* (New York, 1996), 23.

44. David Brion Davis, "Foreword: The Rocky Road to Freedom," in Tsesis, *Promises of Liberty*, xi; Thomas Jefferson, *Notes on the State of Virginia*, ed. William

Peden (New York, 1954), 138; Christopher R. Green, "Duly Convicted: The Thirteenth Amendment as Procedural Due Process, *GJLP*, 15 (Winter 2017), 80; McLennan, *Crisis of Imprisonment*, 17. Thanks to David Konig for sharing ideas from his forthcoming book on Jefferson's legal thought.

45. David R. Upham, "The Understanding of 'Neither Slavery Nor Involuntary Servitude Shall Exist,' Before the Thirteenth Amendment," *GJLP*, 15 (Winter 2017), 139; Fairman, *Reconstruction and Reunion*, 1119; Green, "Duly Convicted," 79–80; *CG*, 38th Congress, 1st Session, 1325. The texts of state constitutions may be found in Francis N. Thorpe, ed., *The Federal and State Constitutions* (7 vols.: Washington, 1909). In emails to the author the historians Peter Onuf and Alan Taylor both referred to Jefferson's prisoner exemption as "boilerplate" language.

46. *Boston Daily Advertiser*, April 14, 1864; *CG*, 38th Congress, 1st Session, 521, 1488; *The Principia*, February 18, 1864; Beverly Wilson Palmer, ed., *The Selected Letters of Charles Sumner* (2 vols.: Boston, 1990), 2: 233.

47. Sidney Andrews, *The South Since the War* (Boston, 1866), 324; *Annual Cyclopedia*, 1865, 19; Eric Foner, *Nothing But Freedom: Emancipation and Its Legacy* (Baton Rouge, 1983), 49–52; Hyman and Wiecek, *Equal Justice*, 319–20; Jerrell H. Shofner, *Nor Is It Over Yet: Florida in the Era of Reconstruction, 1863–1877* (Gainesville, 1974), 50–52; J. W. Blackwell to Andrew Johnson, November 24, 1865, Andrew Johnson Papers, LC; "Official Proceedings of the Colored Convention for the State of Mississippi, Vicksburg, November 22–25, 1865," manuscript, M-82 1866, Letters Received, Ser. 15, Washington Headquarters, RG 105, National Archives.

48. *New Haven Daily Palladium*, December 6, 1865; Daniel R. Goodloe, Manuscript History of Southern Provisional Governments of 1865, Daniel R. Goodloe Papers, Southern Historical Collection, University of North Carolina, Chapel Hill.

49. C. E. Lippincott to Lyman Trumbull, August 29, 1865, Lyman Trumbull Papers, LC; *New York Tribune*, December 25, 1865; Joe M. Richardson, *The Negro in the Reconstruction of Florida, 1865–1877* (Tallahassee, 1965), 44; *Liberator*, December 28, 1865; *CG*, 39th Congress, 1st Session, 153, 332–33, 427; *NAS*, January 19, 1867.

50. *CG*, 39th Congress, 2nd Session, 344–48.

51. *CG*, 39th Congress, 1st Session, 655; Thorpe, *Federal and State Constitutions*, 6: 3281; *New York Times*, July 2, 2017.

52. David M. Oshinsky, "Convict Labor in the Post–Civil War South: Involuntary Servitude After the Thirteenth Amendment," in Tsesis, *Promises of Liberty*, 101–9; Mancini, *One Dies, Get Another*, 20–41; Douglas A. Blackmon, *Slavery by Another Name: The Re-Enslavement of Black People in America from the Civil War to World War II* (New York, 2008), 7; William S. Harris, *The Day of the*

Carpetbagger: Republican Reconstruction in Mississippi (Baton Rouge, 1979), 38–39; Foner, *Reconstruction*, 593; *Colored Men, Read! How Your Friends Are Treated!*, Broadside, July 1876, R. C. Martin Papers, Louisiana State University; Lichtenstein, *Twice the Work*, 18, 193; McLennan, *Crisis of Imprisonment*, 87–135.

53. Foner, *Reconstruction*, 79; Philip S. Foner and George E. Walker, eds., *Proceedings of the Black National and State Conventions, 1865–1900* (Philadelphia, 1986), 180; Steven Hahn, *A Nation Under Our Feet: Black Political Struggles in the Rural South from Slavery to the Great Migration* (Cambridge, 2003), 118–20; *Proceedings of the National Convention of Colored Men, Held in the City of Syracuse* (Boston, 1864), 42, 47; Vorenberg, *Final Freedom*, 81–87.

54. Foner, *Reconstruction*, 63–65; *New Orleans Tribune*, September 9, 1865; Hugh Davis, *"We Will Be Satisfied With Nothing Less": The African American Struggle for Equal Rights in the North During Reconstruction* (Ithaca, 2011), 1–21; Philip S. Foner and George E. Walker, eds., *The Proceedings of the Black State Conventions, 1840–1865* (2 vols.: Philadelphia, 1979), 1: 202.

55. Foner, *Reconstruction*, 114–15; Hahn, *A Nation*, 119–20; Foner and Walker, *Proceedings of Black State Conventions*, 2: 268; *Missouri Democrat*, November 29, 1865; "Colored People of Mobile" to [General Wager Swayne], August 2, 1865, Miscellaneous Papers, ser. 29, Alabama Assistant Commissioner, RG 105, National Archives; Timothy S. Huebner, *Liberty and Union: The Civil War Era and American Constitutionalism* (Lawrence, 2016), 323–47; *Anglo-African Magazine*, December 23, 1865.

56. *Liberator*, February 3, 10, 17, May 26, 1865; *NAS*, May 20, June 3, 1865.

57. Foner, *Reconstruction*, 66–67; *NAS*, February 3, March 4, 1865; Foner, *Douglass*, 378–83.

58. *New York World* in *Washington Daily National Intelligencer*, January 13, 1865.

59. Edwards, *Legal History*, 90.

60. *The Works of Charles Sumner* (15 vols.: Boston, 1870–83), 9: 427.

CHAPTER 2: TOWARD EQUALITY

1. Eric Foner, *Reconstruction: America's Unfinished Revolution 1863–1877* (New York, 2014 ed.), 228–39, *CG*, 39th Congress, 1st Session, 74.

2. Ibid., 39th Congress, 1st Session, 2882; 40th Congress, 3rd Session, 1326; 39th Congress, 1st Session, House Report 30, pt. 2, 174.

3. Mark M. Krug, *Lyman Trumbull, Conservative Radical* (New York, 1965); Foner, *Reconstruction*, 241–42; Thaddeus Stevens to Charles Sumner, August 26, 1865, Charles Sumner Papers, HL; LaWanda Cox and John H. Cox, "Negro Suffrage and Republican Politics: The Problem of Motivation in Reconstruction Historiography," *Journal of Southern History*, 33 (August 1967), 317–18.

4. *CG*, 39th Congress, 1st Session, 110, 256; Appendix, 56–57, 101–2; *New York Herald*, January 31, 1866.

5. *CG*, 39th Congress, 1st Session, 5, 297.

6. Beverly Wilson Palmer and Holly Byers Ochoa, eds., *The Selected Papers of Thaddeus Stevens* (2 vols.: Pittsburgh, 1997–98), 2: 37; *CG*, 39th Congress, 1st Session, 342, 1025; *New York Times*, January 14, February 17, 22, 1866; *New Orleans Tribune*, December 22, 1865; *Chicago Tribune*, December 29, 1865.

7. Earl Maltz, "Moving Beyond Race: The Joint Committee on Reconstruction and the Drafting of the Fourteenth Amendment," *Hastings Constitutional Law Quarterly*, 42 (Winter 2015), 291; Eric Mathiesen, *The Loyal Republic: Traitors, Slaves, and the Remaking of Citizenship in Civil War America* (Chapel Hill, 2018), 140–41; 39th Congress, 1st Session, House Report 30; *CG*, 39th Congress, 2nd Session, 782; Benjamin B. Kendrick, *The Journal of the Joint Committee of Fifteen on Reconstruction* (New York, 1914).

8. *CG*, 39th Congress, 1st Session, 1307.

9. Laura E. Free, *Suffrage Reconstructed: Gender, Race, and Voting Rights in the Civil War Era* (Ithaca, 2015), 114–15; *CG*, 39th Congress, 1st Session, 141.

10. D. Michael Bottoms, *An Aristocracy of Color: Race and Reconstruction in California and the West, 1850–1890* (Norman, 2013), 68; George W. Julian, *Political Recollections 1840 to 1872* (Chicago, 1884), 272; *CG*, 39th Congress, 1st Session, 383, 407; 39th Congress, 1st Session, House Report 30, pt. 2, 158.

11. Garrett Epps, *Democracy Reborn: The Fourteenth Amendment and the Fight for Equal Rights in Post–Civil War America* (New York, 2006), 107–18; *CG*, 39th Congress, 1st Session, 673, 1228, 1288, 2459; *Boston Daily Advertiser*, February 16, 1866; *NAS*, February 3, 1866; James G. Blaine, *Twenty Years of Congress* (2 vols.: Norwich, 1884), 2: 196–98.

12. *U.S. Statutes at Large*, 14: 27–28; *CG*, 39th Congress, 1st Session, 42.

13. Ibid., 39th Congress, 1st Session, 476, 1757–60.

14. Ibid., 39th Congress, 1st Session, 298, 1291; *New York Tribune*, November 17, 1865. On Bingham's career, see Gerard N. Magliocca, *American Founding Son: John Bingham and the Invention of the Fourteenth Amendment* (New York, 2013).

15. *CG*, 39th Congress, 1st Session, 1151; William McWillie to Benjamin S. Humphreys, December 31, 1866, Mississippi Governor's Papers, Mississippi Department of Archives and History.

16. *CG*, 39th Congress, 1st Session, 474–75, 500, 599, 1833; Darrell A. H. Miller, "The Thirteenth Amendment and the Regulation of Custom," *Columbia Law Review*, 112 (December 2012), 1811–54; Richard A. Gerber, "Civil Rights for Freed Persons: The Issue of Private Discrimination Revisited," *Connecticut Review*, 15 (Fall 1993), 25–33.

17. *CG*, 39th Congress, 1st Session, 319, 322, 476, 504, 606, 1117, 1156, 1294; Blaine, *Twenty Years*, 2: 179.

18. Harold M. Hyman and William M. Wiecek, *Equal Justice Under Law: Constitutional Development 1835–1875* (New York, 1982), 412–13; George Rutherglen, *Civil Rights in the Shadow of Slavery: The Constitution, Common Law, and the Civil Rights Act of 1866* (New York, 2013), 57–60; *CG*, 39th Congress, 1st Session, 1117–18.

19. *St. Louis Republican* in *New York Evening Post*, April 3, 1866; James D. Richardson, ed., *A Compilation of the Messages and Papers of the Presidents 1789–1897* (10 vols.: Washington, 1896–99), 6: 399–405.

20. Kendrick, *Journal of Joint Committee*, 46; *CG*, 39th Congress, 1st Session, 157–58.

21. Ibid., 39th Congress, 1st Session, 1034, 1063–65, 1095.

22. Robert Dale Owen, "Political Results from the Varioloid," *Atlantic Monthly*, 35 (June 1875), 660–70; James O. Hollister, *Life of Schuyler Colfax* (New York, 1886), 284; *New York Times*, May 21, 1866; David E. Kyvig, *Explicit and Authentic Acts: Amending the U.S. Constitution, 1776–1995* (Lawrence, 1996), 167.

23. *CG*, 39th Congress, 1st Session, 2459, 2768, 2890–91.

24. Rogers M. Smith, *Civic Ideals: Conflicting Visions of Citizenship in U.S. History* (New Haven, 1997), 309–11; Blaine, *Twenty Years*, 2: 207; Robert J. Kaczorowski, "To Begin the Nation Anew: Congress, Citizenship, and Civil Rights After the Civil War," *American Historical Review*, 92 (February 1987), 53; *CG*, 39th Congress, 1st Session, 2890–96; Earl M. Maltz, "The Fourteenth Amendment and Native American Citizenship," *Constitutional Commentary*, 17 (Winter 2000), 555–74; Catherine A. Jones, "Women, Gender, and the Boundaries of Reconstruction," *JCWE*, 8 (March 2018), 121.

25. *CR*, 43rd Congress, 2nd Session, 1379; *CG*, 42nd Congress, 1st Session, Appendix, 84.

26. Joseph B. James, *The Framing of the Fourteenth Amendment* (Urbana, 1956), 30; *CG*, 39th Congress, 1st Session, 3041; Kurt T. Lash, *The Fourteenth Amendment and the Privileges and Immunities of American Citizenship* (New York, 2014), 26–28.

27. *CG*, 39th Congress, 1st Session, 2765, 2961.

28. Elizabeth Reilly, "The Union as It Wasn't and the Constitution as It Isn't: Section 5 and Altering the Balance of Power," in Elizabeth Reilly, ed., *Infinite Hope and Finite Disappointment: The Story of the First Interpreters of the Fourteenth Amendment* (Akron, 2011), 79–80; *CG*, 39th Congress, 1st Session, 156–59, 1065, 1090.

29. Akhil Reed Amar, *The Bill of Rights: Creation and Reconstruction* (New Haven, 1998), 284; *CG*, 39th Congress, 204, 1088–94, 1151, 1833; 42nd Congress, 1st Session, Appendix, 84; Michael Kent Curtis, *No State Shall Abridge: The Fourteenth Amendment and the Bill of Rights* (Durham, 1986), 138–49;

Richard L. Aynes, "On Misreading John Bingham and the Fourteenth Amendment," *YLJ*, 103 (October 1993), 61–60; Foner, *Reconstruction*, 533.

30. John Harrison, "Reconstructing the Privileges or Immunities Clause," *YLJ*, 101 (May 1992), 1387; *CG*, 39th Congress, 1st Session, 156–59. Linda Bosniak criticizes what she calls "citizenship romanticism" prevalent in recent legal scholarship, which obscures that under certain circumstances, citizenship itself can become a mode of subordination of others. Linda Bosniak, *The Citizen and the Alien: Dilemmas of Contemporary Membership* (Princeton, 2006), 1.

31. *CG*, 35th Congress, 2nd Session, 985; Philip S. Foner and George Walker, eds., *The Proceedings of the Black State Conventions, 1840–1865* (2 vols.: Philadelphia, 1979), 2: 263.

32. *CG*, 39th Congress, 1st Session, 256, 1159, 2766; 42nd Congress, 1st Session, Appendix, 156; William E. Nelson, *The Fourteenth Amendment: From Political Principle to Judicial Doctrine* (Cambridge, 1988), 76.

33. *NAS*, August 29, 1863; *CG*, 39th Congress, 1st Session, Appendix, 57.

34. Laura F. Edwards, *A Legal History of the Civil War and Reconstruction: A Nation of Rights* (New York, 2015), 105; Charles Eliot Norton, ed., *Orations and Addresses of George William Curtis* (3 vols.: New York, 1894), 1: 172.

35. William J. Novak, "The Legal Transformation of Citizenship in Nineteenth-Century America," in Meg Jacobs, William J. Novak, and Julian E. Zelizer, eds., *The Democratic Experiment: New Directions in American Political History* (Princeton, 2003), 93–106.

36. Faye E. Dudden, *Fighting Chance: The Struggle over Woman Suffrage and Black Suffrage in Reconstruction America* (New York, 2011), 70–81, 82; Ellen C. Du Bois, *Feminism and Suffrage: The Emergence of an Independent Women's Movement in America 1848–1869* (Ithaca, 1978), 61; *NAS*, May 13, 1865.

37. Free, *Suffrage Reconstructed*, 6, 105–6, 133–34; Dudden, *Fighting Chance*, 70–71; Martha S. Jones, *All Bound Up Together: The Woman Question in African American Public Culture, 1830–1900* (Chapel Hill, 2007), 135–36; *Proceedings of the Eleventh National Women's Rights Convention* (New York, 1866); Theodore Stanton and Harriot Stanton Blatch, eds., *Elizabeth Cady Stanton as Revealed in Her Letters, Diary and Reminiscences* (2 vols.: New York, 1922), 1: 109–10, 202–3; Epps, *Democracy Reborn*, 216–18.

38. *CG*, 39th Congress, 1st Session, 685, 832, 2882; Appendix, 102; 39th Congress, 2nd Session, 40.

39. Foner, *Reconstruction*, 255–56; *CG*, 39th Congress, 1st Session, 829, 1227, 1321; Blaine, *Twenty Years*, 2: 201; George S. Boutwell, *Reminiscences of Sixty Years in Public Affairs* (2 vols.: New York, 1902), 2: 42; Henry L. Dawes to Ella Dawes, March 16, 1866, Henry L. Dawes Papers, LC; Beverly Wilson Palmer, ed., *The Selected Letters of Charles Sumner* (2 vols.: Boston, 1990), 2: 316.

40. Novak, "Legal Transformation," 109; *Chicago Tribune*, December 12, 1868; *CG*, 39th Congress, 1st Session, 1115–20, 2460; Appendix, 228; Frederic Bancroft, ed., *Speeches, Correspondence, and Political Papers of Carl Schurz* (6 vols.: New York, 1913), 1: 413; Richard H. Abbott, *The Republican Party and the South, 1855–1877* (Chapel Hill, 1986), 216–18; James A. Padgett, ed., "Reconstruction Letters from North Carolina: Part I: Letters to Thaddeus Stevens," *North Carolina Historical Review*, 18 (April 1941), 181–82; Krug, *Trumbull*, 246–47; Christopher W. Schmidt, "Section 5's Forgotten Years: Congressional Power to Enforce the Fourteenth Amendment Before *Katzenbach v. Morgan*," *Northwestern University Law Review*, 113 (Issue 1 2018), 47. For the view that Republicans remained wedded to traditional ideas of federalism see Michael Les Benedict, *Preserving the Constitution: Essays on Politics and the Constitution in the Reconstruction Era* (New York, 2006), 4–9.

41. *CG*, 39th Congress, 1st Session, 1034, 2940; *New York Herald*, September 18, 1866.

42. *CG*, 39th Congress, 1st Session, 523, 529, 2500, 2538, 2929, 3213.

43. Ibid., 39th Congress, 1st Session, 2459, 3148. ("The baseless fabric of a vision" is from Shakespeare's *The Tempest*.)

44. Ibid., 39th Congress, 1st Session, 2332, 2462, 2766.

45. Wendell Phillips to Thaddeus Stevens, April 30, 1866, Thaddeus Stevens Papers, LC; *NAS*, July 14, 1866; Timothy Huebner, *The Civil War Era and American Constitutionalism* (Lawrence, 2016), 360; *New Orleans Tribune*, October 23, 1866; Stephen Kantrowitz, *More than Freedom: Fighting for Black Citizenship in a White Republic, 1829–1889* (New York, 2012), 319–25.

46. *CG*, 39th Congress, 1st Session, 2545, 3042, 3148; Foner, *Reconstruction*, 260–69; James E. Bond, *No Easy Walk to Freedom: Reconstruction and the Ratification of the Fourteenth Amendment* (Westport, 1997), 37, 87–88, 192, 216; Brooks D. Simpson, ed., *Reconstruction: Voices from America's First Great Struggle for Racial Equality* (New York, 2018), 314.

47. *Wisconsin State Register*, June 16, 1866; *New York Times*, October 11, 1866.

48. *CG*, 39th Congress, 2nd Session, 159–60; Foner, *Reconstruction*, 276–77; Robert M. Goldman, *Reconstruction and Black Suffrage: Losing the Vote in Reese and Cruikshank* (Lawrence, 2001), 12.

49. Francis N. Thorpe, ed., *The Federal and State Constitutions* (7 vols.: Washington, 1909), 2: 822; 3: 1449–50, 1461, 1467; 5: 2800; 6: 3593; William M. Wiecek, "The Reconstruction of Federal Judicial Power, 1863–1875," *AJLH*, 13 (October 1969), 333–36.

50. Joseph B. James, *The Ratification of the Fourteenth Amendment* (Macon, 1984); Foner, *Reconstruction*, 277.

51. *New York Journal of Commerce*, June 16, 1866; *Springfield Republican*, June 9, 1866.

CHAPTER 3: THE RIGHT TO VOTE

1. Eric Foner, *Reconstruction: America's Unfinished Revolution 1863–1877* (New York, 2014 ed.), 281–91; Francis B. Simkins and Robert H. Woody, *South Carolina During Reconstruction* (Chapel Hill, 1932), 81; Steven Hahn, *A Nation Under Our Feet: Black Political Struggles in the Rural South from Slavery to the Great Migration* (Cambridge, 2003), 184; Samuel S. Gardner to O. D. Kinsman, July 23, 1867, Wager Swayne Papers, Alabama State Department of Archives and History; Joseph H. Catchings to Benjamin G. Humphreys, August 24, 1866, Mississippi Governor's Papers, Mississippi Department of Archives and History; Sydney Nathans, *A Mind to Stay: White Plantation, Black Homeland* (Cambridge, 2017), 116.

2. 41st Congress, 2nd Session, House Miscellaneous Document 154, 1: 637; *Mobile Nationalist*, April 25, May 16, 1867; Laura F. Edwards, *A Legal History of the Civil War and Reconstruction: A Nation of Rights* (New York, 2015), 130–36; Kate Masur, *An Example for All the Land: Emancipation and the Struggle Over Equality in Washington, D.C.* (Chapel Hill, 2010), 7–9; William Crely to Adelbert Ames, October 9, 1875, Mississippi Governor's Papers.

3. Eric Foner, "Rights and the Constitution in Black Life During the Civil War and Reconstruction," *JAH*, 74 (December 1987), 203; Anne C. Bailey, *The Weeping Time: Memory and the Largest Slave Auction in American History* (New York, 2017), 123; *Washington Daily Morning Chronicle*, January 11, 1867; W. E. B. Du Bois, *The Souls of Black Folk* (Chicago, 1903), 4; *CG*, 40th Congress, 3rd Session, 555.

4. *Boston Daily Advertiser*, January 25, 1869; *CG*, 39th Congress, 2nd Session, 63, 76.

5. Leslie H. Fishel Jr., "Northern Prejudice and Negro Suffrage 1865–1870," *Journal of Negro History*, 39 (January 1954), 19–22; LaWanda Cox and John H. Cox, "Negro Suffrage and Republican Politics: The Problem of Motivation in Reconstruction Historiography," *Journal of Southern History*, 33 (August 1967), 317–19; Schuyler Colfax to Theodore Tilton, January 4, 1868, Schuyler Colfax Papers, New York Public Library; Phyllis F. Field, "Republicans and Black Suffrage in New York State: The Grass-Roots Response," *Civil War History*, 21 (June 1975), 141–46.

6. *CG*, 40th Congress, 3rd Session, 672, 708.

7. Henry D. Moore to Elihu B. Washburne, December 7, 1867, Elihu B. Washburne Papers, LC; James Mack Henry Frederick, *National Party Platforms of the United States* (Akron, 1896), 34; *CG*, 40th Congress, 3rd Session, 1006, 1966; Thaddeus Stevens to Charles Pence, June 24, 1868, Thaddeus Stevens Papers, LC.

8. Alexander C. Flick, *Samuel Jones Tilden; A Study in Political Sagacity* (New

York, 1939), 176; *Official Proceedings of the Democratic National Convention* (New York, 1868), 180; *New York World*, September 13, 1868.

9. *Address of the Colored Men's Border State Convention to the People of the United States* (Broadside: Baltimore, 1868); James G. Blaine, *Twenty Years of Congress* (2 vols.: Norwich, 1884), 2: 412; James M. McPherson, *The Struggle for Equality: Abolitionists and the Negro in the Civil War and Reconstruction* (Princeton, 1964), 424; *Philadelphia Press*, November 6, 1868.

10. *CG*, 40th Congress, 3rd Session, 6–9; *Hartford Daily Courant*, December 17, 1868.

11. Alexander Keyssar, *The Right to Vote: The Contested History of Democracy in the United States* (New York, 2000), 94; *CG*, 40th Congress, 3rd Session, 709, 982–83.

12. Ibid., 40th Congress, 3rd Session, 728, 990; *Proceedings of the National Convention of the Colored Men of America* (Washington, 1869), 1, 20.

13. *CG*, 40th Congress, 3rd Session, 560; Appendix, 294.

14. *New York Journal of Commerce*, February 2, 1869; *CG*, 40th Congress, 3rd Session, 668.

15. Ibid., 40th Congress, 3rd Session, 901, 939; 41st Congress, 2nd Session, Appendix, 411.

16. *Cincinnati Daily Gazette*, March 21, 1866; *Springfield Weekly Republican*, February 6, 1869; Foner, *Reconstruction*, 447; *CG*, 40th Congress, 3rd Session, 1037; Keyssar, *Right to Vote*, 97; *Chicago Tribune*, February 1, 1869.

17. *Milwaukee Daily Sentinel*, January 27, 1869; *Hartford Daily Courant*, February 6, 1869; *CG*, 40th Congress, 3rd Session, 1013, 1037.

18. *Chicago Tribune*, February 10, 25, 1869; *CG*, 40th Congress, 3rd Session, 668–69.

19. *Boston Daily Advertiser*, February 10, 1869; Blaine, *Twenty Years*, 2: 416; Keyssar, *Right to Vote*, 100–101; Hans L. Trefousse, *The Radical Republicans: Lincoln's Vanguard for Racial Justice* (New York, 1969), 416–18.

20. *NAS*, February 20, 1869; George S. Boutwell, *Reminiscences of Sixty Years in Public Affairs* (2 vols.: New York, 1902), 2: 44–52.

21. *CG*, 40th Congress, 3rd Session, 1623; Georges Clemenceau, *American Reconstruction 1865–1870*, ed. Fernand Baldensperger, trans. Margaret MacVeagh (New York, 1928), 278–79.

22. *CG*, 40th Congress, 3rd Session, 862–63; Appendix, 97–99.

23. Henry Adams, "The Session," *North American Review*, 108 (April 1869), 613; *CG*, 40th Congress, 3rd Session, 863.

24. Ibid., 40th Congress, 3rd Session, 722, 1009, 1626–27; William Dudley Foulke, *Life of Oliver P. Morton* (2 vols.: Indianapolis, 1899), 2: 106–9.

25. *Boston Daily Advertiser*, March 1, 1869; *CG*, 40th Congress, 3rd Session, 727, 1010.

26. Foner, *Reconstruction*, 446; *CG*, 40th Congress, 3rd Session, 706, 909, 990; Appendix, 151, 205.

27. James D. Richardson, ed., *A Compilation of the Messages and Papers of the Presidents 1789–1897* (10 vols.: Washington, 1896–99), 7: 8; Foner, *Reconstruction*, 452.

28. William Gillette, *The Right to Vote: Politics and the Passage of the Fifteenth Amendment* (Baltimore, 1965), 150–54; David E. Kyvig, *Explicit and Authentic Acts: Amending the U.S. Constitution, 1776–1995* (Lawrence, 1996), 180–81. The states where black men did not enjoy the same voting rights as white men until ratification of the Fifteenth Amendment were: California, Connecticut, Delaware, Illinois, Indiana, Kansas, Kentucky, Maryland, Missouri, Ohio, Oregon, Nevada, New Jersey, New York, Pennsylvania, Tennessee, and West Virginia,

29. Akhil Reed Amar, *America's Constitution: A Biography* (New York, 2005), 401; McPherson, *Struggle for Equality*, 424–25.

30. Richard M. Re and Christopher M. Re, "Voting and Vice: Criminal Disenfranchisement and the Reconstruction Amendments," *YLJ*, 121 (May 2012), 1583–85, 1624–33; *CG*, 39th Congress, 2nd Session, 324; 40th Congress, 3rd Session, 361, 828.

31. Ibid., 40th Congress, 3rd Session, 862; *New York Times*, October 7, 2016.

32. Richardson, *Messages and Papers*, 7: 56; William Gillette, *Retreat from Reconstruction 1869–1879* (Baton Rouge, 1979), 22–23; *New National Era*, August 31, 1871; *Christian Recorder*, April 9, 1870.

33. *Jackson Weekly Mississippi Pilot*, April 9, 1870; *New York Times*, April 9, 1870; Mitch Kachun, *Festivals of Freedom: Memory and Meaning in African American Emancipation Celebrations, 1808–1915* (Amherst, 2003), 132–33.

34. Foner, *Reconstruction*, 448; Timothy S. Huebner, *Liberty and Union: The Civil War Era and American Constitutionalism* (Lawrence, 2016), 391; *NAS*, May 15, June 5, 1869; *New York Times*, April 10, 1870.

35. Sarah Pugh to Mary Estlin, January 31, 1869, Estlin Papers, Dr. Williams's Library, London; Martha S. Jones, *All Bound Up Together: The Woman Question in African American Public Culture* (Chapel Hill, 2007), 146–47, 197; *Proceedings of the National Convention of the Colored Men of America* (Washington, 1869), 6, 12.

36. Faye E. Dudden, *Fighting Chance: The Struggle over Woman Suffrage and Black Suffrage in Reconstruction America* (New York, 2011), 80; Susan B. Anthony to Charles Sumner, February 8, 1870, Charles Sumner Papers, HL; *The Revolution*, February 11, March 11, June 10, 1869.

37. Ibid., January 20, 1868, March 11, 1869.

38. Ibid., December 24, 1868, March 18, May 20, 27, 1869; Alison M. Parker, *Articulating Rights: Nineteenth-Century American Women on Race, Reform, and the State* (DeKalb, 2010), 119–20; Rosalyn Terborg-Penn, *African American*

Women in the Struggle for the Vote, 1850–1920 (Bloomington, 1998), 27–42; Ellen C. Du Bois, *Feminism and Suffrage: The Emergence of an Independent Women's Movement in America 1848–1869* (Ithaca, 1978), 71–72.

39. Free, *Suffrage*, 162–64; *The Revolution*, December 17, 1868; *CG*, 39th Congress, 2nd Session, 40; 40th Congress, 3rd Session, 710, 727, 1039; *New York Times*, March 11, 1869; *Springfield Republican* in *NAS*, January 30, 1869.

40. Foner, *Reconstruction*, 425–35.

41. Hannah Rosen, *Terror in the Heart of Dixie: Citizenship, Sexual Violence, and the Meaning of Race in the Postemancipation South* (Chapel Hill, 2009), 9, 117, 180; J. W. Bailey to DeWitt Senter, May 15, 1869, Tennessee Governor's Papers, Tennessee State Library and Archives; Kidada E. Williams, *They Left Great Marks on Me: African American Testimonies of Racial Violence from Emancipation to World War I* (New York, 2012), 25; Herbert Aptheker, ed., *A Documentary History of the Negro People in the United States* (New York, 1969), 594–99; *Proceedings of the State Convention of the Colored Citizens of Tennessee* (Nashville, 1871), 4–7, 15; Adam Palmer to Rufus Bullock, August 24, 1869, Georgia Governor's Papers, University of Georgia; *New National Era*, March 21, 1872; 42nd Congress, 2nd Session, House Report 22 [Ku Klux Klan Hearings], Georgia, 611.

42. Shannon M. Smith, "'They Mustered a Whole Company of Ku Klux as Militia': State Violence and Black Freedoms in Kentucky's Readjustment" (Paper Delivered at Conference: Freedoms Gained and Lost: Reinterpreting Reconstruction in the Atlantic World, College of Charleston, 2018).

43. John H. Wager to William H. Smith, August 1, 1869; Alabama Governor's Papers, Alabama State Department of Archives and History; Foner, *Reconstruction*, 342, 431; *U.S. Statutes at Large*, 16: 140–46, 433–40; 17: 13–15; *CG*, 41st Congress, 2nd Session, 3111–13.

44. Pamela Brandwein, *Rethinking the Judicial Settlement of Reconstruction* (New York, 2011), 30–51; Richard M. Valelly, *The Two Reconstructions: The Struggle for Black Enfranchisement* (Chicago, 2004), 107–8; *CG*, 42nd Congress, 1st Session, 375, 501; Appendix, 69–70, 78–79.

45. Ibid., 42nd Congress, 1st Session, 391, 394–95; 2nd Session, 1987.

46. Ibid., 42nd Congress, 1st Session, 448; Appendix, 153–54.

47. Ibid., 41st Congress, 3rd Session, 1271; 42nd Congress, 1st Session, 477, 575–77, 709, 1871; Appendix, 153, 414–15.

48. Gregory P. Downs, *After Appomattox: Military Occupation and the Ends of War* (Cambridge, 2015), 6–9, 40–41; Robert W. Coakley, *The Role of Federal Military Forces in Domestic Disorders 1789–1878* (Washington, 1988), 311–12; Mark L. Bradley, *Bluecoats and Tar Heels: Soldiers and Civilians in Reconstruction North Carolina* (Lexington, 2009), 5–6; Lou Falkner Williams, *The Great South Carolina Ku Klux Klan Trials, 1871–1872* (Athens, 1996); Wang

XI, *The Trial of Democracy: Black Suffrage and Northern Republicans, 1860–1910* (Athens, 1997), 300–301.

49. Ibid., 300–301; August Belmont to G. W. McCrook, June 5, 1871, in Manton Marble Papers, LC; Frederick, *Platforms*, 39; Foner, *Reconstruction*, 508.

50. Clemenceau, *Reconstruction*, 299; *New York Tribune*, February 27, 1869; *New National Era*, March 21, 1872; James A. Garfield to Robert Folger, April 16, 1870, Letterbook, James A. Garfield Papers, LC.

51. Gillette, *Retreat*, 364.

CHAPTER 4: JUSTICE AND JURISPRUDENCE

1. William M. Alexander, *The Brotherhood of Liberty, or Our Day in Court* (Baltimore, 1891), 6–12; *Indianapolis Freeman*, February 15, 1890; J. Clay Smith Jr., *Emancipation: The Making of the Black Lawyer, 1844–1944* (Philadelphia, 1993), 143–44, 178; Susan D. Carle, *Defining the Struggle: National Racial Justice Organizing, 1880–1915* (New York, 2013), 35–36.

2. *New York Freeman*, December 4, 1886; *Indianapolis Freeman*, April 6, 1889; Alexander, *Brotherhood*, 18.

3. Melissa Milewski, *Litigating Across the Color Line: Civil Cases Between Black and White Southerners from the End of Slavery to Civil Rights* (New York, 2018), 48–54, 77; Carle, *Defining*, 1–5, 54–56, 195.

4. Brotherhood of Liberty, *Justice and Jurisprudence: An Inquiry Concerning the Constitutional Limitations of the Thirteenth, Fourteenth, and Fifteenth Amendments* (Philadelphia, 1889), v, 423, 428, 451; Jon-Christian Suggs, "Romanticism, Law, and the Suppression of African-American Citizenship," in Reynolds J. Scott-Childress, ed., *Race and the Production of Modern American Nationalism* (New York, 1999), 67.

5. William E. Nelson, *The Fourteenth Amendment: From Political Principle to Judicial Doctrine* (Cambridge, 1988), 1; Richard L. Aynes, "Unintended Consequences of the Fourteenth Amendment," in David E. Kyvig, ed., *Unintended Consequences of Constitutional Amendments* (Athens, 2000), 120; Pamela Brandwein, *Rethinking the Judicial Settlement of Reconstruction* (New York, 2011), 1–3; G. Edmund White, "The Origins of Civil Rights in America," *Case Western Reserve Law Review*, 64 (Issue 3, 2014), 756.

6. *New York Times*, October 16, 1883.

7. John Niven, ed., *The Salmon P. Chase Papers* (5 vols.: Kent, 1993–98), 5: xx.

8. Pamela Brandwein, *Reconstructing Reconstruction: The Supreme Court and the Production of Historical Truth* (Durham, 1999), 85.

9. Brief biographies of the justices may be found in Kermit L. Hall, ed., *The Oxford Companion to the Supreme Court of the United States* (2nd ed.: New

York, 2005); Andrew Kent, "The Rebel Soldier Who Became Chief Justice of the United States: The Civil War and Its Legacy for Edward Douglass White of Louisiana," *AJLH*, 56 (June 2016), 255.

10. Brotherhood of Liberty, *Justice and Jurisprudence*, 192; John G. Sproat, *The "Best Men": Liberal Reformers in the Gilded Age* (New York, 1968).

11. *New York Tribune*, March 3, 1880; John Sherman, *Selected Speeches and Reports on Finance and Taxation* (New York, 1879), 454; *CR*, 44th Congress, 1st Session, 5585; James G. Blaine, *Twenty Years of Congress* (2 vols.: Norwich, 1884), 2: 419–20; Rebecca J. Scott, "Public Rights, Social Equality, and the Conceptual Roots of the Plessy Challenge," *Michigan Law Review*, 106 (March 2008), 780.

12. *Blyew v. United States*, 80 U.S. 581 (1871), 591–93, 595–601.

13. *Milwaukee Daily Sentinel*, April 22, 1873; Ronald M. Labbé and Jonathan Lurie, *The Slaughterhouse Cases: Regulation, Reconstruction, and the Fourteenth Amendment* (Lawrence, 2003), 6, 75; Michael A. Ross, "Justice Miller's Reconstruction: The *Slaughter-House Cases*, Health Codes, and Civil Rights in New Orleans, 1861–1873," in Elizabeth Reilly, ed., *Infinite Hope and Finite Disappointment: The Story of the First Interpreters of the Fourteenth Amendment* (Akron, 2011), 99–114; Randy E. Barnett, "The Three Narratives of the *Slaughter-House Cases*," *JSCH*, 41 (November 2016), 298–304.

14. *Slaughterhouse Cases*, 83 U.S. 36 (1873), 62, 66, 68, 71, 78–80.

15. Ibid., 68; Nelson, *Fourteenth Amendment*, 163; *CR*, 43rd Congress, 1st Session, 4148; 2nd Session, 1379; Charles W. Calhoun, *Conceiving a New Republic: The Republican Party and the Southern Question, 1869–1900* (Lawrence, 2006), 52.

16. Michael A. Ross, *Justice of Shattered Dreams: Samuel Freeman Miller and the Supreme Court During the Civil War Era* (Baton Rouge, 2003), 204–5; Paul Kens, *The Supreme Court Under Morrison R. Waite, 1874–1888* (Columbia, 2010), 4–5, 25; William J. Novak, *The People's Welfare: Law and Regulation in Nineteenth-Century America* (Chapel Hill, 1996), 230–32.

17. *Slaughterhouse Cases*, 92, 96, 113, 123, 125, 129.

18. Timothy S. Huebner, *Liberty and Union: The Civil War Era and American Constitutionalism* (Lawrence, 2016), 397–98; Ross, *Miller*, xvi, 27, 201–8; Ross, "Miller's Reconstruction," 97–98; *Louisville Courier-Journal*, April 15, 1873; David S. Bogen, "Rebuilding the Slaughter-House: The Cases' Support for Civil Rights," in Reilly, *Infinite Hope*, 119–23; Richard L. Aynes, "Constricting the Law of Freedom: Justice Miller, The Fourteenth Amendment, and the *Slaughter-House Cases*," *Chicago-Kent Law Review*, 70 (1994), 627–89; Barnett, "Three Narratives," 295; Labbé and Lurie, *Slaughterhouse Cases*, 2; *New Orleans Daily Picayune*, April 15, 1873.

19. Norma Basch, "Reconstructing Female Citizenship: *Minor v. Happersett*," in Donald G. Nieman, ed., *The Constitution, Law, and American Life: Critical Aspects of the Nineteenth-Century Experience* (Athens, 1992), 53; Catherine A. Jones, "Women, Gender, and the Boundaries of Reconstruction," *JCWH*, 8 (March 2018), 116.

20. Gwen Hoerr Jordan, "'Horror of a Woman': Myra Bradwell, the 14th Amendment, and the Gendered Origin of Sociological Jurisprudence," in Reilly, *Infinite Hope*, 191–202; Niven, *Chase Papers*, 3: 367–69.

21. *Bradwell v. Illinois*, 83 U.S. 130 (1873), 139, 141–42; Amy Dru Stanley, "The Sovereign Market and Sex Difference: Human Rights in America," in Christine Desan and Sven Beckert, eds., *American Capitalism: New Histories* (New York, 2018), 147.

22. *Cleveland Plain Dealer*, April 17, 1873; Peter W. Bardaglio, *Reconstructing the Household: Families, Sex, and the Law in the Nineteenth-Century South* (Chapel Hill, 1995), 131–35; Nancy W. Bercaw, *Gendered Freedoms: Race, Rights, and the Politics of Household in the Delta, 1861–1875* (Gainesville, 2003), 171–73; Jordan, "'Horror of a Woman,'" 190; Peggy Cooper Davis, *Neglected Stories: The Constitution and Family Values* (New York, 1997), 23.

23. Ellen Carol DuBois, "Taking the Law Into Our Own Hands: *Bradwell, Minor,* and Suffrage Militance in the 1870s," in Marjorie Spruill Wheeler, ed., *One Woman, One Vote: Rediscovering the Woman Suffrage Movement* (Troutdale, 1995), 81–87; Basch, "Reconstructing Citizenship," 55–71; *Minor v. Happersett*, 88 U.S. 162 (1875), 177.

24. Laura F. Edwards, "The Reconstruction of Rights: The Fourteenth Amendment and Popular Conceptions of Governance," *JSCH*, 41 (November 2016), 323–24; Jones, "Women, Gender, Reconstruction," 119–20; *New York Evening Post*, April 15, 1873.

25. Amy Dru Stanley, "Slave Emancipation and the Revolutionizing of Human Rights," in Gregory P. Downs and Kate Masur, eds., *The World the Civil War Made* (Chapel Hill, 2015), 269–73; Scott, "Public Rights," 783–90; David Donald, *Charles Sumner and the Rights of Man* (New York, 1970), 532–34; W. G. Eliot to Benjamin F. Butler, May 28, 1874, Benjamin F. Butler Papers, LC; James Mack Henry Frederick, *National Party Platforms of the United States* (Akron, 1896), 40, 44; Eric Foner, *Reconstruction: America's Unfinished Revolution 1863–1877* (New York, 2004 ed.), 532.

26. Stanley, "Slave Emancipation," 278–88; James W. White to Charles Sumner, January 27, 1872, Albert T. Morgan to Sumner, April 6, 1872, Charles Sumner Papers, HL; *CG*, 42nd Congress, 2nd Session, 429–31; *CR*, 43rd Congress, 1st Session, 50; *New National Era*, December 5, 1872; Barbara Y. Welke, "When All the Women Were White, and All the Blacks Were Men: Gender, Class, Race, and the Road to *Plessy*, 1855–1914," *LHR*, 13 (Fall 1995), 261–76; Jane

Dailey, *Before Jim Crow: The Politics of Race and Emancipation in Postemancipation Virginia* (Chapel Hill, 2000), 106–9.

27. Foner, *Reconstruction*, 368–71; William S. Harris, *The Day of the Carpetbagger: Republican Reconstruction in Mississippi* (Baton Rouge, 1979), 440–46; *New Orleans Tribune*, January 7, 1869; H. S. McComb to Henry C. Warmoth, June 28, July 17, 1871, Henry C. Warmoth Papers, Southern Historical Collection, University of North Carolina.

28. Hugh Davis, *"We Will Be Satisfied with Nothing Less": The African American Struggle for Equal Rights in the North During Reconstruction* (Ithaca, 2011), 103–6; *CG*, 42nd Congress, 2nd Session, Appendix, 4.

29. Ibid., 42nd Congress, 2nd Session, 919; *CR*, 43rd Congress, 1st Session, 416; Calhoun, *Conceiving*, 70; Foner, *Reconstruction*, 533–35.

30. *CR*, 43rd Congress, 1st Session, 337, 412, 3451–54, 4148; 2nd Session, 242, 642–44, 727–29; Donald, *Sumner*, 532.

31. *CR*, 43rd Congress, 1st Session, 407–10; Charles Fairman, *Reconstruction and Reunion 1864–88, Part Two* (New York, 1987), 174.

32. Stanley, "Slave Emancipation," 292; Alfred Avins, "The Civil Rights Act of 1875: Some Reflected Light on the Fourteenth Amendment and Public Accommodations," *CLR*, 66 (May 1966), 875.

33. Benjamin H. Bristow to G. C. Wharton, January 14, 1875, Benjamin H. Bristow Papers, LC; Carole Emberton, *Beyond Redemption: Race, Violence, and the American South After the Civil War* (Chicago, 2013).

34. LeeAnna Keith, *The Colfax Massacre: The Untold Story of Black Power, White Terror, and the Death of Reconstruction* (New York, 2008); Robert M. Goldman, *Reconstruction and Black Suffrage: Losing the Vote in Reese and Cruikshank* (Lawrence, 2001), 51–57; Brandwein, *Rethinking*, 15–17, 91–113; *United States v. Cruikshank*, 92 U.S. 542 (1875), 542, 551, 556.

35. *United States v. Reese*, 92 U.S. 214 (1875), 217–18.

36. *Strauder v. West Virginia*, 100 U.S. 303 (1880), 306; *Ex Parte Virginia*, 100 U.S. 339 (1880).

37. *Wheeling Register*, March 3, 1880; *New York Times*, March 19, 1880; *Virginia v. Rives*, 100 U.S. 313 (1880), 318; *Strauder v. West Virginia*, 310; Michael J. Klarman, *From Jim Crow to Civil Rights: The Supreme Court and the Struggle for Racial Equality* (New York, 2004), 40–41; Benno C. Schmidt Jr., "Juries, Jurisdiction, and Race Discrimination: The Lost Promise of *Strauder v. West Virginia*," *Texas Law Review*, 61 (May 1983), 1406–7.

38. *New York Tribune*, March 3, 1880.

39. Calhoun, *Conceiving*, 148–64; Wang Xi, *The Trial of Democracy: Black Suffrage and Northern Republicans, 1860–1910* (Athens, 1997), 330.

40. *Ex Parte Siebold*, 100 U.S. 371 (1880), 386, 394; *Ex Parte Yarbrough*, 110 U.S. 651 (1884), 652, 661, 663; Richard M. Valelly, *The Two Reconstructions: The*

Struggle for Black Enfranchisement (Chicago, 2004), 69; *New York Times*, March 9, 1880; *Washington Post*, March 9, 1880.

41. *United States v. Harris*, 106 U.S. 629 (1883); Brandwein, *Rethinking*, 154–57.

42. Christopher Waldrep, *Jury Discrimination: The Supreme Court, Public Opinion, and a Grassroots Fight for Racial Equality in Mississippi* (Athens, 2010), 166; *Hall v. DuCuir*, 95 U.S. 485 (1878), 491, 502–4; *New Orleans Times-Picayune*, June 15, 1873; Brotherhood of Liberty, *Justice and Jurisprudence*, 191.

43. Stanley, "Slave Emancipation," 292; Fairman, *Reconstruction and Reunion*, 288–89, 564, 570; *Civil Rights Cases*, 109 U.S. 3 (1883), 11, 17, 20, 22, 24.

44. Linda Przybyszewski, *The Republic According to John Marshall Harlan* (Chapel Hill, 1999), 14–43, 83; Malvina Shanklin Harlan, *Some Memories of a Long Life* (New York, 2002), 112–14; *Civil Rights Cases*, 20, 26, 36, 42, 45, 53, 57, 61; *Pace v. Alabama*, 106 U.S. 583 (1883).

45. *Baltimore Sun*, October 17, 1883; *Hartford Daily Courant*, October 19, 1883; *Chicago Tribune*, October 17, 18, 1883; *Harrisburg Telegraph* in *Harrisburg Patriot*, October 17, 1883; *Milwaukee Daily Journal*, October 16, 1883; *Cincinnati Commercial Gazette*, October 27, 1883; William E. Read and William C. Berman, "Papers of the First Justice Harlan at the University of Louisville," *AJLH*, 11 (January 1967), 59n.

46. White, "Origins," 807; *Cleveland Gazette*, October 20, 1883; *New York Globe*, October 20, November 24, 1883; Steve Luxenberg, *Separate: The Story of Plessy v. Ferguson, and America's Journey from Slavery to Segregation* (New York, 2019), 356; Henry M. Turner, *The Black Man's Doom: Two Barbarous and Cruel Decisions of the United States Supreme Court* (Philadelphia 1896), 48–58.

47. *Civil Rights Cases*, 37; John H. Gauger, "A Delaware Experiment with Reconstruction Nullification," *Delaware History*, 21 (Spring-Summer 1985), 183–85; Donald G. Nieman, "The Language of Liberation: African Americans and Equalitarian Constitutionalism, 1830–1950," in Nieman, *Constitution, Law, and American Life*, 82; Davis, *"We Will Be Satisfied,"* 146–47; Foner, *Reconstruction*, 471; Stephen J. Riegel, "Persistent Career of Jim Crow: Lower Federal Courts and the Separate But Equal Doctrine, 1865–1896," *AJLH*, 28 (January 1984), 28–29.

48. Marianne L. Engelman Lado, "A Question of Justice: African-American Legal Perspectives on the 1883 Civil Rights Cases," *Chicago-Kent Law Review*, 70 (Issue 3, 1995), 1123–95; Carle, *Defining the Struggle*, 37–45; *New York Globe*, October 20, 1883.

49. Brotherhood of Liberty, *Justice and Jurisprudence*, 1, 13–14, 38, 76–77, 156–61, 244.

50. *Baltimore Sun*, December 30, 1889; *Kansas City Times*, May 11, 1890; *Philadelphia Inquirer*, January 9, 1890; *Detroit Plaindealer*, December 20, 1889; *Sci-*

ence: A Weekly Newspaper of All the Arts and Sciences, 15 (January 10, 1890), 26–27.

51. Richard E. Welch Jr., "The Federal Elections Bill of 1890: Postscripts and Prelude," *JAH,* 52 (December 1965), 511–26; Valelly, *Two Reconstructions,* 121; Calhoun, *Conceiving,* 234–58.

52. David A. Bateman, Ira Katznelson, and John S. Lapinski, *Southern Nation: Congress and White Supremacy after Reconstruction* (Princeton, 2018), 77; Patrick J. Kelly, "The Election of 1896 and the Restructuring of Civil War Memory," in Alice Fahs and Joan Waugh, eds., *The Memory of the Civil War in American Culture* (Chapel Hill, 2004), 180–81; Robert Cook, "The Quarrel Forgotten? Toward a Clearer Understanding of Sectional Reconciliation," *JCWE,* 6 (September 2016), 426–27; John W. Burgess, *Reconstruction and the Constitution 1866–1876* (New York, 1902), vii, 217; William A. Dunning, *Essays on the Civil War and Reconstruction* (New York, 1904), 384–85; Eric Foner, "The Supreme Court and the History of Reconstruction—and Vice Versa," *CLR,* 112 (November 2012), 1585–1608.

53. *United States v. Wong Kim Ark* (1898), 169 U.S. 649; T. Alexander Aleinikoff, *Semblances of Sovereignty: The Constitution, the State, and American Citizenship* (Cambridge, 2002), 5–31; Mark Elliott, "The Lessons of Reconstruction: Debating Race and Imperialism in the 1890s," in Carole Emberton and Bruce W. Baker, eds., *Remembering Reconstruction: Struggles Over the Meaning of America's Most Turbulent Era* (Baton Rouge, 2017), 165–66.

54. Rayford W. Logan, *The Negro in American Life and Thought: The Nadir, 1877–1901* (New York, 1954); Michael J. Horan, "Political Economy and Sociological Theory as Influences Upon Judicial Policy—Making the *Civil Rights Cases* of 1883," *AJLH,* 16 (January 1972), 82–86; Adam Winkler, *We the Corporations: How American Businesses Won Their Civil Rights* (New York, 2018); Joseph B. James, *The Framing of the Fourteenth Amendment* (Urbana, 1956), 105, 159, 179.

55. Mark Elliott, *Color-Blind Justice: Albion Tourgée and the Quest for Racial Equality from the Civil War to Plessy v. Ferguson* (New York, 2006), 249–87; Charles A. Lofgren, *The Plessy Case: A Legal-Historical Interpretation* (New York, 1987), 32, 48–52, 173; Scott, "Public Rights," 797–802; Rodolphe Lucien Desdunes, *Our People and Our History: Fifty Creole Portraits,* ed. and trans. Dorothea Olga McCants (Baton Rouge, 1973), 141–44; Luxenberg, *Separate,* 471.

56. *Louisville, New Orleans, and Texas Railway v. Mississippi,* 133 U.S. 587 (1890); *Plessy v. Ferguson,* 163 U.S. 537 (1896), 544, 549, 550, 551.

57. Ibid., 561; *United States v. Wong Kim Ark,* 705; Gabriel J. Chin, "The First Justice Harlan by the Numbers: Just How Great was 'the Great Dissenter?' " *Akron Law Review,* 32 (Issue 3, 1992), 629–55.

58. *Plessy v. Ferguson*, 555, 559, 560, 562; *Cumming v. Richmond County Board of Education*, 175 U.S. 528 (1899).

59. Riegel, "Persistent Career," 17–20; *Dallas Morning News*, May 19, 1896; *San Francisco Chronicle*, May 19, 1896; *Enterprise* (Omaha), May 30, 1896; *Memphis Commercial Appeal*, October 18, 1911; Henry Billings Brown, "The Dissenting Opinions of Mr. Justice Harlan," *American Law Review*, 46 (May-June 1912), 336–38.

60. Foner, *Reconstruction*, 590–91; Francis N. Thorpe, ed., *The Federal and State Constitutions* (7 vols.: Washington, 1909), 4: 2120; Michael Perman, *Struggle for Mastery: Disfranchisement in the South, 1888–1908* (Chapel Hill, 2001), 13–28; Paul E. Herron, *Framing the Solid South: The State Constitutional Conventions of Secession, Reconstruction, and Redemption, 1860–1902* (Lawrence, 2017), 220–23.

61. Valelly, *Two Reconstructions*, 2, 123–26; Francis B. Simkins, "New Viewpoints on Southern Reconstruction," *Journal of Southern History*, 5 (February 1939), 50; George S. Boutwell, *Reminiscences of Sixty Years in Public Affairs* (2 vols.: New York, 1902), 2: 48. France instituted universal male suffrage in 1793, abandoned it in 1799, reintroduced it in 1848, and abandoned it again a few years later.

62. *Williams v. Mississippi*, 170 U.S. 213 (1898), 225; *Yick Wo v. Hopkins*, 118 U.S. 356 (1886), 373; Perman, *Struggle for Mastery*, 70.

63. Smith, *Emancipation*, 273; *Springfield Sunday Republican*, May 3, 1903; *Giles v. Harris*, 189 U.S. 475 (1903), 483, 488; Jamal Greene, "The Anticanon," *Harvard Law Review*, 125 (December 2011), 429.

64. *Charlotte Daily Observer*, April 29, 1903; *New Orleans Daily Picayune*, April 28, 1903; *Baltimore Sun*, April 28, 1903; *Springfield Daily Republican*, May 2, 1903.

65. *Montgomery Advertiser*, May 6, 1903; *Springfield Sunday Republican*, May 3, 1903; *Giles v. Teasley*, 193 U.S. 146 (1904); *James v. Bowman*, 190 U.S. 127 (1903); *Hodges v. United States*, 203 U.S. 1 (1906), 37. In the French-language original, Desdunes used the idiomatic expression "la satisfaction de pousser au pied du mur le gouvernement," which is difficult to translate exactly into English. It suggests forcing the government to do something it does not wish to do. Rodolphe Lucien Desdunes, *Nos Hommes et Notre Histoire* (Montreal, 1911), 194.

Epilogue

1. For example, Richard Kluger, *Simple Justice: The History of Brown v. Board of Education and Black America's Struggle for Equality* (New York, 1976);

Michael J. Klarman, *From Jim Crow to Civil Rights: The Supreme Court and the Struggle for Racial Equality* (New York, 2004).

2. *Bailey v. Alabama*, 219 U.S. 219 (1911); *Jones v. Alfred H. Mayer Co.*, 392 U.S. 409 (1968); Alexander Tsesis, *The Thirteenth Amendment and American Freedom: A Legal History* (New York, 2004), 83–84; William M. Carter Jr., "Race, Rights, and the Thirteenth Amendment: Defining the Badges and Incidents of Slavery," *UC Davis Law Review*, 40 (April 2007), 1311–22; Jack M. Balkin and Sanford Levinson, "The Dangerous Thirteenth Amendment," *CLR*, 112 (November 2012), 1460–70.

3. Ari Berman, *Give Us the Ballot: The Modern Struggle for Voting Rights in America* (New York, 2015); *Shelby County v. Holder*, 570 U.S. 529 (2013), 535; *New York Times*, June 25, 2018; Jamal Greene, "Fourteenth Amendment Originalism," *Maryland Law Review*, 71 (Issue 4, 2012), 978–79.

4. *McDonald v. City of Chicago*, 561 U.S. 742 (2010), 758; *Timbs v. Indiana*, 586 U.S. ___ (2019).

5. Paul Finkelman, "The Historical Context of the 14th Amendment," in Elizabeth Reilly, ed., *Infinite Hope and Finite Disappointment: The Story of the First Interpreters of the Fourteenth Amendment* (Akron, 2011), 35; Christopher W. Schmidt, *The Sit-Ins: Protest and Legal Change in the Civil Rights Era* (Chicago, 2018), 6–7; Pamela Brandwein, *Reconstructing Reconstruction: The Supreme Court and the Production of Historical Truth* (Durham, 1999), 176; Peggy Cooper Davis et al., "The Persistence of the Confederate Narrative," *Tennessee Law Review*, 84 (Winter 2017), 306–7, 341–43.

6. Martha Minow, "Alternatives to the State Action Doctrine in the Era of Privatization, Mandatory Arbitration, and the Internet: Directing Law to Serve Human Needs," *Harvard Civil Rights–Civil Liberties Law Review*, 52 (Winter 2017), 145–50; *Shelley v. Kraemer*, 334 U.S. 1 (1948); George Rutherglen, "The Thirteenth Amendment, the Power of Congress, and the Shifting Sources of Civil Rights Law," *CLR*, 112 (November 2012), 1561–63; Amy Dru Stanley, "The Sovereign Market and Sex Difference: Human Rights in America," in Christine Desan and Sven Beckert, eds., *American Capitalism: New Histories* (New York, 2018), 146–61.

7. *United States v. Morrison*, 529 U.S. 598 (2000), 602, 620–22.

8. Richard Rothstein, *The Color of Law: A Forgotten History of How Our Government Segregated America* (New York, 2017), xii–xv and *passim*.

9. *Adarand Constructors, Inc. v. Peña*, 515 U.S. 200 (1995).

10. Roy P. Basler, ed., *The Collected Works of Abraham Lincoln* (8 vols.: New Brunswick, 1953), 8: 332–33; Clinton Rossiter, ed., *The Federalist Papers* (New York, 1961), 276.

INDEX

ABOUT THE AUTHOR

Eric Foner, DeWitt Clinton Professor Emeritus of History at Columbia University, is one of this country's most prominent historians. He received his doctoral degree at Columbia under the supervision of Richard Hofstadter. He has served as president of the three major professional organizations: the Organization of American Historians, the American Historical Association, and the Society of American Historians.

Professor Foner's publications have concentrated on the intersections of intellectual, political, and social history, and the history of American race relations. His books include: *Free Soil, Free Labor, Free Men: The Ideology of the Republican Party Before the Civil War* (1970); *Tom Paine and Revolutionary America* (1976); *Nothing But Freedom: Emancipation and Its Legacy* (1983); *Reconstruction: America's Unfinished Revolution, 1863–1877* (1988) (winner of the Bancroft Prize, the Parkman Prize, and the Los Angeles Times Book Award); *The Reader's Companion to American History* (editor, with John A. Garraty, 1991); *The Story of American Freedom* (1998); *Who Owns History? Rethinking the Past in a Changing World* (2002); *Forever Free: The Story of Emancipation and Reconstruc-*

tion (2005); *Our Lincoln: New Perspectives on Lincoln and His World* (editor, 2008); *The Fiery Trial: Abraham Lincoln and American Slavery* (2010) (winner of the Pulitzer Prize, the Bancroft Prize, and the Lincoln Prize); *Gateway to Freedom: The Hidden History of the Underground Railroad* (2015) (winner of the New-York Historical Society Book Prize); and *Battles for Freedom: The Use and Abuse of American History* (2017). His survey textbook of American history, *Give Me Liberty! An American History*, appeared in 2004 and is a leading text in the field. His books have been translated into many languages.

Eric Foner has also been the co-curator, with Olivia Mahoney, of two prize-winning exhibitions on American history: *A House Divided: America in the Age of Lincoln* (Chicago Historical Society, 1990) and *America's Reconstruction: People and Politics After the Civil War* (Virginia Historical Society, 1995). He revised the presentation of American history at the Hall of Presidents at Disney World and at Meet Mr. Lincoln at Disneyland, and has served as consultant to several National Parks Service historical sites and historical museums.

Eric Foner is a winner of the Great Teacher Award from the Society of Columbia Graduates (1991) and the Presidential Award for Outstanding Teaching from Columbia University (2006). He is an elected Fellow of the American Academy of Arts and Sciences and the British Academy, and holds honorary doctorates from many universities. He has taught at Cambridge University as Pitt Professor of American History and Institutions, at Oxford University as Harmsworth Professor of American History, at Moscow State University as Fulbright Professor, and at Queen Mary, University of London as Leverhulme Visiting Scholar.

Eric Foner serves on the editorial boards of *Past and Present* and the *Nation*, and has written for the *New York Times*, *Washington Post*, *Los Angeles Times*, *London Review of Books*, and many other publications. He has appeared on numerous television and radio shows, and in historical documentaries on PBS and the History Channel. He has lectured specifically on the Reconstruction amendments at conferences of federal judges, to members of the White House legal staff at Camp David, and at law schools.